W9-BWQ-301

USING RHETORIC

USING RHETORIC

BY

JOHN E. JORDAN

Harper & Row, Publishers

NEW YORK, EVANSTON, AND LONDON

THE TEXT of this book is set in Linotype Baskerville, a recutting of the original type designed by John Baskerville (1706-1775), an English writing master, typographer, and manufacturer of fine printing paper and inks.

 For information address Harper & Row, Publishers, Incorporated, 49 East 33rd Street, New York 16, N.Y.

LIBRARY OF CONGRESS CATALOG CARD NUMBER: 65-11705

FOR MY THREE SONS

Craig, Leigh, and Hugh

The style of an author should be the image of his mind, but the choice and command of language is the fruit of exercise.

EDWARD GIBBON,
Autobiography

CONTENTS

PREFACE

Most instructors who have taught writing courses for any length of time sooner or later get an impulse to write a book making generally available the fruits of their experience. A few even do so, and before they are through think with Huck Finn that if they had " 'a' knowed what a trouble it was" to make such a book, they "wouldn't 'a' tackled it, and ain't a-going to no more." As one of the latter, perhaps I should give my reasons for persisting.

I wanted to write a little book, practical and not too solemn, that would help students understand the necessity of rhetoric. I hoped it would make them recognize that rhetoric is an inevitable and valuable part of their lives, a means of realizing themselves and influencing others, and that they can effectively control this powerful instrument by taking a little pains. My thesis is that the average freshman can write reasonably well if he will make an effort, be himself, and proceed step by step.

I have tried to be realistic about the steps: the student's accepting and benefiting by the convenience of rules, examining and exploiting his own interests, finding a usable subject, addressing it to the readers' needs, clarifying it by logical scrutiny, organizing it as a whole and developing it piece by piece in meaningful relationships from paragraph to sentence to word. Although I now prefer this sequence, I recognize that many of these processes must go on almost simultaneously, and I have put in references back and forth so that instructors can easily assign chapters in a different order if they wish. Since a part of many freshman English courses is an introduction to literature in which students are expected to write about literary subjects, I have often drawn my authorities and examples from literature and have made a point of including, along with contemporary passages, many classic utterances, such as Hazlitt on style, Arnold on culture, Johnson on general language, Newman on a gentleman,

Wordsworth on poetic diction and Robert Louis Stevenson on playing "the sedulous ape." I have ended with some pragmatic advice on how to write examinations, get good grades on essays, and produce term papers. Although this book is not a complete handbook, I believe that it contains enough material on grammar and usage to serve the practical needs of most college students. At the end of each chapter are more assignments than anyone will want at one time; some have literary connections, some aim generally at student interests, and some—which I think can be particularly useful—encourage the student to examine critically and experimentally some element of his own writing.

For much of the content of this book—in ways which I cannot now separate—I am indebted to my own teachers, authors of texts I have used, colleagues with whom I have argued, and students who have continually helped to keep fresh for me the griefs and joys of writing. I am particularly grateful to Professors Bertrand Evans, Josephine Miles, Ralph Rader, Sheldon Sacks and Wayne Shumaker, and to my wife, for reading and improving drafts of this work.

J.E.J.

USING RHETORIC

CHAPTER ONE

Rhetoric, Grammar, Usage

Some readers will be nearly as surprised to be told that they regularly practice the ancient art of rhetoric as was Molière's famous character to learn that all his life he had been speaking prose. For the word "rhetoric" is likely to be associated vaguely in our memories with elocutionary posturing and to survive chiefly in the pejorative sense of flowery rhetoric. Or remembering that a rhetorical question does not really intend an answer, we may stigmatize rhetoric as suspiciously sophistical. Thus rhetoric may connote to us either something empty or something false, and at any rate something remote from our affairs, all the while that we are using it, well or badly.

Historically, rhetoric has been much respected and cultivated. Aristotle wrote a treatise on it, and in Athens of the second century the sophist, or professor of rhetoric, was one of the leading citizens. Cicero and Quintilian were famous Roman rhetoricians. Undergraduate education in medieval times consisted chiefly of the *trivium:* grammar, logic, and rhetoric. Training in rhetoric was an important part of the university curriculum in the Renaissance, and as late as the nineteenth century, colleges had departments of rhetoric. Nowadays, aspects of the subject are distributed among departments of philosophy, psychology, sociology, English, speech, and dramatic arts, and although deprived of its prominence among the academic disciplines and scarcely recognized by its old name, rhetoric still continues to be an important activity.

Etymologically, rhetoric meant the art of oratory; it came to mean the art or science of persuasion. Now it is apparent that we all use language to persuade—ourselves as well as others. Even if our primary purpose is to express ourselves or to communicate information, in so far as we have a hearer or reader, we are seeking to persuade him to take a certain attitude toward what we say. All of the marshaling of an argument, the structuring of a statement, the shaping of a paragraph, the molding of a sentence, and the choosing of a word toward a purposeful end is rhetoric.

THE PLACE OF RHETORIC

Anywhere, except possibly in a Trappist monastery, rhetoric is one of the facts of life. For most people there is a better, more effective way to speak and write—and a need to know how to find it. On one level we recognize the success of the smooth talker, although our traditional image of ourselves as laconic men of action makes us scorn and fear his verbal felicity. One of the paradoxes of our culture is that we admire the strong silent types, while the yap of our radio and TV chokes the ether. We have to realize that an apotheosis of the power of our physical action is not adequate to our needs as individuals or as a nation. Gradually, I think, we are coming to this awareness. I was asked some time ago to teach courses in writing at a research corporation because their scientists, highly trained and intelligent men most of whom were Ph.D.'s, could not get their discoveries across to the vice presidents! Quintilian would have said that they needed to study rhetoric. The term has gone out of favor, but the need remains to be able to express our ideas, to communicate our wishes, to sell our concepts. We are recognizing now that the United States is not gaining friends around the world or making known what is really important about our way of life by producing better refrigerators. The Peace Corps program includes, along with training in techniques of irrigation and other operations valuable to undeveloped areas, training in language—in how to talk about democracy with meaning and persuasion. Aristotle would have said that these young people need a course in rhetoric.

A student once protested to me that he did not want to learn to write like Shakespeare. Although I assured him that he was in no such danger, I regretted his attitude, for what he meant was that he did not think it important for him to make any special effort to rise above the routine and trite. Aside from the small group who perennially aspire to write the great American novel, most Americans are modest in their attitude toward writing. They do not expect to write like Shakespeare or even very well at all. If they do not exactly feel the ancestral contempt for the smooth talker, they are likely to leave writing to Bohemian eggheads. One of the interesting phenomena of recent years has been the articulateness of the "beat" fringe of college generations. Student publications have tended to be *avant garde* partly because the solid, conservative elements in the student body did not feel that writing was their business. My scientist students at the research corporation had erroneously felt that writing was not their business. Probably the young people who join the Peace Corps, for the most part, have not realized the extent to which writing and speaking must be their business.

In our culture effective communication is nearly everybody's business, and from politics to love rhetoric shows a power we must recognize. We Americans tend to scoff at political oratory; nevertheless, we have seen a presidential election influenced materially, perhaps crucially, by a series of television debates. We have never fancied ourselves as great lovers, but we bestow that distinction on the French—a more articulate people. A nation which has built its economy on the persuasion of the "hard sell" and the "soft sell" cannot afford the belittling point of view expressed by one of Alberto Moravia's heroes: "And I am, in fact, inclined to rhetoric—that is, to the substitution of words for deeds."[1] Rhetoric *is* action, a more subtle kind of action, by which words often beget deeds.

At one end of its range rhetoric is concerned with the ordering of ideas: Aristotle said that rhetoric was merely popular logic. At the other end it is concerned with the presentation of ideas in language. Except perhaps in symbolic logic, the two ends are interrelated. Because rhetoric is concerned with the best use of language, it has connections with grammar. Some of these relations will appear later in this book, although we shall be concerned primarily with rhetoric.

The use of language is controlled by three factors: grammar, rhetoric, and usage. Grammar is the science of what is *permissible* in the language, rhetoric is the art of what is *effective*. Grammar concerns itself with the possible ways of saying something, rhetoric with

[1] Alberto Moravia, *Conjugal Love* (New York: Signet Books, New American Library of World Literature, Inc., 1961), p. 11.

the best way. A writer or speaker in choosing the best way must necessarily select from among the possible ways—he must know grammar. His choice must also be influenced by usage, the pattern of ways in which people actually use the language in any time, place, and circumstance. Over the history of the language, usage is the source of grammar; but in any given circle, usage rarely involves all the grammatical resources of the language.

For a simple example of the way in which these three elements work, suppose that a man wanted to say that he was named John. A Frenchman would find it natural to say, "I call myself John"; an American might say, "My name is John." One is no better than the other absolutely, but in English "I call myself John" would not mean the same thing as "My name is John"; it would suggest an assumed name or some other peculiarity in the situation. "I call myself John" is not ungrammatical, but it is outside the idioms sanctioned by usage. "I John myself call" would be ungrammatical because it would be meaningless; it does not conform to any English pattern. "John is my name," on the other hand, would be a possible English formulation, not essentially different in meaning from "My name is John," but different in emphasis. Modern usage makes no distinction between the two forms, and a choice between them would have to be made entirely on rhetorical grounds—probably on whether "my" was important. Usage would influence the rhetorical decision, however, in the choice between "I am named John," "I am John," and "I'm John." For here is a range from formal to informal usage.

Rhetoric, then, exploits grammar and usage. The writer who seeks the most effective expression must know the resources of the language; he must know the rules of grammar and usage.

A WORD ABOUT RULES

Two divergent heresies are abroad among students about grammatical rules. Perhaps the more pernicious is the implicit belief that there is salvation in simply following the rules. Accurate grammar and respectable usage, according to this persuasion, signify an educated man: "Show us the rule in the handbook and we will follow it." Against the oversimplification of that doctrine this book's gospel of rhetoric is directed. Grammar and usage are just the beginning, and the most important things in writing are not covered by rules.

The contrary heresy, which I would like to scotch at the outset, is that the rules of language are an authoritarian nuisance, the work of fuddy-duddies, and should be abrogated by an independent generation. I have some sympathy with the spirit behind this view, but I believe it is nonetheless wrongheaded, because it is based on a misconception of both the value of rules and the character of language. Surely part of our American heritage, and a part which I hope has survived all the forces now making for conformity, is a healthy independence. Perhaps the permissive character of much early training has further conditioned recent generations against rules, with the result that even when maturity dictates that we should accept them we do so with a sense of constraint. We need to change our attitude enough to recognize that even to independent spirits rules can be assets. For in some restriction there is disciplined liberty; without it there is license. Of course, we give logical assent to this idea. We all know that civilization comes only with the acceptance of patterns of living which involve some kind of social control. We all enjoy the benefits of mass production, which are possible only because we follow so many written and unwritten rules of mass consumption. In sports we accept the rules of the game because we realize that without the rules there would be no game. Yet we still are sometimes impatient with speed limits and rules of grammar and usage. Three main courses are open to us whether we are dealing with speed limits or with laws of grammar and usage. We can violate or flaunt them and risk the hazards and penalties involved; we can waste psychic energy in mocking or resenting them; or we can recognize the facts of life, accept the rules and live with them. Margaret Fuller, an American nineteenth-century bluestocking, is supposed to have declared, "I accept the universe." It is a grand gesture, at first glance presumptuous, but essentially a necessary condition to fruitful existence. One must accept something. Even if like Archimedes you want to move the universe, you have to find a solid point outside of it to support your lever. We all inhabit a series of universes, overlapping systems of one sort or another, each with its own order, in which we find our peace. The system of language constitutes one of these universes; the rules of grammar and usage are a part of its order.

The two analogies which we have been using in talking about language, although valid, might be objected to on the one hand as too legalistic and on the other as too pompously philosophical. Language rules are not, like speed limits, decreed by law; and their role in our lives is modest: it would be less pretentious to call them conventions. Conventions are habits of behavior in a society; they have no legal status, although they may in fact be more binding than law. It is only a convention that the president of the United States should throw out the first ball of a baseball season; it is a legal requirement that those admitted to the game have tickets or passes. Which is more likely to be broken? Sometimes convention can override law, as when the practice of shooting off fire crackers on the Fourth of July proves more powerful than the laws against them. To call language practices conventions is not, therefore, to depreciate their significance: it is to recognize that their power is at once more pervasive and less specific than that of mere rules. Continuing the legal analogy, language conventions are more akin to common law than to statutory law. For they are not the result of legislative action, not recorded in carefully drafted statutes; they are accretional, the product of accumulated behavior, clear at the core but blurred at the edges. Unlike the common law, however, they are essentially extralegal, and there is, for English at least, no authoritative machinery for ruling upon them. By the same token, there is really no appeal from them: the court of public opinion has final jurisdiction.

LANGUAGE CONVENTIONS

English grammar is no more than the record of accepted behavior in the use of the English language. There is not, and never has been, any authority except usage. The French have their Academy which decides on the proper form of the language, and I am told that Chiang Kai-shek once designated the speech of a particular learned man as the standard of Mandarin Chinese. From time to time individuals with a tendency toward authoritarianism, or just a penchant for tidying things up, have suggested that English ought to have an academy or some arbiter to straighten out the relative functions of "shall" and "will," preserve the subjunctive, and generally decree linguistic stability. But no such power has ever come into being, and it is doubtful by what authority one could be established and what its effectiveness would be. The result is a certain amount of instability in the English language and rules that are essentially descriptive rather than prescriptive—a record of what has been done and is done, not a codification of what absolutely must be done.

This relative instability comes about because different things are done in different circumstances. A living language changes to reflect circumstances. It is, says E. B. White, like a cow path which shifts to suit the whim of the cows. Social behavior changes in several dimensions—most obviously with time, geographical location, and specific situation. Language also changes in time. We can scarcely recognize the opening of the Lord's Prayer as it looked in Old English about the tenth century:

Faeder ure,
þu þe eart on heofonum,
sī þin nama gehālgod.

We cannot use the ethical dative, as Shakespeare's Petruchio did in *The Taming of the Shrew,* I, ii, 2:

Knock me at this gate.

Thus old forms give place to new "down the ringing grooves of change"—but not entirely, for conventions are hardy and can outlive the era in which they were meaningful. Once a man took the outside position when walking with a lady because she was thus somewhat protected from flying hoofs, spattered mud and slops likely to be thrown into the street from house windows in a day of more primitive sanitation systems. Though circumstances have changed, the custom still survives among modern males who scarcely realize the reason for their behavior. Language is full of such vestiges, older significances now nearly lost in semantic change. We still call a large fire a "bonfire," although it is no longer what the etymology indicates: a bone fire. Someone of whose action we disapprove morally is still "wicked," although the word does not mean wizzard as the Old English *wicca* did. A "spinster," if any of our bachelor girls will admit the term at all, is certainly no longer a female who spins. Sometimes the relevance is still there, but we may not recognize it. How much unnoticed poetry is hidden in words like "daisy," from the Old English *daegeseage*—day's eye! "Pretty" has lost almost all of its connotation of cunning (Old English *praettig*). "Nice" has meant successively foolish, wanton, and coy, but still retains some relation to its original meaning of simple (going back to Latin *nescius*—not knowing).

Thus language changes, though on the whole slowly and gradually. In the early eighteenth century Alexander Pope worried that changes in language would make his poetry incomprehensible:

> Now length of Fame (our second life) is lost,
> And bare threescore is all ev'n that can boast;
> Our sons their fathers failing language see,
> And such as Chaucer is, shall Dryden be.
>
> *Essay on Criticism,* 480–483

Pope's language, however, is not much faded for us. We need to know that the poetic conventions of the time allowed "ev'n" as one syllable and that "join" rhymed with "line"; but we can understand him easily enough. The three hundred years between Chaucer and Dryden wrought more change in language than did the similar expanse of time between Dryden and today because in the earlier period English was still shifting from an inflected to a largely uninflected language and the written form of the language had not yet reacted to the stabilizing effect of mass production. For although scientific advances have encouraged innovations in language as new terms were needed for new discoveries, more significantly these developments have had a standardizing influence through providing the means to present uniform language materials to widespread audiences. Scribal individualities probably kept any two copies of Chaucer's *Canterbury Tales* from being alike; rotary press uniformity can produce millions of identical versions of today's best sellers. The process of linguistic change continues, but slowly; meanwhile many vestiges of past practices are preserved in conventional usage.

Any generation of speakers must, on the whole, accept its linguistic heritage. No agency checks the inventory and throws out obsolete equipment; no surplus store gets rid of, say, excess "n'er's," passé except in "n'er-do-well," but once considered highly poetic. Such winnowing is done gradually and fumblingly by usage. Even organized rational attacks upon such language problems would probably meet the same fate as have the generally futile efforts at spelling reform. Abstractly, there seems no reason for indicating the same sound by different combinations of letters, as in "tough" and "bluff," or different sounds by the same combinations, as in "through," "cough," "though," and "bough." Custom, not logic, however, is the basis of spelling and grammatical practice. Despite the apparent illogicality of different spellings, they follow laws of sound shifts, preserve etymological distinctions, and perform a useful function in separating homonyms. "Bough" might logically be "bow," but that spelling would only compound confusion with at least four other words spelled the same way. A few reformers have taken up "thru" and "tho," but "tuff" and "coff" would seem barbarisms. Linguistic pioneers thus run the risk of being misjudged or misunderstood. On the chronological borders of language, writers without authoritative reputations had better heed Pope's advice:

> Be not the first by whom the new are try'd,
> Nor yet the last to lay the old aside.
>
> *Essay on Criticism*, 335–336

Grammatical conventions also vary in different geographical localities. In the United States dialectal discriminations are most conspicuous in pronunciation. We all recognize a southern drawl and a Yankee twang and the rich flavor of Brooklynese. A trained dialect geographer can sometimes uncannily identify a speaker's habitat within a few miles. My own origin in Piedmont Virginia is evident in my pronunciation of the "ou" dipthong, the peculiarity of which first became painfully obvious to me when I was in the service and my command "about face" was heard as "right face"—once nearly making a squad of men march off a dock. Not all local differences are in pronunciation. When a fisherman on the eastern shore of Virginia announces that he "didn't catch either fish," he doesn't mean that two fish got away, but that he has not caught *any* fish. In some areas a "frying pan" is a "skillet," a "paper bag" is a "paper poke," and a "chesterfield" is a "divan" or "settee" or "sofa." Any (or *either*) reader can add examples from his own locality. Although national magazines and news services as well as coast-to-coast radio and television broadcasts have a standardizing effect which constantly smooths away dialectal differences, enough still remain to remind us of the shifting social character of language structure.

Since language is a social phenomenon, its mutations occur not only in time and place but also in situation. Only a pedant would object to the grammar of the Negro spiritual "It's Me, O Lord, Standing in the Need of Prayer." "It is I" would seem pretentious in this setting, as it would be in answer to your mother's asking who was coming in the back door. Slang, which would be socially acceptable in conversation between students, would not do for a student conferring with the dean. Neither would the dean talk to the student in the same shoptalk he might use with his administrative associates or in the same scholarly prose he employs in his publications in learned journals. We all shift language gears because different situations demand different levels of formality, explicitness, and precision. Although it is possible to work out a hierarchy of gradations from the most lofty academic to the near illiterate, the boundaries between the categories are vague and elastic and each situation is finally unique. In a specific communication, the language world shrinks to its smallest dimensions for us as speakers and writers. There we can see most clearly both the flexibility and the inevitability of language structure; there grammar is conspicuously what is "done," which by implicit agreement is "correct." If one wishes to communicate readily in a given situation, one accepts the unwritten rules of the game.

Each overlapping circle of time, location, or situation circumscribes a certain accepted usage; the common area comprises the most generally accepted usage, available for most purposes, often called Standard English. The sum of all the circles constitutes English grammar, a record of what is possible in the system of the language. This system's intricacies, how its components develop and how they function, constitute a demanding study, to which modern grammarians have made significant new approaches. The more the writer can understand about the mechanisms of his language, the better. What is essential and, mercifully, within the reach of most of us, is an understanding of the way in which the conventions actually work for us.

Of the three chief factors requiring language scrutiny and decision, the only one likely to be important to us as speakers and writers is situation. The changes wrought by time, as we have seen, are generally slow. The only area of our experience in which they are significant is slang, a notoriously ephemeral kind of language. I do not even dare to give examples, because I have no confidence in the currency of my knowledge, and nothing is so square as a faded twenty-three skiddoo. Salinger's use of teen-age slang in *The Catcher in the Rye* is a remarkable tour de force and essential to his characterization, but perhaps fully intelligible only to a teen-ager of the early 1950's. The charm of the novel may well embalm some of the quaint locutions of that era, but if the work endures it will eventually have to be published with a glossary. For the nature of slang is to die; each generation must coin its own slang as a badge of its identity, its psychological warfare against the elders. We are not likely to want to entrust much of our written thought to so perishable a language. Therefore, unless we are trying to produce some special effect of the past or the future by deliberate archaisms or neologisms, we need not concern ourselves particularly with the changes of language in time. We live in our own period and naturally write its language without having to stop and think about it.

Similarly, for most of us as writers the dialectal differences of place still remaining in English are not important. Many of them do not extend beyond the spoken language. True, if we write for a British publisher we have to say "autumn" instead of "fall" and "lorry" instead of "truck," but our editors will probably make such changes silently. Most of us, however, inhabit our locale as we do our age, and adopt its language conventions painlessly. Only if we are members of minority groups with idiosyncratic speech habits, perhaps as a result of the influence of foreign idioms, must we pay conscious attention to conforming to the usage of the whole community.

The Comforts of Being Conventional

The average college student today, then, needs to pay attention chiefly to situation when he makes his choice of appropriate language. In his writing, except some of his personal letters and private memoranda, he would be wise to assume that the situation requires the standard English generally expected by educated readers. By so doing, the writer enjoys all the advantages of convention. He quietly acquires the status symbol that marks him as a member of the intellectual in-group. For such is the effect of conventions: even rebels make unconventionality—beards, sandals, Zen Buddhism or peyote—the conventions of their group. The convenience of an accepted code which reduces his area of decision allows the writer to concentrate on more important aspects of writing.

Habits are great conservers of energy, and language habits are no exception; the beginning of wisdom is to husband our energies for things that matter. Obviously, if we want to get somewhere, we take advantage of established roads and strike off across the open country only when we reach the pathless frontier. The rules of grammar, the formulas of usage, the idioms of language are the established roads. With an excess of pioneer spirit I once climbed a rugged mountain, only to discover that a good road went up the other side. Perhaps I profited from the exercise and the temporary illusion, but for all practical purposes I wasted a great deal of energy. Some prose stylists, like Thomas Carlyle and James Joyce, disdain the highways and triumphantly cut their own ways, as if they could remake the English language. But even they pay a penalty for their perverse originality, and in this area most of us had better enjoy the comforts of unoriginality. Such comforts are not inconsiderable. Men of our era can take advantage of the relative uniformity of dress and need expend little energy in their choice of costume. In writing, our originality and creativity can profitably go into areas beyond the rules of grammar and usage, once we come to terms with the rules and make their observance as habitual as possible.

It is no more profitable to argue about the conventions of grammatical structure than to cite precedent to a basketball referee. In a recent exchange of letters in the *Saturday Review* one correspondent vigorously defended the use of "like" as a conjunction, cited the *Dictionary of Contemporary American Usage* and examples in the *Encyclopaedia Britannica* and respected writers from Shakespeare to Shaw, and ended with a plea that purists not concern themselves with such "trivia" as insisting that "as" is the proper form. Such an attitude is understandable: nearly everybody is against pedantry, red tape, and sin—but definitions vary. "Trivia" may perhaps be defined as little things important to somebody else. The hard truth is that generations of educated people have come to feel that one ought not to write that something "tastes good *like* it should." Any writer who elects to use "like" as a conjunction in a serious piece of writing can count on distracting many readers by calling attention to a form which will ring false. Even if readers are tolerant enough to accept an alternative usage, their concentration has been disturbed. Grammatical usage should not call attention to itself at the expense of the train of thought. Perhaps by any objective standards this distinction between "like" and "as" is trivial, but as we shall see, subjective standards are important to readers. In the long view the author, as Coleridge said, "creates the taste by which he is appreciated." At shorter range it is the reader who determines the rules by which the game is to be played. Therefore, even if a writer believes that "ain't" is a perfectly respectable form and buttresses his opinion with the approval of *Webster's Third New International Dictionary,* he must realize that many, probably most of his readers, will not agree.

Perhaps some day "like" and "as" will be interchangeable as conjunctions, and "ain't" will be widely accepted. No longer is it considered heinous to split infinitives; and Winston Churchill made devastating fun of the old prohibition against prepositions at the end of a sentence: "This is something up with which I will not put." Nevertheless, some prejudice still exists, and it is just as well not to put prepositions at the end of sentences or to split infinitives *if* there are *graceful* alternatives. In all such matters a writer is well advised to be conservative and conventional, saving his independence and originality for areas in which they can be assets—in the necessary art of rhetoric.

Some Shibboleths of Usage

Here are some more "trivia" which will be more or less important to educated readers. The student should consider the wisdom of conforming to the accepted usage.

Can—may The distinction between "can" and "may," although much obscured in contemporary usage, is worth remembering: "can" for ability, "may" for permission or possibility:

Can I squeeze in? (Is there room?)
May I squeeze in? (Am I allowed to?)
I may try to squeeze in. (Possibly I will or I am permitted to.)

Comparisons In precise style comparisons should be completed:

Medical science has developed more effective painkillers than were available even ten years ago.

If the sentence had stopped after "painkillers," it would have made vague sense because it would have implied "than before"; but it would not have specified what was being compared. Conceivably the meaning could have been "more effective painkillers than healing drugs" or "more effective painkillers than is generally recognized."

The expanded version is much clearer. (Here it is safe to imply "than the short version.")

Contractions Although common enough in spoken English and informal writing, contractions are not usually desirable in formal contexts.

Different The colloquial "different than" is still not sure to have a good reception. "Different from" is safer:

The party was totally different from what I had expected.

Due to Passions are probably no longer aroused over the issue, but it is just as well to keep "due to" for adjectival constructions and use "owing to" when a preposition is needed:

He fell, *owing to* the slippery surface of the rock.
His fall was *due to* the slippery surface of the rock.

Fragments Deliberate sentence fragments, intentionally constructed without an expressed subject or predicate and still clear enough, can be used for good cause in informal writing. In formal writing they are much less likely to be admissible. Real sentence fragments, of course (see Chapter Eight), are not acceptable in any writing except dialogue, where they may be needed, for example, for characterization.

Imply–infer Even though in popular usage "infer" often means the same thing as "imply," many readers resent the blurring of a useful distinction:

I inferred that you implied that I was mistaken.

Reason is In the construction "the reason is because" the "because" is redundant:

The reason for my getting up early is that I couldn't sleep.

Subjunctive The subjunctive is not important in modern English, but it still survives in some uses. Its identifying forms are "be" instead of "am," "are" or "is"; "were" instead of "was"; "have" instead of "has"; and in other verbs the omission of the terminal "s" in the third person singular. The subjunctive is used, and will be expected, in certain formulas of invocation or positive assertion ("*be* it upon your head," "suffic*e* it to say"); in clauses beginning with "that" in resolutions, recommendations, and formal suggestions ("he will urge that the chairman reconsider his ruling"); and in conditional clauses which present a hypothesis that is not true ("if I *were* you"). The subjunctive may be used, but is not required, in dubious conditions ("if the prophecy *be* true, we are lost"; "I could not help wondering whether he *were* coming") and in wishes ("I wish I *were* through").

Superlatives Careful usage requires that the superlative be employed only when three or more objects are compared, and not simply as an intensive:

Which of the two ships is the faster? (not "fastest")
This is the best ice cream I ever tasted! (not just "the best ice cream!")

Than In formal writing "than" is preferably used as a conjunction, not as a preposition:

My competitor thought he was smarter than *I*. (i.e., *than I was*—not "than me")

Very Some readers expect "very" not to be used with past participles without the interposition of "much":

I am very glad to see you.
but
I am very *much* annoyed by your action.

Whether Formal English requires "whether" in indirect questions, not "if":

The lawyer asked *whether* he could change his client's plea.

Who–whom Traditionally "who" is the subject form of the interrogative and relative pronoun, "whom" the object; and this distinction is still preferred in a formal style:

Who is that? (subject of "is")
Whom did you call? (object of "did call")
We called the man *who* came last time. (subject of "came")
We called the man *whom* you recommended. (object of "recommended")
but note well:
We called the man *who* you said was a reliable plumber. (subject of "was")

In spoken and informal English "who" is now likely to be used at the beginning of a sentence, or in a normal *subject position,* even though it is actually an object:

Who did you call?

None of these injunctions is worth fighting over, and most of them are, in a way, trivial. They do not deal with the really important things in writing; to concentrate upon them would be defeating. On the other hand, they are venerable shibboleths which take on significance as they are important to educated readers. At worst they are harmless concessions; at best they preserve useful distinctions which increase the precision and resources of the language. The wise writer simply learns them as he would the multiplication table, and goes on to more important things.

ASSIGNMENTS

1. You are in some way subject to several different sets of rules, regulations, and conventions deriving from systems such as your country, state, locality, fraternity, home, school, and social and age group. Write an essay in which you consider what the effects would be if it were possible suddenly to repeal one of these "codes."

2. Write an essay on the advantages of habitual action, illustrating from your own experience.

3. From your reading or conversation make a list of ten words which you believe are not in any circle of usage normal to you. Write an essay in which you describe the circle of usage in which one or more of these is most likely to be found.

4. By discussion with older friends compile a glossary of dated slang and use it for the basis of an essay on the temporal changes of language.

5. Read some "local color" short stories, like those of Sarah Orne Jewett, Mary Wilkins Freeman, or Joel Chandler Harris, and make a list of regional language patterns you found. Experiment with "translating" a section into standard English. Write an essay on the literary effects of the use of the regionalisms.

6. Write an essay arguing for or against an Academy of American English as an authority to rule on questions on the state of the language. Choose any grounds which seem to you valid, but be sure to recognize the existence of other arguments.

7. Pay particular attention to what you read, write, and say for one day. Then write an essay on the role of rhetoric in a day of your life.

8. As a child perhaps you played at making up a private language. Try to do it now, and write an essay on the experience—the difficulties involved, what you learned from it.

9. Pick from your experience some detail which is intrinsically trivial yet which has taken on signficance. Write an essay in which you examine the reasons for that acquired importance.

10. Correct or justify the following sentences:

a. Jet service to Chicago is faster.

b. Your opinions are very different than I had expected.

c. Although I had lost my ticket I asked if I could be admitted.

d. His dislike of Spenser's *Fairy Queen* is due to his difficulty in following the allegory.

e. The reason for his difficulty is his ignorance of Elizabethan affairs.

f. Due to his heavy schedule he was unable to accept our invitation.

g. Whatever the outcome be, he is committed to accept it.

h. The reason I am very pleased is because I received an announcement that I will be awarded a scholarship.

i. He moved that the meeting be adjourned.

j. Between Milton and Shakespeare, Shakespeare is the most original poet, according to a poll I read of.

k. Whether or not you wish to be consulted more than him.

l. He did well, like I expected him to be able to easily do.

CHAPTER TWO

Rhetoric and the Self

As the art of persuasion, rhetoric requires an author to take a stand—to choose a subject and develop an attitude toward it. In so doing he commits himself, defines himself, and enriches himself. A wise student of human nature once declared, "As a man thinketh in his heart, so is he." Since rhetoric is the instrument for ordering and articulating those thoughts, it is literally a means of creating one's self in one's own image. The use of rhetoric, then, is a very personal experience; and yet it must also have a large impersonal element. "Language," according to an Arabian proverb, "takes one into a far country." These complex relations of rhetoric and the author's self are worth some investigation.

Many factors may obscure the personal character of writing. Some of my readers may be wondering, for instance, how they can create themselves in assigned themes, say 500 words on "A Campus Tradition." We will deal with that problem specifically later, but we need to realize that no matter how artificial the situation, a man's writing expresses some part of himself, through what he says or does not say. If an author misrepresents himself deliberately or unwittingly, he still expresses something about his duplicity or ineptness. If he assumes a role—and good authors are, as Keats said, "chameleon"—it must still be a role congenial to him, a voice he can control. Something of the writer's true self is inevitably there. Writing is the most personal thing of enduring character that most of us are called upon to do.

Admittedly, a vast mechanism of routine modifies and restricts the

nt in our writing. We cannot even write a personal
being tempted into formulas of salutation and closing.
n the classes I taught at a research corporation wanted
in prefabricated formats for their reports. They ar-
e is impersonal and much effort is saved by routine.
of science are impersonal; but their relations to the
em are not. True, routine report forms can be writ-
mum of effort—but they can also be read with the
ect. A scientific report does not call for purple prose
ginality of form: the established routines are a pro-
nvenience. They cannot, however, prevent the in-
e writer from revealing itself, if only in some detail.
confessed to me that
nslating

tween
Sincerity is vital to good writing, but
complex way. What does sincerity mean in th
in writing means honesty—not literalism but integrit
be literally true to life, but it must not be essentially false
Affectation and pretention are errors in any field. We recognize them
most clearly as social blunders and quickly feel contempt and pity for
the phoney. Such fakery is just as egregious in rhetoric—more so,
because it is more permanent and more difficult to hide. The folk
wisdom of honesty being the best policy is valid in writing. Here
honesty involves several things, from self-knowledge to self-dedi-
cation.

Know Yourself

"Know thyself," advised Socrates. Taken too literally this is impossible counsel, and I do not urge my readers to embark upon do-it-
yourself psychoanalysis. Nevertheless, when you begin a writing
project face up honestly to what kind of person you are, what your
concerns, interests, attitudes, and aptitudes are. You can know yourself to that extent, and it will pay you to make the effort. What do
you spend most of your time doing? What do you know most about?
In some area you are more or less expert. What is it? Whatever it is—
coin collecting or scuba diving, Civil War generals or blondes, elec-
trotherapy or civil rights—it is an asset, a resource which may be
exploited. In that field you have most of yourself invested and you
can draw upon the account. Are your tendencies liberal or conservative, romantic or realistic, democratic or authoritarian? An accurate

...e he was "a hyphen man." Even
...machine took on character by persistent
...ater goat," finally recognized as meaning "hy-

THE PROBLEM OF SINCERITY

Just as we realize that we put something of ourselves on paper, we must also recognize that much of ourselves we cannot put there. Demands of convention, propriety or the limitations of the medium restrict us. This is the old conundrum of art, the paradox of sincerity and artistry. Art can be truer than life, but it cannot be true to life. Art, for example, must be ordered, no matter how chaotic life is. A student who had read in a handbook about the use of the personality as an organizing device answered my complaint that his essay was confused by saying, "But I have a disorganized personality." Maybe he did, but he still rated an *F* on the paper. Unknowingly he had fallen into what has been called the fallacy of representational form. A novelist who wants to capture the boredom of modern life cannot afford to do so by making his novel boring. Similarly a writer must be clear even in the delineation of confusion.

Art is ordered because it is selective. Out of the vast continuum of existence a very small amount can be recorded, although "of the making of books there is no end." We know and feel more than we can articulate; and we articulate daily more than we could tran scribe, even if we set ourselves to do so. Our writing is a limited

selected version of our real selves. Sir Phillip Sidney ...
to cry out in the agonies of composition,

> Biting my truant pen, beating myself for spite,
> "Fool," said my muse to me, "look in thy heart a...
> *Astrophel and ...*

A fine poetic fancy, and partly good advice—the ma...
write from the heart has given himself a handicap. B...
leading, for not even so fine a Renaissance gentl...
could find a sonnet ready-made in his heart. Althou...
wrote have a kind of sincerity, they also show the e...
ventions of the genre. Always some compromise m...
the inner man and his shape on paper. ...but obviously i... ...his c...

answer can suggest areas of enthusiasm and conviction in which you could write with power. The process of drawing on oneself is circular in a double way. The writer must know himself if he is to write effectively—and by his writing, if he is honest, he comes better to know himself. He draws upon the resources of himself to write—and by his writing he enriches and strengthens himself.

The author's need to know himself does not apply only to his openly autobiographical writing or mean that he should always draw upon his hobbies and interests; for college assignments he could not if he wanted to. More often than he at first supposes, he will find natural connections between assigned topics and his own interests, and such ties will frequently add a vital spark to his work; but he certainly should not try to drag his personal concerns into every theme. What is essential is that he recognize writing as a truly intimate activity, both the fuel and the flame of his own being, not something to be entered into off-handedly or mechanically—even to fulfill a theme assignment. Writing demands and propagates self-knowledge, and in this fundamental way must be sincere.

"Know What You Can Work At"

Thomas Carlyle thought that he was making a pragmatic improvement on Socrates' dictum when he recommended changing it to "Know what you can work at." For our purposes as writers the suggestion is apt. We need to recognize what we can do, and what we cannot. We cannot all work successfully at every kind of writing. Although it is a difficult realization, since most of us will admit any fault except the lack of a sense of humor, a little honesty will force some of us to recognize that we have no light touch, that we had better not try to trifle with whimsy. Some of us have logical or factual minds; others, narrative or dramatic bents. Some of us are happily at home with pack-rat accumulations which to others would appear smothering chaos. Samuel Johnson once defined a lexicographer as a "harmless drudge." The phrase reflects comic self-depreciation, but certainly dictionary making is a kind of drudgery not every writer could stomach. It is only common sense for a writer to try to know what he can work at, and not make his tasks more difficult by attempting to do something that is uncongenial to him or perhaps even impossible to his talents and knowledge.

Inexperienced writers are often tempted to try projects for which they lack the equipment. Freshmen, for instance, are addicted to dealing in irony and satire, although usually they have neither the command of the subtleties of language nor the knowledge of their subjects necessary to produce such effects. Several motives influence young writers to get out of their depths. One is undoubtedly the desire to appear sophisticated, a desire which makes anything simple and obvious seem to them suspect. But the greatest writing has the touch of simplicity and the most profound verges upon the obvious. Consider the "Lord's Prayer" or Lincoln's "Gettysburg Address." Real sophistication has the subtlety to hide art and make the simple appear inevitably right. Remember the beautifully easy ending of *Huckleberry Finn:*

> Tom's most well now, and got his bullet around his neck on a watch-guard for a watch, and is always seeing what time it is, and so there ain't nothing more to write about, and I am rotten glad of it, because if I'd 'a' knowed what a trouble it was to make a book I wouldn't 'a' tackled it, and ain't a-going to no more. But I reckon I got to light out for the territory ahead of the rest, because Aunt Sally she's going to adopt me and sivilize me, and I can't stand it. I been there before.

Another motive that often leads student writers into impossible situations is fear born of an unrealistic attitude toward what can be said in a given number of words. Tailoring an essay to a specified word length is, of course, artificial, and most instructors would prefer to make assignments without such specifications. Students, however, tend to flounder miserably unless they feel that they know what is expected. Furthermore, economic limitations of publishing often force editors to set word limits, so that we might as well face the reality of having to write a certain number of words. Most of us can recognize—even if too late—the temporal illusions that frequently lead us to believe we can do more in a limited period of time than we really can. Similar illusions can beguile students into supposing that 1500 words, say, is a lot of words, that they cannot conceivably write so many unless they have a grandiose subject. Therefore, when they have the option, they choose something like "The Rise and Fall of Japan as a World Power" or "The Life Cycles of Fresh Water Fishes"—not because they are especially interested in the subjects, but because they have a great deal of material available and they feel quite secure about being able to produce the required number of words. Unfortunately this sense of security may be misleading, because such subjects are difficult to treat adequately in just 1500 words. Brevity ceases to be a virtue if it results in superficiality or undeveloped cataloguing of main points. Of course any subject can be dealt with in some fashion at almost any length. The argument here is not necessarily *for* narrowing the subject but *against* choosing subjects primarily because the wordage will be easy. Such choice is dishonest and may mean failure.

Honesty in writing means finally an honest effort. Slovenliness and half-heartedness suck the life from writing. It is possible to take a high moral view of this matter: Robert Louis Stevenson, who had the soul of a sturdy Scottish covenanter despite all his Bohemian adventuresomeness, once declared in *Lay Morals* (chap. 2):

> Every piece of work which is not as good as you can make it, which you have palmed off imperfect, meagrely thought, niggardly in execution, upon mankind, who is your paymaster on parole, and in a sense your pupil, every hasty or slovenly or untrue performance, should rise up against you in the court of your own heart and condemn you for a thief.

Every piece of writing which is "not as good as you can make it" is a cheat imposed upon everyone who will read it. It always rings false, and the ultimate victim of the cheat is the author himself. From a purely practical point of view, less than an honest effort does not pay. The slack author does not achieve self-knowledge and self-realization. He blocks his own growth: if he never works to the limits of his ability he will never extend those limits. And he fails to make the desired effect upon his readers: he does not persuade or move—or get a satisfactory grade.

Realism dictates some modification, however, of this counsel of perfection. The old proverb to the contrary notwithstanding, many things are worth doing only moderately well. One can get a great deal of pleasure from skiing or playing chess without being an expert or even exerting all of his energies. On the other hand, there is a point of noncommitment beyond which pleasure and profit cease. One must care, and take care, or the whole activity becomes too desultory to be rewarding. The highest rewards—and the most pain of effort—come to the writer who can dedicate himself unreservedly to the pursuit of perfection. For most of us such dedication is impossible; but some dedication, some commitment of self, is necessary to the achievement of any success and the realization of any pleasure. Much of our writing, especially college writing, is produced under circumstances of pressure which cause it to be less good than we could make it if we had more time and fewer distractions. Not everything put on paper can be a *magnum opus*. But it need not be "palmed off imperfect" either; it may still be an honest effort on a more modest scale, well enough done to be worth doing. After collecting a set of papers from a class, Robert Frost once asked whether there was anything in the lot anybody wanted to keep. When no one professed that much concern, he protested that he was "no perfunctory reader of perfunctory writing" and threw the whole batch in the trash basket. Few teachers are so bold, but every reader feels the waste of perfunctory writing, writing without commitment. No paper we write should have so little of us in it, represent so small an expenditure of self, that we don't even care what happens to it.

Be Yourself

Anyone who has ever posed for a photograph and been told to look natural knows how impossible it is. Not only would injunctions to write naturally probably prove as futile, but also the natural man might turn out to be a poor writer. Writing, as a skill and an art, is a kind of imposition on the natural; in Willa Cather's words, "It takes a great deal of experience to become natural." Being oneself, then, does not mean being natural in any simple sense. Fortunately, the process is susceptible to conscious control in ways that our facial muscles generally are not when confronted by a camera. One tries to be himself in writing, not only by developing a subject that is within his competence and reflects his genuine interests, but also by making the level of the whole performance appropriate to himself. In matters of vocabulary and syntax the inexperienced writer needs particularly to be careful. One of my students once wrote that his girl was "highly figurative." I congratulated him but gently pointed out that the word did not mean quite what he had supposed. It was obviously a word over his head; he was reaching, and unwittingly revealed his limitations.

On the level with which we are familiar, most of us can do our best writing. The student who invariably gets tangled in involved syntactical creations can frequently be quite impressive with vigorous sentence rhythms native to his ear, which he has scorned because he has some notion, perhaps unformulated, that when he writes he cannot be himself; it does not seem "fine" enough for the occasion. Is it a tribute to our modesty or a sign of our ambition that most of us feel this urge to strain when we write? If we could only relax a little, be more nearly true to ourselves, we could be more successful. "Fine writing" is an abomination unto the reader and a pest forever, and this sentence is an example of the breed.

Being oneself on paper is not at all writing as one talks. Certainly there can be similarities between a spoken and a written style, but nobody really writes as he talks. If he approaches it, he is either a "talking book" (once said of Macaulay) or a sloppy writer. Even written dialogue is condensed and structured beyond actual speech. To try to write as one talks would be to violate the principle of appropriateness to the situation. The relative permanence of the written word demands a formality and order that would appear stiff and precious in oral exchanges. Similarly, the rhythms and patterns of spoken language seem lax, tentative, and uncomposed by the standards of written English. The two worlds meet, but they remain distinct.

Being ourselves does not require that we always accept the limitations of yesterday's horizons or stick to the subjects with which we are currently familiar. Writing is pre-eminently a learning process, and we learn in part by consolidating the old, in part by venturing on to the new. As I look back at my undergraduate days, I find that the subjects about which I remember the most are those on which I wrote term papers, and much of that information I did not have when I launched upon the projects. One may also venture gingerly to use diction and syntax a bit outside the usual range. How then do we avoid getting in over our heads? Not by just thumbing thesauri and dictionaries! These works indeed exist for the purpose of helping us extend our range, but they should be used to check new words rather than to seek them.[1] Taking a word from a list of synonyms without having had any experience of its use in context is dangerous. We will do better to notice words and phrases in our reading, compare them in different settings, and perhaps try them out in conversation before we use them in serious writing. After we have assimilated the new material and are sure that we have com-

[1] See pp. 239, 241.

mand over it, we may be true to ourselves in using it. Otherwise our stilts will be showing. The only reliable way to be taller is to grow.

Before we have grown, sometimes we have to be lifted up, perhaps to stand on the shoulders of somebody else. This support, indeed, is part of growing up, and being ourselves includes exploration of our own literary backgrounds. Pristine freshness is delightful and desirable, and in a sense each writer should see the world with the unspoiled vision of a child, but a child of his own time, with a rich heritage. Even such Romantic glorifiers of the vision of childhood as Blake and Wordsworth—who did much to shake out the set wrinkles of literary convention and remove the "film of familiarity" from life—even they drew much from writers who went before them. Their early work is full of echoes and influences.

Robert Louis Stevenson left us a clearer personal account of standing on the shoulders of the past than do most writers:

> Whenever I read a book or a passage that particularly pleased me, in which a thing was said or an effect rendered with propriety, in which there was either some conspicuous force or some happy distinction in the style, I must sit down at once and set myself to ape that quality. I was unsuccessful, and I knew it; and tried again, and was again unsuccessful and always unsuccessful; but at least in these vain bouts, I got some practice in rhythm, in harmony, in construction and the coordination of parts. I have thus played the sedulous ape to Hazlitt, to Lamb, to Wordsworth, to Sir Thomas Browne, to Defoe, to Hawthorne, to Montaigne, to Baudelaire and to Obermann. I remember one of these monkey tricks, which was called *The Vanity of Morals:* it was to have a second part, *The Vanity of Knowledge;* and as I had neither morality nor scholarship, the names were apt; but the second part was never attempted, and the first part was written (which is my reason for recalling it, ghostlike, from its ashes) no less than three times: first in the manner of Hazlitt, second in the manner of Ruskin, who had cast on me a passing spell, and third, in a laborious pasticcio of Sir Thomas Browne.
>
> "A College Magazine," *Memories and Portraits*

Stevenson's "monkey tricks" are deliberate, conscious imitation—the apprentice exercises of a craftsman learning from masters of the art. The productions of all this effort were a sort of prewriting, fit only to be consigned to "ashes"; but the phoenix of Stevenson's own style rose from them. Not all use of the past is so deliberate, and even after Stevenson had served his youthful apprenticeship of playing the "sedulous ape" he retained some unconscious residue of what he had learned and transmuted it into his own patterns. Thus we all build up the selves we bring to our writing.

STYLE

If we succeed in being ourselves on paper, we have achieved that magical something called "style." This term has been much used and abused. Often it connotes the latest decrees from Paris on women's clothes, in which case it actually refers to the individual taste of Dior or some other designer. As Buffon put it, *le stile c'est l'homme même* —style is the man. Style is the incarnation of the personality, the embodiment of the flavor of the individual, the sum total of all the idiosyncratic details which are combined uniquely in the manner of a man. This includes his style of walking, talking, and taking a bath. We easily recognize styles in popular music and differences between the patterns of, for example, Lawrence Welk and Louis Armstrong. Such differences are personal, and often subtle, but for the most part they manifest themselves and are analyzable in pitch, rhythm, balance, and timbre.

Much of the same is true of writing. "What a piece of work is man," said Hamlet; yet this paragon can be shadowed forth by a collection of marks on a page, an assemblage of words and sentences. Style is finally mysterious, but its materials are commonplace. We can talk about them, and we shall for the rest of this book. They are devices for being true to ourselves on paper, and are more or less available to everyone. Modest young writers sometimes seem to assume that only established literary artists have style, that it is something for a Hemingway or a Faulkner, but not for them. Of course some styles are more marked than others, because some personalities are stronger than others. Some styles are more successful incarnations than others because some writers have better command of the devices of self-expression. But everyone has a style of sorts, just as everyone has a shadow. Wonderful effects can be produced by varying the direction and intensity of the light, but one cannot escape except in darkness.

BENDING ASSIGNMENTS TO FIT YOU

The whole concept of rhetoric as a means of self-expression is pertinent even in the hothouse atmosphere of a freshman composition course. For the benefit of the sceptic let us consider the unpromising assignment mentioned earlier, an essay on "Campus Traditions." How can one use it to know himself, and express himself? By knowing what he can work at, how can the student make the most of such an undertaking?

A freshman new to the campus is not likely to know very much about campus traditions. What he does know and should examine is his own attitude toward them. Does he admire and hallow traditions, or does he tend to mock them? Do they appear to him pageantry which dramatizes and preserves the values of the past or shells of gone-by pomp exploited for propaganda purposes? Once he has established his attitude, he knows the line he can take. If he unconsciously allows himself to remain ambivalent on this question, his essay may be incoherent or even contradictory. It may beat the drums of school spirit in the opening paragraph, and end with a sneer. Of course, he can consciously deal with these two alternative points of view, put his paper into the form of a debate on their validity, and possibly conclude that there is some truth in each position. The point is that he must *know* his position and how he can work with such a topic.

If the student is sceptical about the merits of campus traditions, he need not make a direct attack upon them; he may develop other approaches which undercut them. He may, for instance, consider the relatively ephemeral character of traditions in a college society, where the turnover is large and continuous. He may do a little research in the files of the college newspaper and write on traditions which were once honored on the campus but have quietly faded away. Or he may investigate the origin of some traditions currently observed and perhaps show their relative modernity. He will probably be able to find evidence of deliberate efforts to start traditions and will be able to examine the motivation behind them.

The student, whether generally for or against traditions, will certainly have had some experience with them in his home, high school, church or community. He may draw upon this knowledge by finding some way to relate these to campus traditions. Why does his mother's family always get together for Thanksgiving reunion and his father's never see very much of each other? If he is of a philosophical turn of mind, he may speculate on the "why" of campus traditions. Why do they develop in an academic situation? Is it because academics are wont to be conservative? Or because since they usually work with the past, they delight to honor it? Or because educational institutions are among the most ancient of preserved foundations (Oxford, Cambridge, the Sorbonne, Liège) and even colleges lately sprung up like to imitate their pomp?

A good paper could be made by treating only one tradition. Here again a student should choose within his field of interest and competence. On every campus there are traditions related to a variety of interests: athletics, some cherished song for those interested in music, honored noteworthy personalities for the social-minded. Freshmen are specially concerned with the traditional privileges of and restrictions upon their group, and they might write effectively, even passionately, on the subject. A sophomore transfer from another school might deal with the same subject from his lofty objectivity. The possibilities of personal permutations are almost infinite. An engineering student might do an excellent essay on the calorific value of the annual "Big Game Bonfire," calculating how much work might be done by it or how many homes heated. The student interested in anthropology might compare campus traditions to tribal rites; the business administration major could examine the advertising techniques used in the maintenance of tradition; sociologists and psychologists might consider the effects of tradition in motivating and integrating students into the campus community.

IMPERSONAL PERSONALITY

Our discussion of the "Campus Traditions" theme reminds us again that even though writing is a vital means of self-expression, it has a paradoxical element of impersonality. After all, one must connect one's personality with something outside of oneself. The purely personal approach is limiting and monotonous. No matter how engrossing we find our ideas, generally, except for members of our families, nobody cares much about them simply because they are our ideas. We need to be sure that they are interesting in themselves, that they contain significant substance, that they make some kind of contribution to the edification or amusement of the reader. We are most likely to be successful at this if we commit ourselves to the task but also realize that personal commitment is not enough. We must extend and objectify, not stop with a subjective approach:

I don't like campus traditions; they seem just plain silly. I would rather develop my own values than take easy ready-made ones.

But go on to an objective development:

Much of the appeal of campus traditions is probably due to insecure and immature students who lack the energy and courage to put down their own roots and, therefore, are glad to try to graft themselves onto a common stock.

Commitment must not generate egotism, or even appear to do so since in writing appearances are all the reader has to go by. One way to make a kind of check on the subjectivity of your approach is to look over a page of your rough draft and circle the first person pronoun every time it shows up. Suppose you find a large number of "I" 's, should you attempt to remove many of them, and if so, how? The first person singular is not necessarily a bad word. Consider whether the situation, including the relationships between subject, reader, and writer, properly calls for the author to appear prominently. A subject such as the United Nations would normally be treated in an impersonal manner. The reader would probably not be as interested in the average writer's personal relations to the topic—how he happened to become concerned with the United Nations, his private opinions concerning its success or future—as in the arguments presented to support these opinions. If the author had some status as an authority, of course the situation would change: based on his experience, his opinions would have weight and significance. The status of authority, however, is relative, depending upon the connection between the writer and the reader. Any author is important enough to some readers for his "I think" to be desired and valued. Your mother would gladly read your personal reactions to the United Nations. A foreign student from, say, Nigeria could appropriately write personally of his views about the United Nations because they would be of special interest to an American audience, even though he might disavow any intention of representing his countrymen.

If the situation invites or permits a personal approach, a sprinkling of "I" 's is not objectionable. When you are really bringing yourself into the picture, better admit the fact easily and naturally rather than look for some clumsy disguise such as the third person, the editorial "we" or the passive voice. The personal active "I have heard" is usually more effective than the impersonal passive "it has been reported." Conversely, when the situation does not admit the personal tone, it is preferable to root out the subjective approach and not try to hide the "I" 's behind some circumlocution. The following sentences might appear in an essay on the United Nations:

I believe the UN is doomed.

The UN, I believe, is doomed.

The UN, the author believes, is doomed.

The UN, one is forced to believe, is doomed.

The UN, it has been suggested, is doomed.

If your opinion is important, the first sentence is best: it is frank and forthright. The second suggests a self-depreciatory qualification, "of course, this is just my opinion," which may be modesty, but appears flabby. The third is stiff, perhaps suited to some kinds of formal writing, but generally to be suspected. The fourth provides a kind of false anonymity, and the last goes further by shifting the onus of the opinion to others. Sometimes such a phrase is pure fakery—the writer has no definite outside suggestions in mind but does not want to take responsibility for the idea. If there are specific suggesters, it is better to cite them concretely: "according to a poll of newsmen assigned to the UN headquarters," not "according to informed observers." On the whole, it would probably be preferable to write simply, "The UN is doomed," and follow up with your reason for thinking so: "No nation is willing to surrender sovereignty in matters important to itself."

The "I" 's which spatter your drafts may be even less defensible than some of those in our imaginary essay on the United Nations. They may set up as matters of opinion what properly belongs in the realm of fact. The student who wrote, "Chicago, I believe, is the second largest city in the United States," was merely too lazy to verify his facts. Mock modesty which seeks to exploit the writer's ignorance is an insult to the reader. It would not be much better to write, "As far as I know, there are no campus traditions concerning food." You may not have certain knowledge, but justify its limitations: "The files of the college handbooks and of *The Collegian* for the past twenty years reveal no campus traditions concerning food."

Responsible treatment of facts, proper use of and smooth transition between the personal and the impersonal, the subjective and the objective—these are the marks of maturity in writing and in life. A preponderance of first-person singular references may be appropriate enough to the subject, and yet the subject itself may not be suitable for a mature occasion. If "I" 's sprinkle your pages, the reason may be that you are favoring such anecdotal topics as "My Last Summer's Vacation" or "My First Date." Unless the reader is or can be made interested in *you,* personal anecdotes must depend on strong narrative value. The narrative value may not be great enough to sustain an account of what happened on your first date—probably of interest only to the two people chiefly involved. In addition, since they are the sole authorities on what really happened, the reader has nothing with which to check the authenticity of the record except his notions of plausibility. He is not invited to participate except as a spectator in a performance which is self-centered; and this should not be confused with self-expression. Children are primarily self-centered, but adults learn to extend their concerns. College students should develop their subjects so that instructors have an opportunity to check the responsibility of their writing. You can do this even with a subject like "My First Date" if you transcend the purely narrative by attempting to draw generalizations about the typical awkwardness of a first date or its function as an initiation ceremony in our society or the cultural changes which probably brought you to this experience at an earlier age than was characteristic of your father's generation.

Rhetoric at its best is both eminently personal and transcendently impersonal. It enriches the self by extending the self.

ASSIGNMENTS

1. Make a list of ten subjects conceivably within the range of college students, but on which you think *you* ought not to try to write. Then do one or more of the following:

a. Take one of them and write an essay explaining why you consider it inappropriate for you.

b. Take one and write an essay describing the kind of person you think could write well on it.

c. Take one and see if you can find some way to twist or modify it so that you could write on it—then do so.

2. Make a list of ten subjects on which you think you are qualified to write. Then do one or more of the following:

a. Write an essay in which you explain why you think you are qualified to write on these subjects.

b. Exchange lists with another member of the class and write an essay trying to construct the personality of the author of the list from the choices indicated.

c. Write an essay in which you compare, contrast, and rank the topics on your list in terms of the extent to which they will call for *impersonal* materials.

d. Choose from your list the subject you like best and write an essay on it.

3. Choose from any source ten sentences which you think you could not or would not have written. Rewrite them in diction and syntax which suits you. After you have studied Chapter Eight you might like to try this assignment again.

4. Here are two passages in quite different styles. Examine the passages carefully and find as many specific differences between them as you can. Look particularly at vocabulary and sentence structure. Write an essay in which you describe the differences you find. If you can, suggest how these differences contribute to different tones in the two passages. You might be interested in looking up some information about Bunyan and Thurber and speculating on how their styles fit their personalities.

> As I walked through the wilderness of this world, I lighted on a certain place where was a Den, and I laid me down in that place to sleep: and, as I slept, I dreamed a dream. I dreamed, and behold, I saw a man clothed with rags, standing in a certain place, with his face from his own house, a book in his hand, and a great burden upon his back. I looked, and saw him open the book, and read therein; and, as he read, he wept, and trembled: and, not being able longer to contain, he brake out with a lamentable cry, saying *What shall I do?*
>
> JOHN BUNYAN, *The Pilgrim's Progress*

> There was nothing more that I could say or do. I went home. That night, however, I found that I had not really dismissed the whole ridiculous affair, as I hoped I had, for I dreamed about it. I had tried to ignore the thing, but it had tunnelled deeply into my subconscious. I dreamed that I was out hunting with the Winships and that, as we crossed a snowy field, Marcia spotted a rabbit and, taking quick aim, fired and brought it down. We all ran across the snow

toward the rabbit, but I reached it first. It was quite dead, but that was not what struck horror into me as I picked it up. What struck horror into me was that it was a white rabbit and was wearing a vest and carrying a watch. I woke up with a start. I don't know whether that dream means that I am on Gordon's side or on Marcia's. I don't want to analyze it. I am trying to forget the whole miserable business.

JAMES THURBER, "The Breaking Up of the Winships"[2]

5. Using the information you have garnered on the characteristics of the two styles illustrated above, try to write a paragraph of your own using the devices you find typical of one of them.

6. Find a paragraph in a style which interests you, copy it, read it aloud several times, analyze it, and "play the sedulous ape" by trying to write something of your own imitating that style. Write another paragraph explaining whether you found the imitation difficult or easy and why.

7. Read over something you have written and ask yourself how much of you it reveals. Which face have you put on for the occasion? Write an essay on the face you chose and why.

8. "Fine writing" is hard to demonstrate out of context. See if you can find some examples of strained, elaborate style—maybe in your own writing.

9. For one of the following subjects, make a list of ways in which it impinges upon your personal interests enough for you to be able to write about it with commitment:

a. If the United States is going to make a satisfactory showing in Olympic competition, we must relax our conception of amateur standing.

b. American colleges would do well to adopt the British tutorial system.

c. College students participate in Civil Rights demonstrations out of a variety of motives.

d. The reception of singing groups such as the Beatles reveals a hunger for novelty in American popular music.

e. The private helicopter may replace the private automobile within a generation.

10. For one of the following personal subjects, make a list of ways in which it can be objectified and made of general interest.

[2] James Thurber, "The Breaking Up of the Winships," *Let Your Mind Alone!* (New York: Grosset & Dunlap, 1960).

a. Your favorite book.
b. Your last birthday.
c. Your college plans.
d. Your idea of a perfect evening.
e. Your most difficult course.

CHAPTER THREE

Rhetoric and Knowledge: Getting a Subject

Proverbially the best way to learn anything is to teach it. All of us have had the experience of discovering when we tried to explain something to somebody else that we really did not understand it ourselves. Hammering out an explanation is a good way to clarify our own ideas. Thus rhetoric functions as a way of knowing not only ourselves but also our subjects, simply because most of us need to verbalize our concepts.

Student writers frequently lament pathetically, "I know what I want to say, but I can't seem to get it down." The odds are that they really have only the fuzziest idea of what they want to say and are too lazy to work it out. There is more sense in the remark of the old lady who declared, "How do I know what I think until I hear what I say?" Honest writing is a way of finding out what we think. More than that, it is a way of making us think. As Coleridge succinctly put it, "Words think for us." Words provide a means of arresting the flux of thought and getting it down in black and white. Often it is helpful to look at the early steps of writing as just that, a way of getting down ideas and information in some more or less concrete form so that we can cope with them. At this preliminary stage we are not trying to order them or worrying about how best to present them; we simply want to know what they are. We need to evolve a technique that will help us discover rather than encourage premature formulation of undeveloped ideas.

HOW TO BEGIN

Beginning anything is usually difficult; we are all plagued by a certain amount of inertia. Students often moan that they can't get started with their writing, or they don't know how to begin. Probably nobody can tell them how they should begin, for different authors have quite different ways of getting started. It used to be fashionable to invoke the muse; Schiller depended upon the odor of decaying apples which he kept in his desk. Some writers wait for inspiration, others work with time-clock regularity. Some can compose only in the early morning, others after they are in bed at night. Some worry an idea around in conversation, others hatch it in secret incubation. The technique of beginning is an individual matter, and every writer should use the one that works for him. The following suggestions are addressed to the freshman who sits and stares hopelessly at a typewriter.

Perhaps part of his difficulty is that he is confusing two different kinds of beginning: there is the beginning of his essay, the paragraph which actually stands first on the paper; and there is the beginning of the writing process. The two are not the same. The functions of the beginning on the paper are worth going into later, but that is the *reader's* beginning. Where does the writer actually begin? He does not necessarily begin at the beginning of the piece of writing. Some authors like to get a jump-off sentence, but if one does not come, a writer cannot afford to wait for it. The likelihood is that whatever he puts down at the head of a rough draft will have to be changed anyway. Indeed, the first paragraph is often better written last. Neither does he normally begin with the title, although that will stand at the head of the finished work. A catchy title can be the inspiration for an essay; but the danger is that the essay will not fit the preselected label and the writer will not be able to bring himself to abandon it—condemning the paper to a fate like that of a girl bearing a masculine name because her parents expected a boy. Children are better named after they are born, and essays after they are written. At any rate, a writer does not wait until he gets the perfect title before he starts.

If you have trouble getting under way, try jotting down ideas and facts in the area in which you think you want to write. At this point you probably do not have a real subject, just a subject area.

Even if you think you have a subject, if you are full of something you want to say, the odds are that you still have to clarify, organize, and select from the subject area. This is also true when you are writing on an assigned topic. Although your instructor may have phrased the assignment so that he has done some selecting for you, you still have to find your *specific* subject.

Put your ideas down in the order that they occur to you; if you shuffle them around in your mind and hold one back for some other place, you are very likely to forget it as your thoughts go off in some other direction. One of the most frustrating experiences in writing is the certainty that you had some excellent idea which has now escaped you. Inevitably the ideas will come out in rough groupings, but do not commit yourself to these. If the paper is to be a short one, you may write your jottings on one piece of paper, and then experiment with rearranging them by means of arrows and brackets. If the paper is to be longer, you might find it helpful to put your materials on individual pieces of paper or cards, so that you can easily group them in different ways.[1]

PATTERNS OF GENERALIZATION

As you play with your jottings of ideas and facts, you will soon see that they can be put into several patterns. Some of these will not be useful—they may not suit the occasion, they may require more time or information to develop than are available, they may be foreign to your interests or capabilities. In any event, two things are certain about such an initial listing: you will have both more and less than you need. Your collection will sometimes be misleadingly incomplete. What seems at first glance an almost perfect subject may be invalidated by facts not in your possession. Although whatever pattern you select will require much filling in, you will find that not everything you have put down can be used, nor will it all fit into any one pattern—without violence. This is a difficult lesson for students to observe; they usually seem to be of an economical turn of mind and loath to waste ideas. Unfortunately for this understandable attitude, all along the steps of the writing process there must be

[1] See the suggestions on note-taking in Chapter Twelve.

a sloughing off of excess materials, a winnowing of the grain. Walter Pater has put it strongly but well:[2]

> For in truth all art does but consist in the removal of surplusage, from the last finish of the gem-engraver blowing away the last particle of invisible dust, back to the earliest divination of the finished work to be, lying somewhere, according to Michelangelo's fancy, in the rough-hewn block of stone.

This winnowing must be done rigorously and ruthlessly; nothing must be left which is not an essential part of the pattern selected. A common fault of student essays is that they are often little more than loose collections of tangentially related ideas. It is not enough that an idea have some demonstrable relevance to the subject; it must have a necessary and inevitable place in the development of the paper. This concept is difficult to apply, for a developing subject can engulf extraneous material which the author is reluctant to recognize as nonessential—perhaps because he has become interested in it or because he is enticed by an easy way of filling up the required number of words. He must harden himself to cut out what is not an essential part of the whole, however beguiling the excrescence may be.

Logically, what is this thing we call a "pattern"? It is really a serviceable generalization, or complex of generalizations. Students are often gun-shy of general statements. Probably at some time they have found "too general" written in the margins of their papers, and have picked up the notion that to generalize is bad. Not so. *Vague* and *unsupported* generalizations have been the cause of their readers' complaints. The ability to generalize is one of the basic tools of knowledge, the means by which we make sense of the plethora of experience. Without it we could not see the forest for the trees, or even have the concept of tree. Some primitive people have no word for "tree," but only words for "palm tree," "breadfruit tree," "papaya tree," and so on. Civilized man lives by generalizations. The only excuse a writer has for troubling a reader is that he can offer him some meaningful generalization.

Your rough jottings are in the middle of a generalization cycle. They sprang from the parent generalization, the subject area. Al-

[2] Walter Pater, "Style," *Appreciations* (New York: Macmillan, 1902), p. 16.

ready a selective and synthetic process has been going on. Out of the whole range of experience you have put down ideas which occurred to you in a certain area. These in turn constitute the data from which, plausibly, several other, perhaps narrower, generalizations can be drawn. The first step is to choose one which is congenial to you and appropriate to the situation. Then ask: "Is it sound? Is it supportable? What other material do I need to support it?"

An example. Suppose, for example, that you are going to write an essay dealing somehow with the subject of censorship. You might jot down the following bits of material as you think of them:

1. Censorship of books.
2. Censorship of movies.
3. Censorship of news reports.
4. Moral censorship.
5. Political censorship.
6. Security censorship—war and peace.
   —Does the situation change the acceptability?
7. Philosophy behind: protection, of the individual, of the nation.
   —Compare John Stuart Mill's contention that society has no right to protect the individual against himself ("On Liberty").
8. Philosophy behind: removal of temptation.
   —Compare Mark Twain's conclusion, "Lead us into temptation" ("The Man That Corrupted Hadleyburg").
9. Censorship on the campus.
10. Beginnings of censorship—Roman censor.
11. Mechanisms of censorship.
12. Enforcement of censorship.
13. Cost of making censorship effective. Does ineffective censorship encourage bootlegging?
14. Pornography: alleged increase of, behind current drives for censorship.
    —Definition of? Who decides? Recent edition of Henry Miller's *Tropic of Cancer* as a test case. Hardcover edition expensive: to defray possible legal costs to publisher? Profiting on human desire for the illicit?
15. Personal experiences with censorship:
    —Parents used to censor TV programs.
    —Read expurgated and unexpurgated editions of *Lady Chatterley's Lover.*
16. Dangers of censorship:
    —Suppression of the minority opinion.

—Sets up a czar of some kind.
—May be used to mislead—first official reports of U-2 incident later admitted to be inaccurate.

17. How far compatible with freedom?
18. Differences between censorship of facts (e.g., military information) and of ideas. Line hard to draw (e.g., birth control information).
19. Classifying books and movies as for adults only—acceptable alternative to power to forbid exhibition? Used in England.
20. Voluntary systems of censorship—TV codes, Hollywood "Hayes Office."
21. Self-elected censors: pressure groups, library boards.

Here, obviously, is a great deal of material. By forcing yourself to think along these lines, you have turned up more leads than you probably would have expected. If you were undertaking a book on censorship, you might use all this and more. But if, as is more likely, you are writing an essay of 500 to 1500 words, you will have to be rigorously selective. Look over the list. If possible, give it a day or two to ferment. You will probably find when you come back to it that you can think of more points, attach more examples to the ideas you have down, and see more connections between them. For this reason, it is well not to make your initial list too laconic. If, for instance, you put down under number 8 only "Mark Twain"—as one is tempted to do at the time—later you may forget what reference you had intended.

As you look over the list, observe that the first three items have to do with media in which censorship is most commonly exercised or urged: books, movies, and newspapers. These are not all the possible media. Do the various restrictions on advertising amount to censorship? In time of war private letters are often censored. Public utterances by men in office are sometimes subject to censorship. United States military officers, for example, are generally expected not to make policy statements in areas of civilian authority. The next three items, on the other hand, have to do primarily with the scope of censorship, the kind of things in books, movies, and so forth, which is usually censored. The *what* of censorship is further raised in number 14 and implied in 18. Numbers 7 and 8 deal with the *why* of censorship; numbers 11, 12, 13, 19, 20, and 21 are concerned with the *who* and *how*. Number 10 opens up the *when* and *where;* numbers

16 and 17 touch on the *why not* of censorship; and numbers 9 and 15 suggest immediate personal approaches to the subject.

Thus as we look over the list we begin to see generalizations along the lines of the traditional five "w" 's and an "h" of a good news story: the who, what, when, where, why, and how. We are not, however, writing anything so simple and straightforward as a news story, and we would not be likely to use all of this information on this scale. Furthermore, it is obvious that these six elements might be of varying significance and relevance in different subject areas. Nevertheless, this familiar sextet may serve as a convenient nudge to the memory in suggesting material for an attack upon a subject area. If you jot down all the information from *who* to *how* about something, you are likely to get to know enough about it to find a subject.

DISTINGUISH FACT AND FEELING AT THE START

If you look again at our list of jottings on censorship, you will notice that the material covers a spectrum from fact to feeling. Some of the entries represent data—they are factual; they lead to specific and concrete information. Henry Miller's *Tropic of Cancer* was for a number of years banned in the United States. There exist expurgated and unexpurgated editions of D. H. Lawrence's *Lady Chatterley's Lover,* and one can be literally accurate about the differences between the two versions—but not about the differences these differences make. Thus even the most factual entries can shade off into the realm of feeling. Some are clearly not fact but feeling. Number 17, "How far compatible with freedom?" frankly calls for an opinion, and may invite an emotional response. Some entries are slanted in their formulation. Take number 16, "Dangers of censorship." Such phrasing assumes that there *are* dangers involved. What would have been the difference had you written "Objections to censorship"? Would the case not have been left more open? Objections can be well founded or not; they can be made by responsible persons or opinionated cranks. Since words can "think for us," we must watch them closely in the initial stages of our writing process—lest they abuse us as we seek to use them. As phrased, number 16 expresses an opinion. There is nothing wrong with this as long as you are aware of what is happening. Your jottings will inevitably and properly contain material of different degrees of factual solidity. Some of the feelings and opinions adduced here will probably later produce the energy which molds some of the facts into an essay. The only requirement is that the writer distinguish as clearly as possible between the two orders of material.

Numbers 19 through 21 suggest some fuzziness in our basic term: What do we mean by censorship? If, as happens in some dictatorships, all material to be published must first be submitted to a censor who has power to prevent publication, that is clearly censorship. If there is no authority to prevent publication, but power to prevent distribution through public mails, is that still censorship? What if there is no power of outright prohibition at all, but merely various kinds of disapproval with attendant pressures and penalties? If a man is free to publish his opinions, but will lose his livelihood if they are not socially acceptable, does that pressure constitute censorship? Sharp definition of crucial terms is something that needs to be done *near the beginning* of any writing project. It is one of the ways in which honest rhetoric leads to awareness. We are speaking now of definition for the benefit of the writer, so that he will know what he is talking about. Definition for the reader is something else.[3] Obviously a whole paper could be devoted to just defining censorship, in which case definition would be the subject and the writer's convictions as to the correct definition would be the thesis. Even when no such elaborate definition seems necessary, the writer should still make sure that he and his reader understand each other, make sure by establishing clearly the sense in which he is using any controversial or ambiguous terms. He must start by working out such clarity in his own thinking.

LIMITING THE SUBJECT

Most of the items on our list are interconnecting. A study of the history of censorship, for instance, would take in most of the points, although the emphasis would be on the chronological narrative, the "when." Any full treatment of the censorship of books (number 1) would similarly include historical material and go into which books were censored, why (numbers 4, 5, 7, 8, 14), how (numbers 11, 12, 19, 20, 21) and with what effects (numbers 16, 17). The center of the essay, however, would remain the operation of censorship on *books.*

[3] See pp. 132–136.

It is possible, then, to make any one of these points the center and relate it to as much of the other material as is pertinent to the line of development. It is also possible to combine several related items into a discussion of some element they have in common. For instance, instead of a specific discussion of the censorship of books, movies, or newswriting, one might treat the general matter of media that have been, are, or can be censored. In either case the development of the theme involves generalizations: the former on the basis of all available material about the censorship of books, the latter on the basis of information on censorable media of communication. Both would require a great deal of investigation—perhaps more time and effort than are available for most college projects—and might have to be cut down to a more manageable size. How can the area around a usable center be plausibly limited?

Let us make it clear first that a limited subject is not necessarily a miniscule subject. We warned in Chapter Two against the tendency of student writers to choose inappropriately grandiose subjects in order that they might be certain of having plenty of material to produce the required number of words. Perhaps we should also warn against the opposite prudential tendency to whittle the subject down to some completely manageable splinter. One of my colleagues protests against the idea that students cannot be allowed to write about death, but must restrict themselves to treating the right rear handle of the coffin. Although one cannot, indeed, say very much about a subject as large as death in 500 words, one may elect to say the things that seem important to him about the whole concept without reducing the scope to something as specific as infant mortality in eighteenth-century Ireland. In "Of Beauty" Bacon treats an equally profound subject in briefer space. To find something interesting to say in brief scope about a large subject is perhaps more difficult than to cover a neat little topic. The temptation with the large subject will be to settle for the obvious or the general. If a writer is to deal successfully with such a subject, he must find some way of getting hold of it, which is to limit it. Just so William Hazlitt limited the larger topic of death by focusing on the fearful human reaction to it and writing on "The Fear of Death."

To limit a subject is to stand in its center and draw a line around it. We are all stimulated by the idea of being in the middle of something, at its heart's core. The classical formula for writing an epic was to plunge *in medias res*—into the middle of things. The center is the point at which all radii meet, the vantage place from which the author can look out at all aspects of his subject. But being in the middle of things can be very confusing if one cannot discern the boundaries. And, as a matter of fact, unless you know where the limits are, you cannot be sure that you *are* in the center. To know anything is to know the boundaries of it, and rhetoric promotes knowledge in forcing us to that recognition. The precise area of our subject may and probably does appear vague when we begin to think about it, but we must clarify and limit before we can go very far. Some subjects are like spiral nebulae; their boundaries are practically indeterminate and have to be assumed on the best evidence available. Other subjects are like circles inscribed by a pair of dividers: one may adjust his radius to suit his convenience and come up with a usable subject, provided he has a real center.

Centers vary in their realness. The geographical center of the Pacific Ocean is an arbitrary and shifting point, probably of no significance. The geographical center of the United States has some curiosity value, especially since it has been moved around by the achievement of statehood by Alaska and Hawaii, but not much importance. The financial center of Wall Street or the political center on Constitution Avenue are vital realities. Such a subject as book censorship offers a tangible center around which it is easy to draw restricted circles with clear boundaries. Limitations can be introduced in a number of ways. The limiting factor may even be personal: "What I Think about Book Censorship." Such a treatment, of course, would need to solve the problem of objectifying the subjective, which we discussed in the last chapter. Limitation may be philosophical: "The Case Against Book Censorship." The most obvious limitations for a historical treatment are temporal and spatial: "Censorship of Books in the Last Ten Years" or "Censorship of Books in California." The area can be cut down by specifying what is being censored or by whom: "Censorship of Pornographic Books" or "Censorship by Public Library Boards." Of course combinations of limiting themes are also possible, even "Censorships of Pornographic Books in the Last Ten Years by California Public Library Boards." One might reduce the subject still further by treating the case history of a particular book, say, *A Dictionary of Slang and Unconventional English,* in the public library of one city. Even in such a limited area, anything other than a literal transcript of library board rulings would require generalizations on the pattern of censorial behavior.

More theoretical generalizations, such as those dealing with the range and rationale of censorship, can also be limited in much the same way. For instance: "The Scope of Censorship Activities in the League of Decency," or "Reasons for News Censorship in the United States during World War II." The latter might be developed interestingly on the thesis that wartime censorship was intended not only to deny information to the enemy but also—and perhaps more significantly—to deny our own citizens information which might injure the nation's morale.

THE THESIS

One must have some thesis to weld the mass of facts and ideas into a meaningful generalization. The tension of a thesis as the attractive force at the center gives the subject its cohesive unity and keeps it from being loosely linear. A list of official pronouncements about the need for censorship all put together would still be only a list. The thesis is your reason for presenting the list to the reader, the motive which orders the material so that it becomes more than just a list. Notice that I did not say that the thesis was your reason for gathering the material. Although you must have had some reason which imposed a kind of preliminary order on the enterprise, you cannot intelligently and responsibly get a thesis until after your jottings have informed you of what you think.

While you are working around in the subject area, your mind might fix on a fact, e.g., one official pronouncement of the purpose of military censorship, which suggests to you that more such might be available and that it would be worthwhile to collect and compare them. Or you might start with the general idea of trying to discover what justification was offered the public for military censorship. Your idea leads you to discover new facts which produce new theories which open up new sources of further facts. Proceeding by such a chicken-egg alternation you will finally hatch a chick which suits you. Suppose you come across post-office placards of an enemy general with megaphonic ears or a sinking freighter with the legend, "Somebody talked." You may get the idea to explore the use of suggestion in explaining the need for censorship, with the thesis that the security function of censorship was obviously paramount. But perhaps you cannot find enough examples of this kind of thing, and then in memoirs of high-ranking officers you come upon statements that the enemy spy system was so efficient that all of our troop movements were expected to be known. You would have to readjust your thesis.

So it usually goes, if a writer keeps his eyes and mind open to all kinds of evidence. If he freezes to his preliminary generalization, he may find himself able to support it only by the use of distortion and omission; or he may even write an essay which really supports another generalization which he has not recognized. A student who writes on the thesis that book censorship constitutes unfair restriction on trade would at least have to deal with the fact that the label "Banned in Boston" usually assures a book financial success; he might end up showing that censorship provides free advertisement which stimulates book trade.

A sound thesis is the real beginning of the essay. Everything which comes before is a necessary preliminary. The elaborateness of the preliminaries can vary considerably with the difficulty of the field and the experience and temperament of the writer. Some skillful authors may be able to survey the area, sort and arrange the material, and come up with a sharp thesis almost as if by intuition without putting anything on paper. Less experienced writers often must go through the steps in a more painful way. All must in some way go through this process of accumulating, screening, organizing, and generalizing before they are ready to write, before they really have a focused subject.

Perhaps the term "focus" or "focused subject" will help to clarify this crucial step in writing. A subject is in focus when it is sharp and clear, has an obvious center, a specific area, and plain boundaries. You have a focused subject when you have something to say, not just something to write about. Usually you can tell whether you have a focused subject or not by trying to put it in a sentence. If you find yourself saying "I am going to write about censorship," you are obviously a long way from a real subject. Your statement is too vague, loose, and comprehensive. If you say, "I am going to write about the effects of book censorship by customs officials," you have limited your area adequately, but you still have no point, no thesis. All you are promising is a list of "effects." You should be able to commit yourself to something about those effects, even if it is no more than that they are significant. If you say, on the other hand, "I am going to show that book censorship by customs officials is necessary and desirable" or "I am going to show that book censorship by customs officials is an unwarranted restriction on the rights of the reading public," you have a partly focused subject. You have a point; you promise to say something. But the exact area of the subject is not yet clear. "Necessary and desirable" or "unwarranted restriction" are too vague without elaboration. Furthermore, as the subject takes shape, it should be able to stand alone, apart from the "I am going to write." The following sentence indicates an adequately focused subject: "Book censorship by customs officials is necessary and desirable because it protects the American public from pornography and enemy propaganda." This sentence shows that you have something to say and know in general terms how you are going to say it. You have enough to get started writing. You can and probably will make small adjustments in the focus as you write. You might, for instance, decide that you wanted to add other justifications for censorship than those covered by the causal clause in your focus. Fine: the focus should be regarded as a sharp and clear preliminary statement, not an unbreakable contract.

Usually it is worth the effort to force yourself to formulate in one sentence what you are planning to say, even though the temptation will be to slip into two or three short sentences. The grammatical structure of the sentence, if it is properly written, can reveal the direction of your idea and the relation of its parts. The main point will normally be in the independent clause, and the supporting elements in subordinate clauses and phrases. If you have said that book censorship by customs officials is "necessary and desirable," are both these terms required? Are they in the proper order? Do you mean "desirable and even necessary" or "necessary, and desirable even if it could not be shown to be necessary"? The clause "because it protects . . ." indicates that your development will be chiefly causal; and you can see immediately that you are making a basic assumption—that the American public needs to be protected from pornography and enemy propaganda. You will have to come to grips with this position; a clear formulation at the outset should call it to your attention and protect you from the fallacies of unrecognized and unexamined assumptions.

PREDICATION

Hammering the subject into focus in one solid sentence also helps to make clear what the predication of the essay is to be. A normal sentence has a predicate; so must a sharp focus; so must a strong essay. A writer must decide what he wants to *assert,* what—of all the many things which can be said on the subject and which he might say on different occasions—he elects to say at this time. He must determine unequivocably which one, of all the possible facets, he will hold up and emphasize, which of all the handles he will grip and there exert his force. For the dynamics of a piece of writing depend upon a definite and specific predication, and without such a positive direction the paper tends to meander, to "cover" the subject in a flat and ineffective sprawl. Although several possible papers in the same subject area could contain the same assortment of facts and arguments, they could also differ significantly because of the orientation of these facts and arguments, the end to which they are directed, the assertion they support. It is extremely important that the author make an explicit decision of what he wants to predicate, keep it before him, and allow it to control his essay. The focus sentence can help to do this.

Consider, for instance, three sentences which seem at first glance to lead into the same subject:

> A college student should not take more than three classes at the same time.
>
> A college student should concentrate his efforts in a few courses in order to be able to go into these more deeply.
>
> A college student who takes more than three courses at a time is likely to get hurried and superficial coverage.

Further examination shows that although essays growing from these sentences would use much of the same material, they ought to have quite different orientations because the sentences promise different predications. The first makes a negative assertion: "should not take more than three classes at a time." An essay really focused on this assertion would develop *all the disadvantages* of the student's doing so: scheduling difficulties, limitation on extracurricular activities and job opportunities, splintered curricula, inadequate time for any one class; with the constant emphasis on the recommendation that students should not take more than three classes. An essay focused on the second sentence, however, would make a positive assertion in terms of principle—concentration of effort. Its organization should stress the value of concentration, demonstrate that a student carrying only a few courses could and would go into them more deeply and gain thereby. The third sentence does not urge any action at all; there is no "should" in its predication. It makes a generalization that a program of more than three courses usually leads to shallow coverage. Its development will have to try to support this generalization by as much evidence as possible. All the other arguments against more than three courses at a time, which are appropriate to the first essay, have no place here, except perhaps in an aside which recognizes that they exist but excludes them from this paper. The author is not arguing for or against any program; he is presenting observations. A good essay could be written using any of these focuses, provided the author faces up to his obligation to make a predication.

A focus, a thesis, a pattern, a predication—each of these emphasizes a different aspect of the preliminary process of ordering ideas to write about them. To put it another way, a satisfactory subject is (1) clear, (2) solid, (3) limited, and (4) directional. In the following sentence the central assertion of the focus is left blank:

Hamlet is a(n) ____________ play.

Which of the following insertions would make a subject upon which a good essay could be written:

Elizabethan	philosophical	unactable
Renaissance	blood-revenge	immoral
great		

Here is a great range of possibilities, some of which meet our criteria readily, others of which would surely require modifications. To say that *Hamlet* is an Elizabethan play is obviously to make an almost empty assertion. As a statement of fact it is impeccable, but not much can be made of it without revised emphasis. If the point is that *Hamlet* is peculiarly representative of the Age of Elizabeth, the focus needs to be clarified to make that aspect stand out. As stated, the focus lacks either substance or clarity. "*Hamlet* is a Renaissance play" is open to much the same objection unless seen perhaps in a context of counterclaims that the play is modern. We cannot really tell where the thesis is aiming; it lacks the important element of direction.

Many of the difficulties that inexperienced writers have in finding appropriate endings for their essays stem from their not having directional theses. A thesis should be going somewhere. If you know your destination, you will be more likely to know when you get there. "*Hamlet* is an immoral play" needs a little more direction regarding just where it is going. Immoral by what standards, from what point of view? On the one hand it could be maintained that the tragedy embodies a high moral teaching of the destiny of man and his responsibility to do his duty as he sees it, no matter what the cost. However, the editor of a popular magazine recently answered a reader's complaint that a story was full of lust, sex, violence, and murder by saying that the same was true of *Hamlet*. Does that make it an immoral play? Perhaps by some standards. At any rate, a satisfactory focus making such an assertion ought to include some indication of the grounds of the argument. The thesis that "*Hamlet* is an unactable play" needs the same kind of qualification concerning the direction of approach to an apparently perverse conclusion. An interesting essay could be developed along the lines suggested by Charles Lamb and other Romantic critics: *Hamlet* cannot be presented satisfactorily on the stage because no production can handle the complexity and subtlety of Shakespeare's conception.

Undoubtedly, the safest focus of those suggested is "*Hamlet* is a blood-revenge play," because it is the most precisely and narrowly limited. There is a sound body of clearly delineated material to work with: one need only establish the characteristics of the Elizabethen Senecan tragedy and show them operating in *Hamlet*. "*Hamlet* is a philosophical play" is less manageable; it would be neater to focus on a particular philosophy and argue, for instance, that the drama reflects Stoic thought. The larger focus is fuzzy, and may mean no more than that *Hamlet* is a thoughtful play—which would seem to be a superfluous thesis. Broadest of all is the formulation, "*Hamlet* is a great play." Would that make a good focus? On the one hand, it would be ridiculous to say that one could not write an essay on such a generally accepted thesis—although T. S. Eliot called the play "most certainly an artistic failure." On the other hand, why write on such a vague and worn theme? Unless the motivation is strong and valid, such general theses should be viewed with suspicion.

The clear, solid, limited, and directional subject which the author finally settles upon is after all a generalization derived from the varied material in the subject area which he has assembled and shuffled through to find out what he knew about it and what was useful to him. The limited subject we finally brought to a focus from our list of jottings on censorship owes something to numbers 1, 5, 6, 7, 8, 11 and 14, and perhaps others as well. When the writer begins to write, he must reverse the process and work backwards from the generalization, giving it substance for his readers through analysis and the presentation of supporting details. More than likely, the evidence which was sufficient for him to arrive at his working generalization will not be enough to support it when he presents it to the reader, who must be presumed to be alert and critical. Therefore, the writer must seek more information, organize it in the most effective way possible, and direct it to his readers—the next steps in the writing process.

ASSIGNMENTS

1. Friends seeking assistance are likely to ask you, "What do you know about _____?" anything from termites to electric shavers. Fill in the blank with something you think you might be asked about, and then make a list of what you do know on that matter. Do you know more or less than you thought? Do you need to know more than you do to write authoritatively about it? Work out three focused subjects for 500-word essays in this subject area. Write one of the essays.

2. Reread a paper that you have recently written and try to recall the details of its composition. Write an essay on the writing of that paper. How did you approach the subject? Where did you get your material? Was the process economical and effective? Can you recommend any improvements?

3. In as many of the following subject areas as you can, find a focused subject which you think might make a good essay:

a. The character of Falstaff.

b. The value of space exploration.

c. The cost of a college education.

d. The function of poetic language.

e. The decline of Hollywood.

f. Manifestations of prejudice.

g. Poe's theory of the short story.

h. Effects of automation.

4. Take one of the above subject areas about which you know the most and see how many different focused subjects you can find in it. Experiment with changing the subject by changing the predication.

5. Take one of the focused subjects which you like and examine it as a generalization which must be proved to your reader. Make a list of the points you could adduce to support the generalization.

6. By now you should be ready to write an essay on the above subject. Go ahead and do so. If you are not ready, consider why. If the results are interesting, you might like to write instead on why you are not ready.

7. Take a famous assertion and use it as the starting point for an essay. You will probably find that you need to be careful about definition and qualification. For example:

All men are created equal.

Beauty is as beauty does.

You can't fool all the people all the time.

We have nothing to fear but fear itself.

Discretion is the better part of valor.

8. Consider the differences in predication in the following focused subjects. Write an essay developing the one which pleases you most.

a. The function of poetry is to please.

b. Poetry instructs by pleasing.

c. A good poem provides a unique pleasure.

d. Poetry pleases the initiated reader.

e. Great poetry instructs as it pleases.

9. See if you can construct a focused subject from which this chapter could have been written. Then read an essay in one of your texts or elsewhere and try to put *its* thesis into one sentence. If you have difficulty, consider whether the fault is in you, the subject, or the essay.

10. Take one of the following broad subject areas and construct in it a focused subject which is solid, clear, directional, limited, and appropriate for a 500–1000 word essay. Try to express the focus in one sentence.

a. Style

b. Death

c. Superstition

d. Science

e. Popularity

11. Exchange with another member of the class the focused subject prepared for assignment 10. Then do the following:

a. Try to write the essay with your classmate's focus.

b. Show your essay to the author of its focus and get the essay he wrote with your focus.

c. Write a paragraph on whether or not the essay produced was what you had in mind when you wrote the focus.

d. Consider whether any discrepancies result from a lack of solidity, clarity, direction, and limitation in your focus.

CHAPTER FOUR

Rhetoric and the Reader

When a writer has his clearly focused subject, he knows in general terms *what* he is going to say; he still is not ready to write until he thinks about *to whom* he is going to say it. He needs a clear target for his rhetoric. Writers have problems like those of launchers of uncontrolled missiles, who must select their targets and plot their courses in advance, calculating the weapon's trajectory and making due allowance for such variables as wind direction and velocity, effects of earth's rotation, and possible enemy evasive and defensive maneuvers. Once they have pushed the button they can only hope they will be on target. Similarly, writers must make all possible provisions to send their missiles—or missives—on true courses through their readers' minds, taking into account the winds of distraction and various evasive and defensive behavior—apathy, carelessness, stupidity, stubbornness. After a writer has chosen a course and launched his essay, there is no opportunity for second thoughts—except in second editions. One must have experienced the sickening sensation of seeing some oversight multiplied in print to realize fully the irrevocability of the written word. Perhaps a spoken word cannot be recalled, but at least it can be modified in the give and take of a face-to-face relationship. Not so the unblinking black and white fixed on the page. A writer must be on target when he fires.

THE ADDRESS

A weakness of much student writing is that it has no target; it is not addressed to anybody. Week after week countless themes are like so many shots fired at random. Worse than that, many of them are not even directed "To Whom It May Concern"; the tacit assumption seems to be that nobody *is* concerned. And in such an atmosphere, often nobody is.

When a writer virtually ignores the existence of his readers he creates a lot of trouble for himself. For one thing, without directing himself to a critical reader, a writer is likely to be careless of unvoiced assumptions and unexplained logical leaps. Many sentences get marked "not clear" simply because their authors did not realize the necessity of making sense to someone who might not be able to fill in the context not put down on the paper:

Not clear

If satellites continue to clutter up space, we will soon be able to get to the moon by jumping from rocket to rocket, ~~like~~ just as Eliza in *Uncle Tom's Cabin* crossed the Ohio River on ice floes.

A weary dialogue between student and instructor goes something like this: "But I meant . . ." "But that's not what you said." The students are usually not incapable of saying what they mean; they just overlook the fact that they must work at directing their meaning *to somebody outside themselves.* William Saroyan's one-act play *Hello Out There* says something important to writers, and to all people involved in the difficult and rewarding business of communicating with each other. From the center of our beings we speak, trying always to break through, to make contact with somebody out there. Unless we are fully aware of the need to do this, our writing will be so many futile words piled up futilely—a sort of miniature Tower of Babel.

It is psychologically important for a writer to remember that there *is* a reader, even if he is not definitely sure of exactly who the reader is. For a writer can count on a common ground of humanity—

> The Colonel's lady an' Judy O'Grady
> Are sisters under their skins!

And many of the readers of this book may also be able to count on a common ground of literate, middle-class Americans. Nevertheless, audiences are different and make different demands, just as military targets are different, some calling for a sharpshooter's rifle bullet, others for a nuclear warhead. Writing is likely to be most effective when it is designed especially for a particular audience. A specific address is, of course, easiest when the reader is a single person whom the writer knows well. We have all had such experiences in writing personal letters: in fact, most of us have written love letters we not only designed particularly for one individual but would rather nobody else saw. But this experience is not typical of the writer-reader relationship, for most readers cannot be counted upon to be as sympathetic and perhaps even clairvoyant as one's beloved. In the language of love a few dashes, asterisks, and exclamation points can be most eloquent. In more mundane communications things have to be spelled out. But at least a love letter can give some idea of the kind of purposeful address, the genuine concern for the reader which a writer ought to have. Balzac once recommended to a young man who had aspirations to be a writer that he get engaged to a girl who lived some distance away and write to her daily.

As a somewhat less drastic measure, I suggest that inexperienced writers try to make themselves aware of their purposeful attack upon some segment of the world out there by forcing themselves to put an address on every piece of writing they undertake. Put the address on first, of course, before you begin to write. My students sometimes cheat themselves by putting the address on last, which is to defeat the purpose of the device. You would not write a letter and then decide to whom to send it, would you?

Several kinds of addresses commend themselves to student writers. Canniness sometimes dictates an address to the instructor, for obviously he is the real target, and his grades a convenient way of scoring hits. Lest the motive of getting a good grade appear unworthily mercenary, let us recognize that it is indirectly equivalent to pleasing the reader, which is one of the most ancient and respected reasons for writing. Horace declared that poets wish *aut prodesse aut delectare*—either to profit or to please. Wordsworth held that "The Poet writes under one restriction only, namely, the necessity of giving immediate pleasure to a human Being possessed of that information which may be expected from him . . . as a Man." Normally an author pleases his readers or he does not get read. All the different manipulations of address are, in crass terms, lures designed in response to a kind of consumers' preference survey. Commercial writers try to find out what their potential readers like, and provide it or at least an acceptable substitute. Otherwise they collect rejection slips. Student writers are in the peculiar position of having captive audiences: instructors who must read their papers whether they like them or not. Unless, however, the writers are mindful of the necessity of pleasing or satisfying their readers, they get rejection slips in the form of poor grades.

Yet since class essays are the forced growth of a hothouse situation, the instructor tries not to read them as an individual. If he did so, students would be at a disadvantage, since usually they cannot really know him or reach his level of maturity. It is generally safer for students to follow the instructor's directions but choose some other addressee more within their competence. It is most satisfactory, by and large, for students to direct their essays to the other members of the class and their contemporaries in general.

For practice exercises, however, it is often helpful to try to aim at different audiences. One device is to aim at the readers of a given magazine. Choose a magazine with a more distinctive audience than *Reader's Digest* and one not too far from your experience—*The New Yorker* is likely to be dangerous. You might start with something like *Field and Stream* or for fun have a go at *Jack and Jill* or—only if you have a gift for that sort of thing—*Mad*. Then work up through the *Saturday Evening Post* to the *Saturday Review* and *Harper's*. Read through several issues of the magazine and decide what kind of people read it. If you like, imagine a typical reader and concentrate on him. Then stop and ask yourself how you arrived at this image and, as if you were unravelling a "who-dun-it," list the clues to the identity of the reader. Sometimes it is interesting to compare your image of a magazine's reader with the images of other members of your class. Be very specific concerning exactly what in the orientation, development, and style of the articles in a given journal indicates the intended audience. It is, of course, possible that you will find contradictions and anomalies: the editors may make mistakes in their conception of their audience or they may attempt to lure a variety of readers. But these inconsistencies will sharpen your perceptions. The important thing is to become aware of what kind of items appear on your list, for these are probably indications of the author's purpose and of the audience he is trying to reach. They are the kinds of things which you will exploit when you reverse your role and start with an image of a reader whom you want to reach. Many of your items will relate to the level of presentation, which we take up next.

LEVELS

One of the facts of life is the existence of different levels. From the amoeba to man, from the earth's core to cosmic dust, from folk tunes to Beethoven, from Skid Row to Park Avenue we can observe stratification. The stratifying factor may be density, complexity, sophistication, or something else. These differences in level are so commonplace that most of us take them for granted and make often unconscious adjustments for them in our behavior, just as when we climb a mountain our lungs and heart provide for the changing oxygen content in the atmosphere. The adaptation may not be as automatic, but we do the same kind of thing when we shift from ballads to Beethoven. Our techniques or expectations or standards change. As writers—and as readers—we also need to adjust to different levels. We have already mentioned differences in grammatical propriety and formality of style (Chapter One), and different degrees of subjectivity (Chapter Two). Level dictates, however, not just choice of language and syntax, but also choice of argument, illustrations, development, pace, structure—of everything to adapt a piece of writing to its audience. After long experience we may be able to make these adaptations almost unconsciously; but for a time, at least, we must adjust as deliberately as we would reset our car's carburetor if we suddenly moved from Death Valley to Denver.

Almost any subject can be treated on almost any level, depending upon the interests and capacities of the writer and the readers. A funeral is one thing to a bereaved mourner, another to an anthropologist, still another to an officiating minister, yet another to an escorting traffic patrolman, and something else again to a mortician. William Blake said, "A fool sees not the same tree that a wise man sees." In fact, no two people see quite the same tree; but individuals with similar orientations and backgrounds will see close enough to the same tree to find substantial points of agreement. I once took a cousin who is a lumberman to visit Muir Woods National Monument, and discovered that the giant coast redwoods, which were to me graceful, venerable, awe-inspiring symbols of eternal beauty, were to him chiefly remarkable as so many board feet of lumber. He had spent a great deal more of his time walking through woods than I had and had conditioned himself to estimate timber values. Any writer who wanted to reach him and his fellows through, say, the *Lumberman's Journal* would have to use very different tactics from those employed by a writer who wished to speak to me and others of like persuasion through the pages of *The Conservation Monthly*. That is not to say that one could not preach conservation to lumbermen and a realistic attitude toward the world's lumber needs to conservationists: enlightened members in both camps recognize the justice of the other position. A writer would, however, need to be aware of the orientation of his prospective readers and be sure he was seeing the same trees they did.

Treatment

Imagine a writer planning an essay on the feeding habits of fish for the *Journal of Ichthyology*, the *Saturday Evening Post, Field and Stream,* and *Boy's Life*. What differences in level would be required by the respective readers? Differences in the handling of the subject surely would be needed. The ichthyologists would expect a scientific treatment, probably an ecological survey of the relationship of various species of fish to the organisms upon which they feed. Readers of the *Saturday Evening Post* would prefer a more popular approach, such as a collection of data about fish with curious feeding habits: the angler fish, which carries about a wormlike appendage to trick his prey; the archer fish, which shoots down his dinner; and fishes which use electric shock to stun their meals. Or perhaps these readers would be interested in economics: a discussion of the effects on the fishing industries of changes in the feeding grounds of herring or tuna. The devotees of *Field and Stream,* on the other hand, would most likely think of a fish's feeding habits in terms of making a catch. They would want to know at what time of day a certain species is wont to feed, in what kind of water, and on what sort of prey or bait. The *Boy's Life* audience would be interested in the same aspects of the subject as the *Post* and *Field and Stream* readers, but treated somewhat less technically and oriented directly to boys.

Presentation

Along with these various developments of the subject would go different levels of presentation—differences in *texture, tone, structure,* and *diction.*

TEXTURE

The scientific essay would be solid in texture. It would require a great deal of detailed information, carefully documented. Charts of population density and graphs of the relation of water temperature gradients to feeding patterns would be appropriate. In the more popular treatments documentation would be sparser and more selective. Generalization would probably be supported by illustration and example rather than by accumulation of exhaustive evidence. A popular address invites relatively colorful, active, open-textured treatments which move rapidly and carry the reader from high point to high point. The writer for the ichthyologists' *Journal,* on the other hand, can assume that his readers are interested in nearly everything about fish, and therefore he can hold his audience with a denser, more detailed treatment than would be wise for the popular writer.

TONE

A major difference in tone would be in the personality or impersonality of the treatment. As we saw in Chapter Two, the appropriateness of the subjective approach depends upon a complicated interaction of the subject, writer, and reader. The *Post* article would probably be impersonal overall, but might well include interviews with fishermen or imbedded elements of personal narrative. The scientific treatment almost surely would be entirely objective and impersonal because convention dictates such treatment of such a subject in such a journal and the readers will expect it. The *Field and Stream* article might well be built around the personal experience of one knowledgeable fisherman because the emphasis has shifted from the clear realm of fact to the more subjective one of lore. The *Boy's Life* version would probably be anecdotal in character. The tone of the popular presentations could be light—a jocular treatment of the fisherman's problems in catering to fish—or serious —how economic privations when salmon feed elsewhere can make

Alaska a "disaster area." In the ichthyological publication a light touch, generally, would be inappropriate.

STRUCTURE AND DICTION

Clearly the four publications would demand differences in structure and vocabulary. The ichthyologists would expect technical terminology. Fish would be identified by their Latin names and the essay would bristle with scientific language. The syntax might also be somewhat complicated, the paragraphs relatively long. While the *Saturday Evening Post* writer might throw in a few Latin names occasionally for authentication, he would be careful to parallel them with common names. He might use such words as "salinity" and "thermal gradients," but if he ventured so far as "ecology" he would be sure to define the term—perhaps unobtrusively. The *Field and Stream* author might have a semitechnical language of his own, a fisherman's jargon including "leaders" and "whipping." His syntax would probably be relatively simple and his paragraphs short. The *Boy's Life* writer would doubtless also use simple sentences and paragraph structure and a generally available vocabulary, although his diction—especially in dialogue—might tend toward teen-age slang.

Diction clearly intelligible to one set of readers interested in the feeding habits of fish might, then, be more or less opaque to another set. I am reminded of an official highway sign I saw recently marking a low underpass. It read precisely: "Impaired vertical clearance." Right next to it someone with an apparently more realistic view of the vocabularies of most truck drivers had put up a crudely lettered sign which read: "Low Overhead. Look up!" That second sign-maker had a good grasp of the necessity of an appropriate level. Not only had he tailored the diction to the likely capabilities of his readers, but he had adjusted the tone to the exigencies of the situation by converting the coolly objective original into a direct appeal to action—"Look up!"

THE READERS' NEEDS

Once an author has put himself on the level of his readers, he can make contact with them by recognizing and providing for their specific needs. A reader needs to know and understand certain facts—he must have them explained to him. A reader needs to judge and accept certain hypotheses—he must be convinced of them. A reader needs to follow sequences in time, to recognize arrangement in space, and to appreciate character and quality—he must be told and shown what they are. To use the traditional terms of rhetoric, his needs can be met by the modes of exposition, argumentation, narration, and description. These modes are not distinct, because in most situations readers have all of these needs more or less simultaneously. Rarely, then, does a piece of writing use one of the approaches exclusively. An essay explaining Swift's use of scale in Lilliput (primarily exposition) would probably include some description of the Lilliputian landscape and people, some narration of Gulliver's adventures in Lilliput, and some argumentation in support of the explanation offered. Furthermore, many of the elements of good writing are common to all of the modes. Still, the different needs have individual characteristics worth considering.

Explaining to the Reader

The basic mode is exposition. Its name comes from the Latin *expono* (*exposui, expositum*) meaning to put forth, and its function is well suggested by the modern slang phrase, "to put it on the line." To set something forth, to explain it, requires absolute clarity and precision. Clarity and precision are merits in any kind of writing, although some modes allow the writer to "by indirection find direction out." Not so exposition. Subtlety is not its forte. Ambiguity, a virtue in some kinds of writing—notably modern poetry—is out of place in exposition. Its method is logic, its tone cool and analytical, and it puts on frills at its peril.

How can we guarantee clarity and precision? Perhaps we cannot on subjects of peculiar complexity. Generally, however, the fuzziness and obscurities which creep into our writing are avoidable. I suggest that a way to avoid them is to write as if we were putting down instructions for packing a parachute we expected to use.

First, we would have to know how to pack a chute ourselves—the knowledge element of rhetoric again. Obviously we cannot explain anything clearly unless we understand it clearly. Just as obviously, explaining it clearly will not help if our own information is wrong; our exposition might be technically impeccable and we could still break our necks. Suppose, however, that we know precisely and accurately how to pack a parachute, what then?

Second, we have to know what the person who is going to read our instructions knows about packing parachutes. Here the question of audience which we discussed above becomes crucial. Does the reader know what a shroud is, or do we have to tell him? Conceivably it might do no harm to tell him anyway, but there is a significant expository principle involved: parsimony or economy. The best way to explain anything is usually the shortest way that is clear to the reader. Too much brevity can be defeating. We have all suffered from messages like a telegram reading, "Arriving 8:45 tomorrow. Meet me. Love, John." Maybe there is only one vehicle arriving at only one station—but if there happens to be a train and a plane at the same time, or a bus, or any combination at different depots, or something at 8:45 in the morning and at 8:45 at night, we wish the sender had squandered a few words. On the other hand, too many words would be an unnecessary expense in sending a telegram. Too many words is always an unnecessary expense, in printing costs or in readers' energy. Too many words cloud the issue. To tell the parachute packer things he already knows or does not need to know is likely to encourage him to pay less attention to your instructions, to skim them selectively. Maybe he will miss something vital.

Finally, after we know exactly what needs to be said, we must know how to say it exactly, without any possibility of confusion or ambiguity. Such knowledge is ultimately the whole art of the right words in the right places, and will be the subject of the rest of this book. An alert awareness of the problem is, however, more than half the battle. Most of us can be clear if we are concerned enough to be really critical of what we write. Suffice it here, therefore, to emphasize the necessity of making no statement which the parachute packer can possibly interpret in more than one way. Perhaps it will help if we can only realize the complete dependence of that packer on the words we put down for him. Navy recruiters for candidates for Bomb Disposal School used to say, "It's good duty; you're on your own; nobody looks over your shoulder." Whether it is good duty or not, the reader is on his own with our prose. We cannot look over his shoulder if we want to. It is up to us to take every possible precaution to see that he cannot make a fatal mistake.

Try being dependent on your own prose and see how far you can trust it. Write out a set of detailed directions for putting on your clothes, and tomorrow morning follow them exactly—no cheating.

If you get down to breakfast without raising any eyebrows, you passed. Better yet, write out a set of instructions for the class and see if every member interprets them in the same way. It is not easy, as I know from humbling experience, to give an assignment or question that is foolproof. Try writing a question for your next test and see if you can phrase it in such a manner that you are willing to guarantee that nobody can possibly misunderstand it.

Exposition is used, of course, for more than instructions and directions. It covers a range from the *Declaration of Independence* and the *Origin of Species* to your next term paper. It is the necessary art of setting anything forth with maximum effectiveness, which means at least clearly, precisely, accurately, and economically.

Convincing the Reader

Although traditionally a distinct rhetorical mode, argumentation is not really separable. For to explain or describe or narrate anything effectively, a writer usually commits himself and in fact argues for the version he presents. Where, however, there are manifest alternatives, an author has the option of leaving the choice to his readers or supporting one interpretation. Argument, then, is by definition one-sided. Since its purpose is to convince, its method is properly logical; but since it is also intended to move or convert, its appeal may be emotional, its tone warm. Honest argument employs expository clarity and precision. Dishonest argument deliberately blurs and attempts to deceive. For the honest arguer the following suggestions may be helpful.

Be wary of overstating your case. Carried away by the intensity of their own convictions, writers, particularly young writers, are wont to be overenthusiastic. Enthusiasm is a good thing, and young men ought to dream dreams; but sound argument needs to be tempered with judgment. Do not write "always" if your evidence will support only "most of the time," or "beyond doubt" when you have some sneaking doubts—or maybe *because* you have doubts. For overstatement may result, not so much from an overwhelming conviction of the strength of one's position, as from a conscious or subconscious wish that it were stronger. This is "whistling in the graveyard" writing, not very far from the "big lie" technique—the implication that anything said loudly and vehemently and persistently is true, that error can simply be brazened out. An intelligent reader will not buy this technique; he may react negatively to even a suspicion of it. Despite all the triumphs of propaganda in our time, the writer may still believe Abraham Lincoln's famous creed: ". . . you can't fool all of the people all of the time."

Be sure to deal with other points of view than your own. Students often take too literally the one-sided character of argumentation, forgetting that you argue against as well as for. The writer must take his stand and support it to the best of his ability, but he does not do this effectively by acting as if no other opinions were possible. The reader needs to be assured that the writer has considered these alternatives and discarded them for good reason. If the reader thinks of one alternative which the author did not mention, he immediately loses confidence in the author. He cannot be sure that if the writer had considered that possibility, he might not have changed his position. He cannot be sure how many other alternatives the writer has ignored. The good writer of argumentation, therefore, must use the debater's technique of preparing both—or all—sides. Since argumentation is one-sided only in purpose, perhaps it would be better to say it is one-directional. But, then, so is most good writing; the man who jumps on his horse and rides off in all directions does not get very far.

Suppose, for instance, you were writing an essay the purpose of which was to argue that the changes of heart which result in the marriage of Mr. Darcy and Elizabeth Bennet in Jane Austen's *Pride and Prejudice* were unbelievable. You might tend to exaggerate the unpleasantness of Darcy's early pride and Elizabeth's reaction to it, and thus overstate the magnitude of the shift of feelings. Actually, Miss Austen early in the novel plants evidence of Darcy's admirable qualities and of his own growing admiration for Elizabeth. And Elizabeth herself is too honest and too perceptive ever to have been totally unaware of either, much as her own pride may have made her scorn them. Besides recognizing qualifications in the abruptness of the change of feelings, you need also to allow for different points of view concerning what degree of irrationality can be believable in such matters: all is fair—and possible—in love.

Perhaps the trick of successful argumentation is to steer a course between oversimplification and overelaboration. Most questions are more complex than they appear on the surface, and any effective arguments concerning them must recognize that complexity. Complexity and confusion, however, can be near akin, and they are likely to be so in the hands of a writer who cannot distinguish valid qualifications and necessary defensive maneuvers from all manner of tangentially related ideas. We have all had a painful experience, particularly in conversation, with an arguer who is continually being led away to elaborate the structure of the substrata of the foundation of some flying buttress on his thesis. The first law of argumentation is to *keep to the point.*

Showing the Reader

The etymology of "describe" is interesting. The word derives from the Latin *de scribo,* meaning to write from, or literally, to copy. Now if we are going to write from something, we have to establish a clear relationship to it. That is the secret of good description: it is predominantly relational. When our purpose is to describe, we seek to put ourselves and our readers in a meaningful relationship to our subject. This relationship is a matter partly of attitude and organizing concept, and partly of actual physical position. Where do we stand as we view the object? Where does the reader stand as he sees it?

Often we must literally tell our readers what their physical point of view is:

> Seen from above, Uncle Amos's head looked like a well-polished hard-boiled egg and even had a jagged line across it like the crack of an egg cooked in too-hot water.

Here the angle of vision is important, for unless the reader places himself strategically, he is not in a position to appreciate the descriptive simile. Frequently the reader's position must be shifted, travelogue fashion. Our job then is to be sure that the reader realizes his stance is being shifted, and also that his view is not disturbed by too obvious machinery. Guides are indispensable, but should be unobtrusive. I remember vividly an impeccably mustachioed guide who took me through a Loire Valley chateau, all the while rolling off innumerable dates in orotund French; but I'm afraid I don't remember much about the chateau.

While we are establishing our reader's physical attitude, we are also arranging his mental attitude toward our subject. My chateau guide had a professional reverence for his subject and sought to propagate that attitude. A very different attitude pervades the mock reverence of Alexander Pope's description of a woman's toilette:

> Here files of pins extend their shining rows;
> Puffs, Powders, Patches, Bibles, Billet-doux.
> Now awful Beauty puts on all its arms;
> The fair each moment rises in her charms,
> Repairs her smiles, awakens ev'ry grace,
> And calls forth all the wonders of her face;
> Sees by degrees a purer blush arise,
> And keener lightnings quicken in her eyes.
>
> *The Rape of the Lock,* I, 137–144

The description, we might say, is colored. Description almost always is, even when the writer makes a deliberate effort to describe impartially. He cannot see through any eyes but his own, and he is inevitably forced into some selection which indicates bias. He cannot describe everything at once: he must start somewhere, and therefore create some emphasis. Far better that the writer recognize and admit his coloration, to himself at least. Then he can face up to his rationale of presentation.

There must be some rationale, some system of orderly presentation. This seems an obvious thing to say, but somehow writers who take for granted that they have to organize exposition and argumentation seem to suppose that description has a kind of built-in organization. It does not. All of the elements of any subject of description are not of equal importance. If we gave the reader all of the pieces, like a jig-saw puzzle, and let him put them together, he would ultimately find that some aspects stood out prominently, others were insignificant. Such a procedure, however, would be time-consuming and wasteful—the reader would have a right to complain. Furthermore, it would be unsafe, since without our guidance the reader might get the wrong perspective.

Another relation, then, that the writer of description must be concerned with devolves from his selective function: the relation of the parts to the whole. How should he start? In what order should he describe the various elements of his subject? Should he use the newspaper caption system—left to right? Should he describe the more important aspects first? Should he fit together the pieces and leave the reader to draw his own conclusions about the whole, or should he begin with a general view? Obviously he should decide to do whatever is appropriate to his subject, his readers, and his purpose. If the description is of a process, the writer will probably want to follow it through, step by step. This is the kind of description regularly used in writing up chemistry experiments. If, on the other hand, the description is of a panoramic scene, the writer will probably try to give some sense of the whole sweep of the vista, pick out the salient features, and then fill in some of the details. Too scattered a presentation of fragments of a picture would give the reader something like the effect of looking through a venetian blind.

When we describe, we are actually interpreting, organizing the details into a pattern which seems logical to us. We must find some controlling concept, some dominant motif which fits our purpose and establishes our relation to whatever is being described. Students asked to describe their home towns or neighborhoods usually provide a variety of factual details: population, climate, elevation, industry, history, geography. But often all these facts do not add up to a picture of the town because they are not organized and interpreted to portray the *character* of the place. Is the town bustling or sleepy, spic and span or sprawling and ugly, quiet and conservative or loud and rowdy? And how do all the details, from the façade of Main Street and the line of the church steeple to the personality of the mayor, fit into this picture?

Suppose you were describing the Prioress in Chaucer's *Canterbury Tales*. She has a broad forehead, blue-grey eyes, an impeccable wimple, and a brooch inscribed *Amor Vincit Omnia*. She speaks school French, sings through her nose, is most meticulous about table manners, feeds cake to pet dogs which she hates to see hurt. Well enough, but you cannot be content with such a list. What does it all add up to? What turns this collection of facts into a unified picture? Professor Lowes summed it up as "the delightfully imperfect submergence of the woman in the nun." Such an idea pulls together and interprets the descriptive details.

In *straight* description we need to be careful that our controlling concept does not so condition our perception as to make our presentation distorted or thin. To describe a modern home in terms of its functional efficiency may be the best way to organize the details, but is functional efficiency adequate as a descriptive motif for the modern house? Not if it leads us to ignore other significant aspects.

Beauty, for instance, can live in the simple, clean lines of a functional design. On the other hand, efficiency may be something sterile, bare, inhumanly ugly. Our description will be inadequate unless our interpretation accounts for all the relevant facts.

A particular kind of description, however, emphasizes the inevitable personal element, which to different observers can make the same scene "ruggedly picturesque" or "hideously jumbled," the same movie "refreshingly frank" or "disgustingly sordid." When this personal element of selection and organization takes over, the result is *impressionism*. Then the coloration becomes the important thing, the description becomes imaginatively creative, and the reader must be interested not so much in what is described as in the description itself. A justly renowned example is Walter Pater's portrait of Leonardo Da Vinci's painting, "La Gioconda," or "Mona Lisa":[1]

The presence that thus rose so strangely beside the waters, is expressive of what in the ways of a thousand years men had come to desire. Hers is the head upon which all "the ends of the world are come," and the eyelids are a little weary. It is a beauty wrought out from within upon the flesh, the deposit, little cell by cell, of strange thoughts and fantastic reveries and exquisite passions. Set it for a moment beside one of those white Greek goddesses or beautiful women of antiquity, and how would they be troubled by this beauty, into which the soul with all its maladies has passed! All the thoughts and experience of the world have etched and moulded there, in that which they have of power to refine and make expressive the outward form, the animalism of Greece, the lust of Rome, the mysticism of the middle age with its spiritual ambition and imaginative loves, the return of the Pagan world, the sins of the Borgias. She is older than the rocks among which she sits; like the vampire, she has been dead many times, and learned the secrets of the grave; and has been a diver in deep seas, and keeps their fallen day about her; and trafficked for strange webs with Eastern merchants: and, as Leda, was the mother of Helen of Troy, and, as Saint Anne, the mother of Mary; and all this has been to her but as the sound of lyres and flutes, and lives only in the delicacy with which it has moulded the changing lineaments, and tinged the eyelids and the hands.

Telling the Reader

Narration is perhaps the most primitive of the modes. It is simply the telling of a story, and probably goes back to some caveman's first

[1] Walter Pater, *Renaissance* (New York: n.d.), pp. 103–104.

attempt to tell his mate of the saber-toothed tiger that got away. As children we called our first piece of writing "a story," and by now are probably more or less adept at the mode. But a few reminders may be in order.

Just as the distinctive element of description is relation, particularly in space, the characteristic note of narration is sequence in time. We need, therefore, to remember to keep our readers clearly oriented in time, whether we begin our narrative at the beginning, or at the end, or in the middle. Beginning at the beginning is sometimes effective in maintaining suspense and building up to a climax. Beginnings, however, are often difficult to make exciting, and the reader may not be interested in the uneventful early stages unless he has some intimation of what is in store. Of course in a sense things do not have any real beginning but grow out of something else—but along that line of thought madness and boredom lie. Avoid tracing the beginning back *ab ovo* unless the need seems imperative.

Wherever we begin in the action, we can jump back to earlier times with flash-back techniques or look ahead by means of anticipatory touches. These devices are also useful in dealing with simultaneous action, for one of the difficulties of narration is that it is linear whereas in life events overlap and pile up on each other. "Slow down. One thing at a time," we say to an excited child telling of some experience. As we become skilled narrators, we can manage to do more than one thing at a time. By the use of foreshadowing we can anticipate the end at the beginning: a lugubrious tone or little sombre touches in the opening of an account of a beach picnic, for instance, can forecast a tragic ending. By echoes and parallels we can recall, relate, and project, and thus build up a structure of cross references that point up, for example, the inevitability or the irony in a set of circumstances, provided we are careful to make every detail meaningful in orienting and conditioning the reader. What kind of story would you expect to develop from this start?

My younger brother got his first hot-rod at the age of twelve—and he wasn't much older himself. This was in 1960; he was a very naïve sixteen and the car was a late 1948 model Plymouth. That is, she was one of the last cars off the assembly line that year, but "late" wouldn't be much of an exaggeration in a more morbid sense. Stevie had some family problems with this purchase. My father was a bank cashier with no hot-rod sympathies. He considered an automobile a necessary evil of modern society, traded every two years, and scarcely looked under the hood in between. My mother had never learned to drive and was nervous about cars. She was also nervous about Stevie.

The light tone of the unexpected turn in the first sentence suggests that nothing very serious is forthcoming. Yet the "very naïve" character of the brother—fitting in with his youth and his diminutive name—the mock-ominous "late," and the foreshadowed difficulty with the unmechanical and nervous parents suggest difficulties ahead.

The devices for controlling and displaying time in narration are simple. Foremost is the use of tense. Narration typically is written in the past tense, but modulations backward and forward are possible and sometimes useful. Consider the following scrap of narration:

Rome was (*past*) not built, nor won, in a day. John had known (*past perfect*) that for a long time, and now he was planning (*imperfect*) his campaign carefully. He must be careful, he realized. Tomorrow he would begin (*future*). By then he would have (*future perfect*) crossed his Rubicon. He smiled wryly to think (*infinitive*) that by then he might also be in jail. He wiped his forehead and threw away the handkerchief. It was a silly gesture, but it seemed a way of cutting his ties with the past. He was at last his own man. His own man—his own fool! Why do (*present*) that? That handkerchief may have his initials on it! Panicky, he turns to look back through the gutters, all his bravado gone, limp as the crumpled cloth he seeks.

Notice that the predominant past tense is varied with glances backward by past perfect and forward by future perfect, and is finally shifted—not very successfully—into the present. The use of the present tense, called the historical present, is appropriate for some narrative moments of high intensity, but should be used with caution. Notice also that the chronological movement of the passage is helped along by such indicator words as "now," "tomorrow," "then," and "the past."

Observe something else about the narration in the above passage. The story has to be told from some point of view, be seen from the perspective of some observing intelligence. Here the anonymous author tells the story in the third person. This is perhaps the easiest system, for it allows the author the most freedom. He can be omniscient, know as much as he wants and tell as much as he wants.

There's the rub, however: omniscience is a remote quality, and the author may wish a more intimate effect. Furthermore, if for purposes of suspense he does not want to tell all, he can hold back with more grace if he adopts a limited point of view. He can still keep the third person, but stand behind, as it were, one of his characters. This author limits himself to John's knowledge: he does not step in and tell us whether or not the hankerchief did have initials on it—as some omniscient authors might. He could, conceivably, shift to other characters at other points in the story. Even more immediate and limited is the first-person point of view, the "I was there" narrative. John could have told his own story, and been restricted not only to what he knew but to what he could articulate. This technique can be awkward if the author is forced to put his narrator in places he probably would not have been so that he can get information he would not normally have. Sometimes the first-person narrator resorts to such things as eavesdropping, intercepting letters, listening to people talk in their sleep, and pumping children, in order to get the pieces of the story. Such devices, however, may add a certain verisimilitude and credibility. The first-person narrator can be involved in the story himself or merely be an observer; if the former, the very fact that he has survived to tell the tale modulates the suspense. It is reassuring to children, for example, that despite the dangers of his position in the apple barrel, Jim Hawkins must have escaped somehow.

Just as a successful author of children's books takes into consideration the need to reassure his readers, all good writers try to anticipate and provide for the desires, expectations, capabilities, and vulnerabilities of their readers. To do this a writer must have a reader in mind, write on his level of interest and comprehension, orient him in time, place, and attitude, and tell him what he needs to know in such a way that he will accept it.

ASSIGNMENTS

1. The following paragraph is not clear at several points because the needs of the reader are ignored:

> A great deal is said piously by deans and commencement speakers about life. Nonsense. The campus is perforce an artificial construct, hammered together by a mismatched crew. Academic purpose pro-

poses and fiscal means disposes. There is nothing vital about the whole operation. It is no microcosm, but a completely unnatural combination. At the outset unnatural selective procedures work. The population is atypical, the social drives unnaturally restricted and directed to artificial goals. Rewards are really deferred. The whole atmosphere is one of suspended animation—someday the Prince will come.

a. Explain the difficulties and suggest improvements.

b. Comment on the appropriateness of the level of the paragraph for an address to college freshmen.

c. Write a rebuttal to the main ideas expressed in the paragraph.

2. Write a set of instructions in list form on how to perform one of the following activities:

a. How to locate and draw a book from the college library.

b. How to become enrolled in courses.

c. How to vote in your state.

3. Take the list you prepared in assignment 2 and write an expository essay using that information. Pay particular attention to what you have done to turn a list into an essay.

4. Choose an essay in a text or magazine for an examination of its possible audience. Then do the following:

a. Mark every element in the text which you think shows it to be for a particular audience.

b. Classify the elements you have marked as aspects of content, syntax, and diction.

c. Write an essay on the audience to whom you think the essay is addressed. Be as specific as possible and use your analysis for documentation.

5. Write a brief description of one of the following:

a. The room in which your class meets.

b. An individual well known on the campus.

c. The oldest building on the campus.

6. Look at the essay you wrote in assignment 5 and ask the following questions:

a. What was your attitude toward your subject?

b. Did it get across in your essay?

c. Did you use any dominant motif? For example, was the room predominantly "cluttered," the individual "crusty," the building "quaint"? If so, did the motif serve effectively as an organizing device, or unfortunately as an oversimplification?

7. Write a piece of argumentation on one of the following subjects:

a. Exposition is the mode of writing most important to college students.

b. _______ (fill in an author of your choice) ought to be read in freshman English.

c. The love of money is the root of all evil.

8. Look over the essay you wrote for assignment 7 and make a list of the points at which you took specific cognizance of other opinions and indicate the ways in which you dealt with the difference.

9. Write a brief narrative on what happened in this class yesterday. Then do the following:

a. Examine your account to see how you have dealt with time. Were there references to what happened before yesterday and what might happen after? Check your tenses and your temporal words.

b. Rewrite the account from another point of view.

10. Write a paragraph reporting on the college dining facilities for each of the following:

a. The official catalogue of the college.

b. A letter to your family.

c. A letter to a friend at another college.

d. The alumni magazine.

CHAPTER FIVE

Rhetoric and Logic

In the process of getting to know what he wants to say and to whom, a writer inevitably picks up ideas about *how* to say it. Although some of these ideas may be useful, unfortunately they are not all trustworthy, and even those of which an author is most fond may be suspect. These notions along the way are various, fragmentary, and possibly incompatible with each other, since some of them are probably vestiges of false starts more appropriate to other subjects and addresses. The author must scrutinize the validity of these ideas for his thesis, being sure he understands the implications of that thesis and its potential for development. To do this, he needs some knowledge of logic.

Of course logic enters rhetoric at many points—we recall that Aristotle said rhetoric was but popular logic. One of the differences between grammar and rhetoric is that grammar can appear illogical and still be approved by the sanction of usage, but rhetoric must either be logical or somewhow get the reader to accept its own logic. We have already discussed the logic of the relationship of the subject to the author and the reader—and we shall discuss later such essentially logical processes as classification and definition. In this chapter as we look at some of the basic methods of logic, we shall see that the writer can benefit from a knowledge of logic in three main ways:

1. By putting his ideas into logical form the writer can brush aside the verbal camouflage and find out exactly *what* he is saying.
2. By observing the laws of logical inference he can assure the *validity* of what he is saying.

3. By penetrating through to his assumptions and testing their origins, he can improve the *accuracy* of what he is saying.

REDUCING THE OBFUSCATION OF LANGUAGE

Although rhetoric is popular logic, there is also something in rhetoric that is at war with logic. The smooth formulation—decked with metaphors, varied by synonyms which perforce are not exact, and rounded out to please the reader—all this can obscure logic and lead the writer into positions he would not intentionally accept. Valuable as are the arts of style in their place, they need to be laid aside by the writer in the privacy of his own mind, as he attempts to view his ideas in their barest and most prosaic actuality.

Consider, for instance, the thesis, "Since the future of society is in the hands of youth, college students ought not to spend their time studying the past"; or the opposite, "Since the past is the key to the future, college students should spend their time studying the past." We are all likely to be befuddled by such metaphorical language—"the future . . . in the hands of youth" and "the past . . . the key to the future." What exactly do these phrases mean? Unless we scrutinize them carefully they lead us unwittingly into statements which we could not justify. A logical formulation of the ideas underlying the first thesis will make this clear. Logically it is a species of *enthymeme,* a syllogism with one of its propositions suppressed:

> People concerned with the future are not concerned with the past.
> College students are people concerned with the future.
> College students are not concerned with the past.

When we bring this suppressed major premise out into the light, it looks dubious:

> People concerned with the future are not concerned with the past.

Is it true as stated? The development of an effective essay on this subject hinges on that point. The writer has to find out whether or not it is true as stated, and, if not, how it can be accurately stated and whether the conclusion is still valid. These are the basic problems: the *accuracy* of the premises, and the *validity* of the conclusion. If the premises are accurate and the inferences are valid, the conclusion is true and the essay can be developed. Of course it matters little whether or not a writer knows an enthymeme by name or is generally familiar with the technical terminology of logic; but what does matter is that he understand the precise nature of such problems; and some knowledge of terminology helps. He can get a good start by seeing his basic ideas as propositions in logic.

LOGICAL FORM: PROPOSITIONS

A proposition is a statement of a relationship between two terms, a statement that may be either true or false, but considered as a whole must be one or the other—by authority of the fundamental laws of thought which are considered to be self-evident: the principle of contradiction (a thing cannot be and not be simultaneously), the principle of identity (whatever is, is), and the principle of the excluded middle (a thing either is or is not—there is no middle ground). That is, even if a proposition contains much truth, if there is *anything* wrong with it, it is false *as a statement.* Of course writers regularly deal with issues that are not clear-cut. They cannot reduce everything to black and white, but that is no excuse for sloppiness. They can recognize that any statement is *as it stands* true or false; and if it is not true, they can look for ways of modifying and qualifying it to make it true.

The simplest form of proposition is the categorical proposition, which asserts that one thing is or is not another, the subject term is or is not what is predicated of it.

Subject term—S	*Copula*	*Predicate term—P*
People concerned with the future	are not	concerned with the past.

A categorical proposition is a judgment of inclusion or exclusion; in traditional logic it carries the sense of one thing's being (or not being) in the class of another, and can be indicated $S < P$ or $S \nless P$:

S	$\nless$	*P*
People concerned with the future	are not in the class of	people concerned with the past.

Propositions, then, have *quality*—they are either affirmative or negative—and also *quantity*—their terms are universal, particular, or singular. Take the following, for example:

S	$<$	P
College students	are	people concerned with the future.

The subject term appears to be universal, to mean *all* college students. The predicate term is clearly particular: it can mean no more than that college students are *some* of the people concerned with the future. The first term then is *distributed,* in that it includes, is distributed over, all the members of the class; the second is *undistributed,* since it does not cover the whole class.

Singular terms refer to unique individuals, places, or events:

George Washington was the first president of the United States.

Singular terms are considered to be distributed, since they fill up their classes: All of George Washington was the whole first president. Generally a distributed term can be recognized because it carries or implies a word such as "all," "each," "every," "no," or "none." "All" can, however, be misleading if it is used collectively:

All the angles of an equilateral triangle equal 180 degrees.

"All" here does not mean "each," and the subject term is not distributed. Neither is "all" a reliable indicator in such expressions as

All girls are not beautiful.

This means, hopefully, *some* girls are not beautiful: the subject term is undistributed. To avoid this ambiguity, a negative universal proposition is usually indicated: No $S < P$, instead of $S \nless P$.

A writer cannot use propositions safely unless he can distinguish between distributed and undistributed terms, for the quantity of the terms is of first importance in controlling what inferences can be drawn from the statements. Most categorical propositions fall into four forms, two affirmative and two negative, with the following patterns of distributed and undistributed terms:

A propositions (so called after the first vowel in *affirmo,* I affirm):

All $S < P$	(S distributed, P undistributed)
All dogs are pets.	(The whole class of dogs is included, but not necessarily the whole class of pets.)

E propositions (after the first vowel in *nego,* I deny):

No $S < P$	(S distributed, P distributed)

No dogs are pets. (The whole class of dogs is outside the whole class of pets, making pets distributed.)

I propositions (after the second vowel in *affirmo*):

Some $S < P$ (S undistributed, P undistributed)

Some dogs are pets. (Neither the whole class of dogs nor the whole class of pets is considered.)

O propositions (after the second vowel in *nego*):

Some $S \nless P$ (S undistributed, P distributed)

Some dogs are not pets. (Some part of the class of dogs is outside the whole class of pets.)

Sometimes it is helpful to diagram propositions. In the most generally accepted system—developed by a nineteenth-century English logician, John Venn—the terms are represented by interlocking circles, the subject term always on the left, and the relation between them shown by shading or *X*'s.

A propositions: All $S < P$

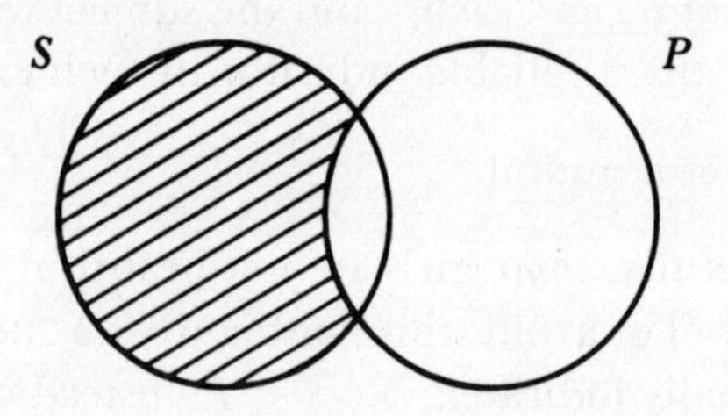

The shading indicates that there is no *S* outside of *P*.

E propositions: No $S < P$

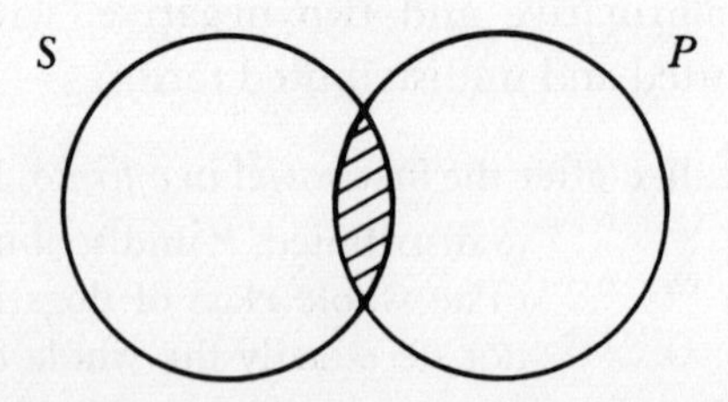

The shading indicates that there is no *S* inside of *P*.

I propositions: Some $S < P$

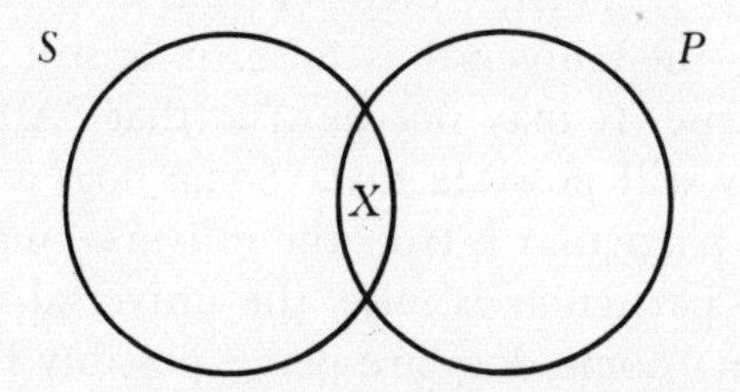

The X indicates that there is some *S* in *P*.

O propositions: Some $S \nless P$

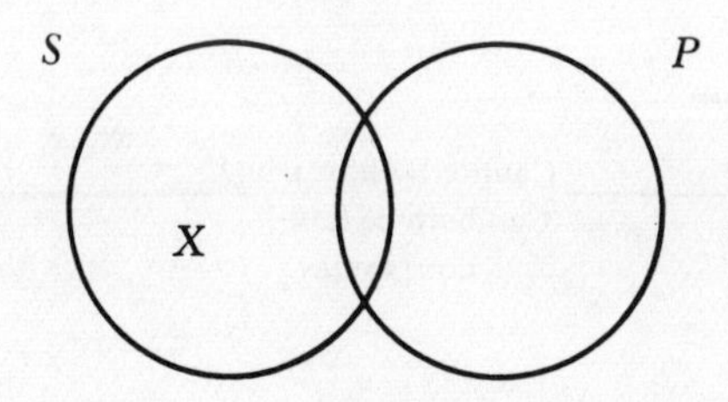

The X indicates that there is some *S* outside of *P*.

RELATIONS BETWEEN FORMS OF PROPOSITIONS

Obviously there are relationships between the *A, E, I, O,* propositions which can cast some light on their truth or falsity. *A* and *E,* for instance, are *contraries:* these propositions with the same terms cannot both be true, although both can be false. *I* and *O,* called *subcontraries,* may both be true, but it does not follow that if one is true the other is also: "Some dogs are pets" does not mean that, therefore, "Some dogs are not pets"; it merely asserts that some are. If however, one subcontrary is false, the other must be true: if "Some dogs are not pets" is false, then "Some dogs are pets" must be true. $A - O$ and $E - I$ are *contradictories.* The difference between contraries and contradictories is the difference between black and white and black and nonblack. Contradictories have a reciprocal relation: if one is true, the other is necessarily false; if one is false, the other is necessarily true. If "All dogs are pets" is true, then "Some dogs are not pets" cannot be, and vice versa. $A - I$ and

E – O, called *subalterns,* have a universal-particular relationship. If the universal (*A* or *E*) is true, then its particular (*I* or *O*) must be true. However, if the universal is false, it is still possible for the particular to be true. It may not be true that "All dogs are pets," but it is obviously still possible that "Some dogs are pets." On the other hand, if the particular is true, the universal may or may not be true; while if the particular is false, the universal must be false. If we know only that "Some dogs are pets," possibly further investigation will show that "All dogs are pets," possibly not. If, however, we know that "Some dogs are pets" is not true, we know that "All dogs are pets" cannot be true. These various relations can be summed up in the square of opposition (see diagram below).

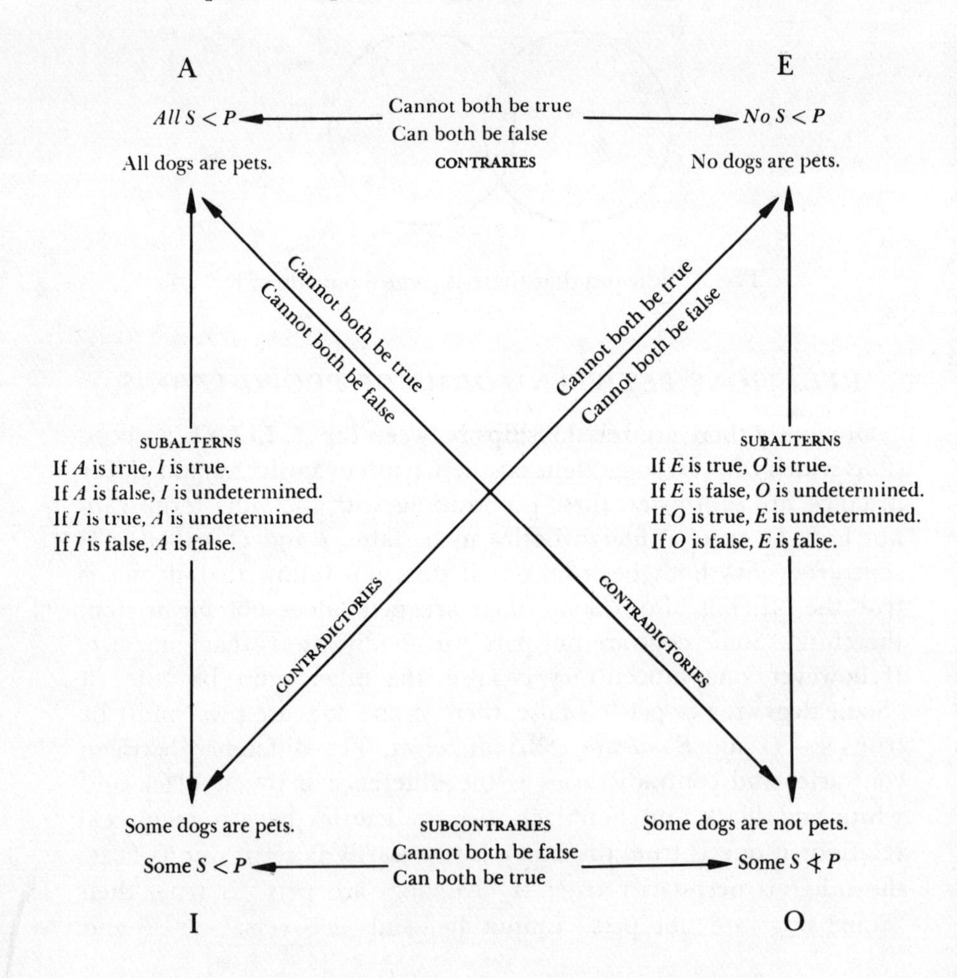

A writer can get along without memorizing all the details of the square of opposition, but he can often benefit from recognizing some of these logical relationships. To go back to the subject we discussed in Chapter Three, he can first of all realize that "Book censorship by customs officials is necessary and desirable" has a double predicate and might better be split into two propositions scrutinized separately. "Book censorship by customs officials is necessary" is essentially an *I* proposition because it has an undistributed subject which amounts to "some censorship." If "some censorship is necessary" is true, the subcontrary "some censorship is unnecessary" may also be true. If so, what are the grounds for discrimination? Why particularly by customs officials? If "some censorship is unnecessary" is true, possibly its subaltern "no censorship is necessary" is also true. Is it?

A good grasp of the square of opposition can also protect writers from fallacies which result from confusing these all-some relationships with whole-part relationships. What is true of all members of a class is true of one member of the class, but what is true of the whole is not necessarily true of all its parts, and vice versa. The whole must be recognized as an entity, not just all the parts. To argue that because all the features of a face are individually beautiful the face must be beautiful is to ignore how they might actually be put together, and to commit the *fallacy of composition.* Similarly, to reason that because Shakespeare was a great poet and dramatist a particular passage must be admirable even if we cannot understand or appreciate it—as some Bardolators have done—is to apply to the part what is true only of the whole, and to fall into the *fallacy of division.*

Although precise logical form cannot by itself provide solutions to these difficulties, it can call attention to them and lay the groundwork for solutions to come through the logical processes of eduction, deduction, or induction.

EDUCTION

Just by looking carefully at a proposition, we can make some immediate inferences about it by *eduction,* that is, by *leading the inferences out* of the statement itself. For if a proposition is true in one form, it will be true transposed into certain other forms. We can *obvert* the proposition by changing the quality of the copula from affirmative to negative or vice versa and contradicting the predicate term:

$$\textit{If } S < P \quad \textit{then } S \nless \text{non}P \quad \text{or} \quad \text{no } S < \text{non}P$$

and

$$\textit{If } S \nless P \quad \text{or} \quad \text{no } S < \text{P} \quad \textit{then } S < \text{non}P$$

To apply this second pattern of obversion to the suppressed proposition of our enthymeme, we see that

If People concerned with the future are not in the class of people concerned with the past.

Or No people concerned with the future are concerned with the past.

Then All people concerned with the future are in the class of those unconcerned with the past.

Put this way, the absoluteness of the proposition is more apparent, and we are perhaps even more dubious about its truth than we were before.

Further clarification can come from *converting* the proposition by transposing the subject and predicate terms, being careful to keep the same quality and quantity:

$$\textit{If } S < P \textit{ then } \text{some } P < S$$

(Note that since, as we saw, the predicate term in an *A* proposition is undistributed, it is converted as some *P* to preserve the quantity.)

$$\textit{If } \text{no } S < P \textit{ then } \text{no } P < S$$

If No people concerned with the future are concerned with the past.

Then No people concerned with the past are concerned with the future.

This conversion gives us another view of our statement, which by now certainly seems to need qualification—perhaps as follows:

> Some people concerned with the future are not much concerned with the past.

How could we determine whether that statement is true? We might know it by induction, from observation, our own or that of people we trust; or we might deduce it from other generalizations we accept.

DEDUCTION

Deductive thought is natural and easy: all of us regularly make deductions from generalizations, often almost intuitively and with little consciousness of the steps involved.

> Gather ye rosebuds while ye may,
> Old time is still a-flying,
> And that same flower that smiles to-day,
> To-morrow will be dying.

Underlying this familiar stanza of Robert Herrick's is the sequence of propositions:

> All flowers fade and die.
>
> These rosebuds are flowers.
>
> Therefore these rosebuds will fade and die.

Most of us know from experience, inductively, that rosebuds will fade; but if we were presented with a flower concerning which we had no experience, we would be justified in reasoning that the new flower would share the mortality of all flowers. This pattern of reasoning is called a syllogism.

The Categorical Syllogism

The categorical syllogism starts with a general statement, the major premise, which contains a predication in which we are interested, the major term or predicate term; it then adds a connected statement, the minor premise, which contains a subject in which we are interested, the minor term or subject term. What connects the subject and predicate terms is the middle term, which appears in both the major and minor premises. We are not interested in it except as a connecting link between the subject and predicate terms that will therefore allow us to relate them in the conclusion. The classic pattern is as follows:

Major premise:

M (*distributed*) $<$ P

Middle term is in the class of the major (predicate) term. (*A* prop.)

Minor premise:

S (*distributed*) $<$ M

Minor (subject) term is in the class of the middle term. (*A* prop.)

Conclusion:

S (*distributed*)   <   *P*

Therefore the minor (subject) term is in the class of the major (predicate) term. (*A* prop.)

By adding another interlocking Venn circle below the subject and predicate terms to bring in the middle term, we can diagram this syllogism, and the diagram will serve as a check on the validity of the conclusion. If we diagram the premises first and then find that the conclusion is already correctly diagramed, we know that the syllogism is valid.

All of the middle term is in *P*. (Shading shows no *M* outside *P*.)

S

P

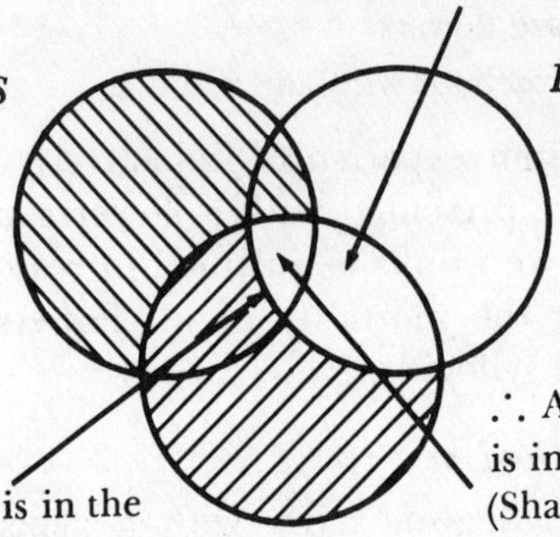

All the subject term is in the middle term. (Shading shows no *S* outside *M*.)

M

∴ All of the subject term is in the predicate term. (Shading shows no *S* can be outside *P*; therefore the conclusion is valid.)

Any categorical syllogism in the above pattern, with three *A* propositions (called *AAA* mood) and the arrangement of terms shown, can be diagramed in the same way and is valid; whether or not it is also true depends upon the truth of the premises. Terms are arranged in one of four "figures." The example diagramed is in

Figure 1:	Major premise:	*M*iddle term–*P*redicate term
	Minor premise:	*S*ubject term–*M*iddle term
	Conclusion:	*S*ubject term–*P*redicate term

Other figures are as follows:

Figure 2:	*P–M*	Figure 3:	*M–P*	Figure 4:	*P–M*
	S–M		*M–S*		*M–S*
	S–P		*S–P*		*S–P*

Shuffling around the order of the terms in these four figures, and using different combinations of kinds of propositions in other moods, will produce a great variety of different syllogisms, some of which are valid, some not. Let's try a syllogism which happens to be in the *EIO* mood and in figure 3, to see if it will get us to the conclusion we were seeking about some people concerned with the future not being concerned with the past:

M *P*
The younger generation is not much concerned with the past. (*E* prop.)
M *S*
Some of the younger generation are concerned with the future. (*I* prop.)
S *P*
Some people concerned with the future are not much concerned with the past. (*O* prop.)

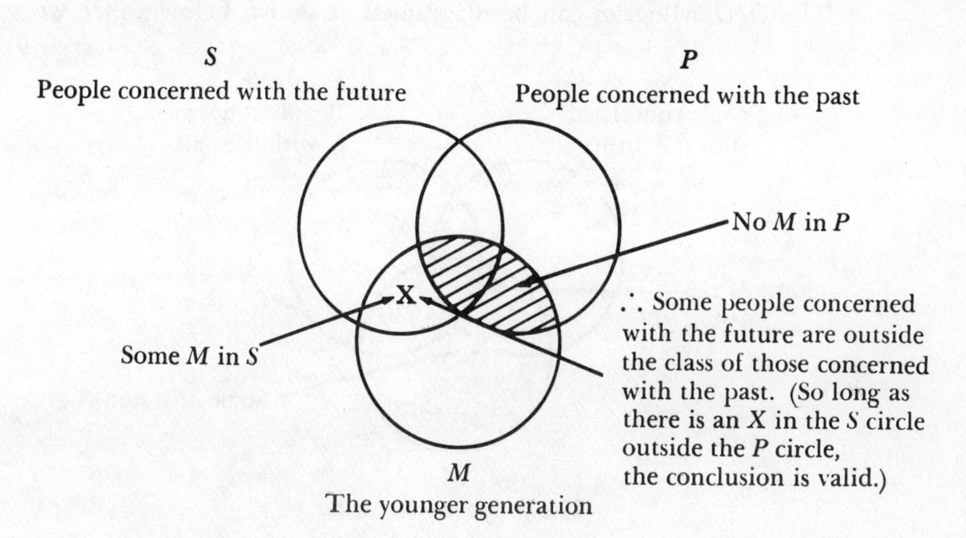

The *EIO* syllogism is valid, but this argument is not sound. The major premise needs scrutiny, because although it may be true that the younger generation by and large is not much concerned with the past, it can hardly be said that *none* of the younger generation is much concerned with the past. What is generally true is not necessarily true in all circumstances, and to treat it as if it were is to fall into the *fallacy of accident*. Therefore, although the syllogism is valid as stated, the conclusion is not reliable. That is, the conclusion may still be true, but this syllogism has not proved it because the major premise is not accurately interpreted. Its middle term is not logically distributed, for even if it means *most* of the younger generation, this still amounts to *some* of the younger generation, and the major premise is more accurately an *O* proposition:

M (*undistributed*) *P* (*distributed*)
Some of the younger generation are not much concerned with the past. (*O* prop.)

M (*undistributed*) *S* (*undistributed*)
Some of the younger generation are concerned with the future. (*I* prop.)

S (*undistributed*) *P* (*distributed*)
Some people concerned with the future are not much concerned with the past. (*O* prop.)

The *OIO* syllogism can be diagramed as shown below. Since we

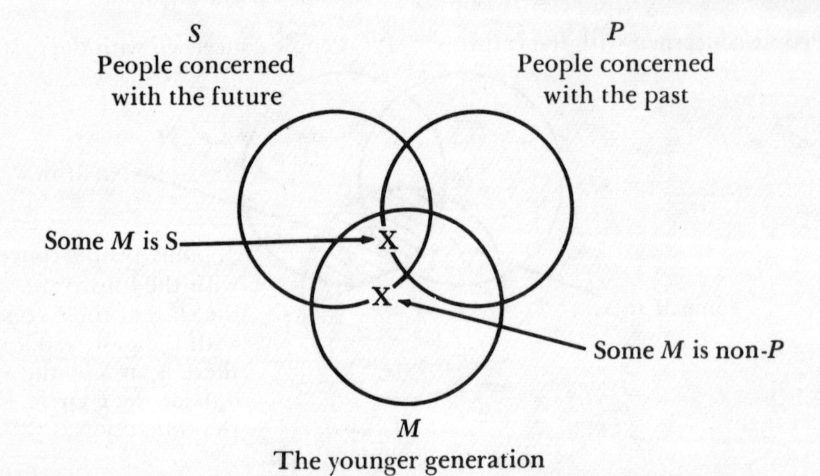

cannot be certain whether or not the "some *M*" that is outside *P* is in *S*, we have to put the *X* on the line between the *S* and *M* circles; and since we cannot be sure whether or not the "some *M*" which is in *S* is also in *P*, we have to put that *X* on the line between the *M* and *P* circles. We are left with no evidence regarding whether or not there is some *S* outside of *P*. Conceivably the "some" of the younger generation not much concerned with the past might not include any of the "some" concerned with the future—they *might* all be concentrating on the present. Therefore the conclusion is not valid. It may be true, it probably is true, but there are no grounds here stated for asserting that it is true. We simply do not know: logic begets a healthy humility.

Basic Rules of Deductive Logic

The syllogism we just looked at is not valid, and no *OIO* syllogism in this figure can be valid, because the middle term is undistributed in both the major and the minor premises, so that there is no certain common ground for making a connection between the subject and predicate terms. One of the basic rules of deductive reasoning is that in a valid categorical syllogism *the middle term must be distributed in at least one premise.*

Since in our informal, unrecognized syllogistic reasoning—and it goes on all the time—we rarely put the propositions in rigorously precise logical terms, our casualness, not to say sloppiness, often causes other troubles. One danger is that the meaning of terms will change imperceptibly. Sometimes we use an approximate synonym which is not really equivalent and therefore destroys the validity of the reasoning:

M 1 *P*
Pornographic books should be banned.

S *M*2
Ullyses has erotic passages.

S *P*
Ullyses should be banned.

Nothing can be proved by this syllogism, since "erotic passages" is not synonymous with "pornographic." The syllogism has in fact two middle terms, and therefore has fallen into the *fallacy of four terms,* which leads us to another basic rule of deductive reasoning: a valid categorical syllogism *must have only three unequivocal terms.*

At the other extreme is the argument which has no real middle term at all, but merely presents as a premise a different formulation of the conclusion. The *fallacy of begging the question* can sometimes be almost obscured in a plethora of words:

All honest men support Senator X in his campaign for reelection because Senator X, I am proud to say, is and always has been the kind of man who can unfailingly count on the sincere support of the honest men of this great state.

In our casual deductions frequently we will unconsciously make a term more inclusive in the conclusion than it is in its premise, and thereby invalidate the syllogism. That is what is wrong with the line of reasoning shown below.

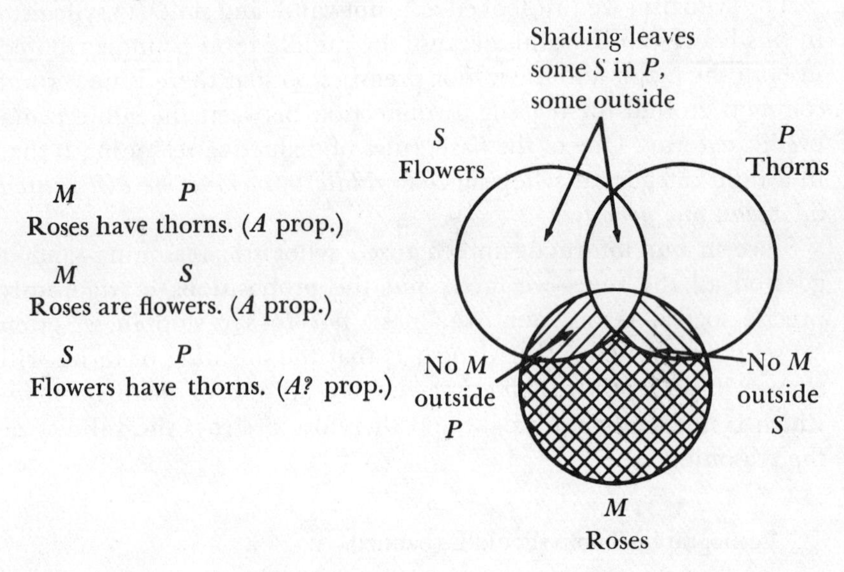

Both premises are true, but the conclusion is false because the subject term shifts from undistributed to distributed: in the minor premise it actually means *some* flowers; in the conclusion it appears to mean *all* flowers. As the diagram shows, the only valid conclusion is "Some flowers have thorns," and the conclusion is properly an *I* proposition. This shifting of the subject term from particular to universal is called the *fallacy of the illicit minor*. The same shift of the predicate term results in the *fallacy of the illicit major:*

M *P (undistributed)*
All great historians are much concerned with the past. (*A* prop.)

S *M*
No college students are great historians. (*E* prop.)

S *P (distributed)*
No college students are much concerned with the past. (*E* prop.)

Obviously great historians are only *some* of the people much concerned with the past, and nothing in the syllogism rules college students out of the rest of that group. The conclusion is invalid—as it is for all *AEE* syllogisms which have their terms arranged in figure 1. Another fundamental rule of deduction, therefore, is that a valid categorical syllogism *cannot distribute any term in the conclusion which is not distributed in its premise.*

Two other basic rules concern negative statements: *if one of the premises is negative, the conclusion must be negative;* and *if both of the premises are negative, no valid conclusion can be reached* (see diagram below).

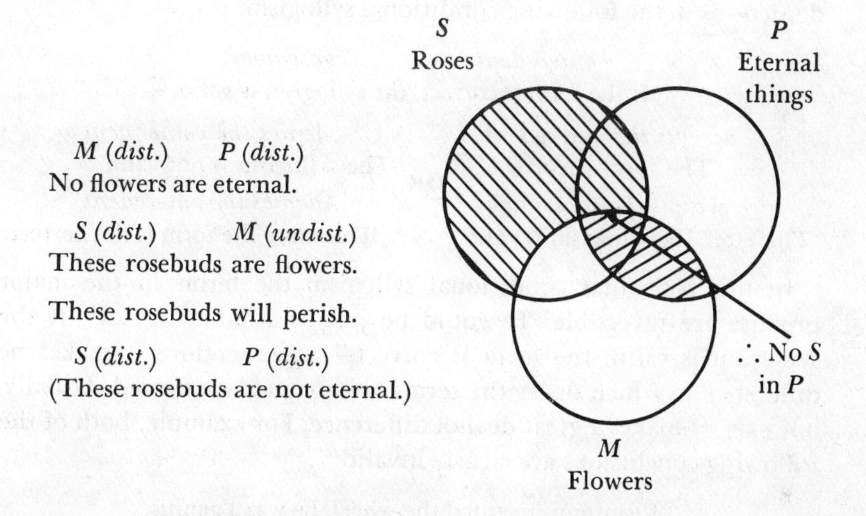

Notice that although the idea in the conclusion is expressed positively—"will perish"—it is actually a negation of the predicate term —not in the class of eternal things. In the following syllogism the minor premise is also negative in meaning, although positive in expression:

No declared atheist has ever been elected president of the United States. (That is, all declared atheists are not in the class of those who have been elected president of the United States.)

Senator X is a Methodist. (That is, Senator X is not in the class of declared atheists.)

Senator X will be elected president of the United States.

The conclusion obviously does not follow because both premises are negative and all that can be said from them is that Senator X is *not* in *one* class of those who have *not* been elected to the presidency.

Conditional and Alternative Syllogisms

Since categorical statements are often arrived at only through a hypothetical chain of reasoning, writers must also deal with syllogisms containing alternative or conditional premises. These differ from categorical syllogisms in that one or both premises enunciate two elements, either alternatives or antecedent and consequent, and the argument can move in two ways, depending on which alternative is accepted or whether the antecedent or consequent is accepted or denied—as in the following conditional syllogism:

antecedent *consequent*
If the form is correct, the syllogism is valid.

accepts the antecedent
The form is correct.
accepts the consequent
Therefore the syllogism is valid.

OR

denies the consequent
The syllogism is not valid.
denies the antecedent
Therefore the form is not correct.

In this particular conditional syllogism the terms in the major premise are reversible: It would be just as accurate to say "If the syllogism is valid, the form is correct," and therefore it makes no difference in which order the terms are accepted or denied. Usually, however, it makes a great deal of difference. For example, both of the following conclusions are clearly invalid:

If Einstein invented the wheel, he was a genius.

accepts the consequent
Einstein was a genius
accepts the antecedent
Then Einstein invented the wheel.

denies the antecedent
Einstein did not invent the wheel.
denies the consequent
Einstein was not a genius.

For a conditional syllogism to be valid, the minor term must accept (posit) the antecedent, and the conclusion must accept the consequent; or the minor term must deny (sublate) the consequent, and the conclusion deny the antecedent. Similarly, the valid alternative syllogism must accept one alternative in the minor premise and deny the other in the conclusion, or deny one in the minor and accept the other in the conclusion:

Either we will win this game or we will lose the championship.

accepts 1st alt.	*denies 1st alt.*
We will win this game	We will lose this game.
denies 2nd alt.	*accepts 2nd alt.*
Therefore we will win the championship.	Therefore we will lose the championship.

What is more likely to cause difficulty for writers is an argument with more than two alternatives, for here a valid conclusion can be reached only by *denying all alternatives except one.* Sloppy or wishful thinking can produce the invalid conclusion in the left column below:

We lost the game because of bad luck, injuries, or a superior opponent.

accepts 1st and 2nd alts.	*denies 1st and 2nd alts.*
We had bad luck and many injuries.	We had good luck and no injuries.
denies 3rd alt.	*accepts 3rd alt.*
Therefore our opponent was not superior. (*invalid*)	Therefore our opponent was superior. (*valid*)

Validity and Truth

All these rules, we should never forget, are concerned with the formal validity of the syllogism—not necessarily with its truth. If the rules are observed, the logical machine will work correctly and the conclusion will be valid. Unless the premises are accurate, however, the conclusions will not be reliable—although they may be true by accident:

Professors who know their subjects are good teachers.
Professor X knows his subject.
Professor X is a good teacher.

The syllogism is perfectly *valid,* which is to say that it follows the logic of the syllogism accurately. But the conclusion is not reliable, because the major premise can be debated. Probably all that one can say positively is that most professors who know their subjects are good teachers. Professor X might be in a minority who for some reason are unable to communicate their knowledge. The minor premise might also be wrong—Professor X might not be a real authority on his subject. Nevertheless, despite the flaws in the premises, the conclusion might be correct. Professor X might be a good teacher for other reasons: his personality, his interest in students, his willingness to spend time on teaching. A syllogism, it is important to note, *will not work backwards.* Because a conclusion is true, it does not follow that the premises are true; and if the premises are not true, the conclusion is not reliable no matter how valid the operation of the logical machinery.

Constructing Syllogisms

What should a freshman do with these rules of logical inference? Aside from being interested in them for their own sakes—they form an ancient and fascinating discipline—he may as a writer find them helpful in making him aware of and able to scrutinize his many buried syllogisms. He may also sometimes deliberately start with a generalization and deduce conclusions from it in developing an essay, as in this train of thought:

College students should not be encouraged to accelerate their educations.
M
(That is, nothing which will encourage college students to accelerate
P
their educations is desirable.) (*E* prop.)

S *M*
Year-round operation of colleges will encourage students to accelerate. (*A* prop.)

S *P*
Therefore year-round operation of colleges is not desirable. (*A* prop.)

As a focused subject, however, this order would be more likely to be reversed: "Year-round operation of colleges is undesirable because it will encourage students to accelerate their education to their disadvantage." Often, as we bring our subjects into focus we *have* the conclusion of a syllogism and are looking for the "because," trying to line up sound premises to support the conclusion. For instance:

M	*P*
????	Senecan revenge tragedy
S	*M*
Hamlet	????
S	*P*

Hamlet is a Senecan revenge tragedy.

What we are looking for here is a middle term, an adequate connection between the two points which interest us.

All Renaissance plays which contain ghosts, violence and revenge are Senecan revenge tragedies. (*A* prop.)

Hamlet contains ghosts, violence and revenge. (*A* prop.)

Hamlet is a Senecan revenge tragedy. (*A* prop.)

The middle term is distributed, there are three clear terms, the subject term is distributed in both the minor premise and the conclusion: this is an *AAA* syllogism with the terms in figure 1, and the argument is valid.

If we were writing such an essay on *Hamlet,* most of our effort would probably go into demonstrating the truth of the minor premise by a careful examination of the play, by evidence from observation. We would probably accept the major premise from authorities, who had themselves made careful examinations of many plays and arrived at the conclusion by induction.

INDUCTION

Induction is the method of reasoning from particulars to generalizations or universals. From the facts that the sun rose in the east yesterday and the day before that, and in our experience and recorded history has always risen in the east every morning, we can conclude by *analogy* that it will arise in the east tomorrow and go further to generalize that it always does and will rise in the east every morning. Induction works on the basic principle of uniformity, that the same cause will always produce the same effect. We can never be sure of an induction, however, in the same way that we can be sure a deduction is valid if the machinery is sound. The best we can expect of an induction is a high degree of probability. Probability varies with the *verifiability* of the observations and the *relevance* of the data to the conclusion.

Much of what we consider to be true comes to us through observation, through sensory experience. "Seeing is believing," we say. Yet any magician can demonstrate that we cannot believe what we see, or what we think we see; and any court room will demonstrate that witnesses do not always see the same event in the same way. Much of what we think of as observation is actually an interpretation of observation: the sun, of course, does not really rise in the east at all —it only appears to do so. Even so simple a matter as observing the extent to which Shakespeare presents ghosts in *Hamlet* poses a problem in interpretation: does Hamlet's dead father actually appear in the Queen's chamber, or is the Prince having hallucinations? Even those observational truths which we consider to be self-evident—"the whole is equal to the sum of its parts" or "a circle is round"—are, in fact, matters of definition. We define a circle as round, although most of us have never seen a perfectly round circle and do not have the sensory acuity to perceive one if it could exist. We must learn to be sceptical of the truth of our observations.

Yet much of our knowledge is based ultimately on our sensory experiences, and as writers we want to use these experiences because they are concrete and vivid, they add color and substance to our work. If we are going to draw any general conclusions from them, however, we need to show that the observations are verifiable, that the phenomenon can be observed again, and by other people. The more times it can be observed by more different people under more different circumstances, the more probable it becomes and the more reliable as a basis for inductive reasoning.

If it is possible to observe all the instances of a phenomenon, it is possible to make a complete induction. When we have the examination scores of all the students in a class and observe that they all failed abysmally, we can conclude that the examination was too difficult for that class. To answer the question why it was too difficult requires an hypothesis based on other, less complete data: was the class of below average intelligence, not working, lacking in preparation, inexpertly taught, or was the test unreasonable? Rarely are our data as complete as a list of test scores. Scholars seeking the character of a Senecan revenge tragedy might investigate all known plays of Seneca and all extant Renaissance plays which show the possibility of Senecan influence, and come up with a relatively complete induction; but they would still lack the evidence of lost plays. Usually we have to deal with data even less complete. We therefore take only sample evidence and close the gap between the particulars and the generalization by the *inductive leap*. If we can assume that our observations are accurate and our particulars true, the problem is to determine how far and where we can leap.

Suppose a friend told you that he got an *A* grade in English 10 with little effort. You might decide that anything your friend could do you could do, and determine by simple analogy that you also could easily get an *A* on the course. If you wanted to go on to the inductive generalization that English 10 was a soft course, you would have to accumulate data:

Students X, Y, and Z got *A* grades on English 10 last term.
Students U, V, and W got *A* grades on English 10 the term before.
Students N, O, P, and Q said the course was easy.
Students L and M got *C* grades without even opening the book.
Therefore (*leap*), English 10 is a soft course.

The probability of this conclusion depends on the spread and relevance of the analogies. Are these data relevant to something about the course, or something about the students cited? The discovery that students L–Z were all English majors and publishing writers would make you dubious about the relevance of their testimony. Generally the larger the number of instances, the safer is the induction; the reason for this is simply that a larger number of incidents may be expected to cover a wider range of experiences. However, the records and opinions of 200 students with high IQ's would be less indicative for this conclusion than would a smaller sample carefully taken from students of different capabilities and interests. We must, of course, also be sure that these data are relevant to the exact same course. If the course is taught by different instructors, a sampling should cover them all, or the only probable conclusion might be that Professor X's English 10 is a snap course. If the course has been changed this term, none of the data from the past may be relevant.

Other facts which might enter into the conclusion but which have limited relevance would be:

English 12 is recognized to be a soft course.
English 10 is generally called an entertaining course.
Professor X never assigns term papers.

Such facts may have some application to the matter, but do not directly support the conclusion: two courses in the same department can vary widely in difficulty; a course can be entertaining and still not easy; and a course can be difficult even if it does not require a term paper. Weak in itself, such evidence added to the weight of more relevant data can, however, provide some support by the cumulative effect. To know what data *are* relevant requires some assumptions regarding what makes a course easy, some hypothesis concerning causal relations.

CAUSE

The concept of cause is complicated. Aristotle recognized four kinds of causes: material, formal, efficient and final. The *material* cause of a watch is the steel, gold, jewels, enamel, and glass or plastic of which it is made; the *formal* cause is the design by which these materials are organized; the *efficient* cause is the watchmaker who built it; and the *final* cause is the purpose of telling time.

For an easy course the material cause would be the subject content, the formal cause the organization and presentation of the material, the efficient cause the professor, and the final cause the educational theory behind the course. Effects of these different orders of cause can cancel each other out: the most complicated subject can be made to appear easy by a gifted teacher, and the simplest material can be made difficult by an inept instructor. A gifted teacher might, however, prefer to keep his students reaching, and offer a rigorous course. And a very poor teacher might give a snap course simply because his requirements were low. The ability of the teacher, then, is not a *sufficient* cause for an easy course—it will not produce an easy course all by itself, although it can be a *necessary* cause in consort with other conditions. Perhaps an unusually liberal grading standard might be a sufficient cause for an easy course. In each kind of causes there may be causal chains from *remote* to *proximate* cause. The professor who gives an easy course may do so because he had one when he was an undergraduate, or because he believes that undergraduates are overworked and wishes to give them more leisure because he is actually opposed to the course system anyway. Such causal chains are interesting, but usually we are concerned with the proximate or immediate causes.

Since as writers we will frequently be developing essays causally, starting with a thesis and showing it should be accepted *because* of what follows, we need to know something about the mechanisms for ferreting out causes. Some fruitful procedures work by *elimination* of antecedents which *might* be causes but are *not*. Ignoring these procedures leads us into false assumptions that apparent sequences are causally related, that a rain dance or washing the car makes it rain—the fallacy of *post hoc ergo propter hoc.* How do we know, on the other hand, that seeding clouds can make it rain?

If in a normally dry period ten rain storms occurred at different times of day, in different areas, in different phases of the moon, with different initial barometric pressures, and were preceded by a great variety of human behavior, but shared *one significant* common circumstance—the seeding of the clouds—we could eliminate all the diverse elements and conclude that the common element was the cause. John Stuart Mill, who explored the logic of causality in the nineteenth century, called this the *method of agreement.* By his *method of difference,* which can be used concurrently or separately, we could note that for a given number of days during a dry period it did not rain except when the clouds were seeded, and the only significant difference between the days it did rain and did not was the cloud seeding; the circumstance which is different can then be considered the determining factor. If we could account for the gathering of clouds by shifts of adjacent pressure areas and through similar inductions could relate all the associated effects with some antecedent, but had left over one effect and one antecedent—the actual precipitation and the antecedent cloud seeding—we could then relate the left-over effect with the left-over antecedent by using what Mill called the *method of residues.* The only catch to these methods is in determining *significant* agreement and difference, for rarely can we eliminate all factors but one, and we may pick the wrong one. The classic example is the story of the man who found he got drunk on gin and water, bourbon and water, scotch and water, rye and water—and decided to give up water. It is just possible that all of these rains occurred on Friday, and although we would hardly conclude that the common circumstance of the day of the week was meaningful, we could not be sure until we could produce rain on other days.

If we were dealing with a phenomenon in which it was impossible or impracticable to eliminate certain antecedents or certain instances, we might get a line on causation by the *method of concomitant variations.* For that matter, we could not observe whether it would rain or not if there were no barometric pressure, but we could notice a correlation between changes in pressure and weather conditions. Since this method is quantitative and invites statistical application, it should be used with caution by the statistically unsophisticated. Proverbially, figures don't lie, but liars do figure—and figures can make liars of well-meaning writers. Correlations can be established between all kinds of concomitant variations—say the price of rum and the salary of college professors. This does not mean either that the professors demanded higher salaries because of the increased cost of rum or that they drove up the price of rum by the demand occasioned by their higher salaries.

AUTHORITIES

All of us have to depend a great deal upon authorities. In the nature of things many of the major premises of a writer's syllogisms—recognized or unrecognized—will be derived from some outside source and accepted by him. What is it safe to accept? First, we have to resist the temptation simply to accept as authorities people whose ideas agree with our own, and dismiss as crackpots people whose ideas do not. This crackpot technique of abusing the opposition, impugning their intelligence, motives or morality, takes the argument from issues to personalities and is a species of the fallacy of *argumentum ad hominem*. Defense attorneys and advertising agencies may go looking for authorities to support predetermined positions; the writer in search of the truth tries to consider opinions from recognized authorities in the field.

Both of those attributes are important: *recognized* and *in the field*. For we have to be wary of self-elected and self-seeking "authorities" who issue dicta of dubious value and spokesmen of real competence in some fields who pronounce in other realms—movie stars discoursing on health foods, baseball players on automobiles, and astronauts on politics. We may personally agree with the opinions of these worthies on these subjects and, indeed, they may very well be right, but we cannot depend upon their authority. It is sobering and sometimes helpful to remember that whenever we cite an authority we are leaning implicitly on this line of reasoning:

> *Whatever* X says *on this subject* is true.
> On this subject X had said this.
> Therefore, this is true.

That buried major premise often needs qualification, as we realize if we face it.

As writers, we may not deliberately use all of this logical machinery, for we have absorbed much of it and call it common sense. By whatever means, however, we must look to the logic of our writing, remembering that rhetoric is popular logic—popular in order to persuade pleasantly, and logical in order to persuade soundly.

ASSIGNMENTS

1. Put the following sentences into logical form as propositions:

a. It never rains but it pours.

b. George Washington slept here.

c. The youth of a nation is one of its chief resources.

d. It is not yet certain whether or not we will go.

e. Given an opportunity to comment, I will express my opinion vigorously.

f. No further information can be expected at this time.

g. All students are not industrious.

h. Some ballots have not yet been received.

2. For all the categorical propositions above indicate whether the subject and predicate terms are distributed or undistributed and identify them as *A, E, I,* or *O* propositions. Draw Venn circle diagrams for *b, f,* and *h.*

3. Obvert and convert the following propositions:

a. Every holiday is welcome.

b. No job is too small.

c. Some men are geniuses.

4. Obvert the following proposition and explain why it cannot be logically converted:

Some men are not geniuses.

5. Make a square of opposition using the terms in the following proposition:

All hills are high.

6. Comment on the logic of this passage from Sydney Smith's "Noodle's Oration":

> What would our ancestors say to this, Sir? How does this measure tally with their institutions? How does it agree with their experience? Are we to put the wisdom of yesterday in competition with the wisdom of centuries? (*Hear, hear!*) Is beardless youth to show no respect for the

decisions of mature age? (*Loud cries of hear! hear!*) If this measure be right, would it have escaped the wisdom of those Saxon progenitors to whom we are indebted for so many of our best political institutions? Would the Dane have passed it over? Would the Norman have rejected it? Would such a notable discovery have been reserved for these modern and degenerate times? Besides, Sir, if the measure itself is good, I ask the honourable gentlemen if this is the time for carrying it into execution—whether, in fact, a more unfortunate period could have been selected than that which he has chosen? If this were an ordinary measure, I should not oppose it with so much vehemence; but, Sir, it calls in question the wisdom of an irrevocable law—of a law passed at the memorable period of the Revolution. What right have we, Sir, to break down this firm column, on which the great men of that day stamped a character of eternity? Are not all authorities against this measure—Pitt, Fox, Cicero, and the Attorney and Solicitor General? The proposition is new, Sir; it is the first time it was ever heard in this House. I am not prepared, Sir—this house is not prepared, to receive it. The measure implies a distrust of his Majesty's government; their disapproval is sufficient to warrant opposition.

7. Fifteen students live together in an old house; nine of them have contracted a mysterious malady. From the following data draw such conclusions as you can by Mill's methods as to the probable source of the difficulty.

Student	*Major*	*Class*	*Age*	*Job*	*Ate in House*	*Ill*
A	Physics	Fr.	17	None	Yes	No
B	Classics	Soph.	18	Lab. janitor	Yes	Yes
C	Botany	Soph.	19	Library	Yes	No
D	Bacteriology	Sr.	19	Gym janitor	Yes	Yes
E	Physics	Jr.	20	Reader	Yes	No
F	Chemistry	Jr.	19	None	Yes	Yes
G	Dramatic art	Jr.	19	Lab. janitor	Yes	Yes
H	Bacteriology	Sr.	20	None	Yes	Yes
I	Zoology	Fr.	17	Library	Yes	Yes
J	Zoology	Fr.	18	Service station	Yes	Yes
K	English	Soph.	17	Lab. janitor	Yes	Yes
L	Sociology	Sr.	22	Lab. store room	Yes	Yes
M	History	Jr.	18	Library	Yes	No
N	Speech	Fr.	16	None	No	No
O	Anthropology	Soph.	18	Gym janitor	No	No

8. Characterize the fallacies in these statements:

a. Any fair person must be in favor of the Fair Housing Bill.

b. Since Judge X has taken an oath to support law and order and has devoted his life to justice, he cannot be guilty of a crime himself.

c. The opinions of the Rev. Mr. Y on religious matters cannot be disinterested.

d. Since "the king can do no wrong," Charles I was unjustly treated.

e. It is unnecessary to refute the opinions of Mr. X on city government: he is a well-known ward heeler and even a confessed bigamist!

f. I have it on the authority of that eminent Neapolitan tenor, Pietro di Cosimo, that Italian secondary school education is the best in the world.

g. Censorship has been used in some form in most cultures of which we have any knowledge; it must, therefore, be desirable.

h. It has been said of Harvard, and it can be said of most colleges that they are great depositories of wisdom because the freshmen bring so much and the seniors take so little away.

i. General Motors is a respected company with the finest facilities and a reputation for building good automobiles; therefore my 1960 Chevy is a good car.

j. There were no corrections at all marked on the essay paper; therefore, it must have received a grade of *A*.

9. Make three syllogisms and diagram them using Venn circles. If possible, take them from the theses of essays you have written recently. Do they turn out to be valid? Are the premises true? By what sort of evidence?

10. Consider the following proposition:

Overeating is likely to cause one to dream.

Support it if you can by these kinds of evidence:

a. From your own knowledge (demonstrate its credibility and beware of *post hoc ergo propter hoc*).

b. From authorities (show their credentials).

c. From accumulated witnesses (demonstrate relevance and reliability).

11. What's wrong with the following syllogisms? Consider both validity of form and accuracy of premises.

a. Star-crossed lovers cannot live happily ever after.
Romeo and Juliet are star-crossed lovers.
Romeo and Juliet must die.

b. Flowers smell sweet.
Roses are flowers.
Roses smell sweet.

c. Industry is rewarded.
He is not industrious.
He will be unrewarded.

d. If it rains I stay at home.
It did not rain.
I did not stay home.

12. Construct at least one syllogism underlying each of the subjects listed in assignment 2 of Chapter Six. Consider what kind of evidence would be needed to support each premise. What are the basic assumptions? Are they tenable?

CHAPTER SIX

Rhetoric and Structure: The Outline and Its Uses

A piece of writing is a physical structure, a complex of symbols on paper, designed to evoke in the mind of the reader an intellectual structure. As we saw in talking about rhetoric and knowledge, for the writer the conceptual design and its physical form often evolve together by interplay of influence. Since, however, the only means of recording and transmitting the intellectual structure is the final physical structure, for the reader the pattern of ideas is entirely dependent upon the pattern of words. As John Donne put it of an analogous situation:

> Love's mysteries in souls do grow,
> But yet the body is his book.
> "The Ecstasy," 71–72

A writer must struggle to embody the mystery of his idea in the substantial form of his essay; and between the germinal thought and the elaborated theme, between the thesis sentence and the finished piece, he needs architectural assistance. Such aid is most readily found in a good outline.

An outline is in part a pious statement of intention, in part a skeleton to flesh out, in part a blueprint to follow, in part a cut-down model on which to try out ideas. It is not, except under unusual circumstances, a deep freeze to preserve bits of prime verbiage for later embellishment of the finished work. If you think of an outline as a skeleton upon which to build up structure—like a sculptor's armature for supporting and directing the shape of a clay statue—you might remember that a skeleton does not show through except in cases of emaciation. Yet bone structure is of fundamental importance, none the less. If you think of an outline as an architect's drawing, you might remember that even architects make mistakes and very few buildings are put up without some changes in plans during construction. An outline is not a strait jacket, it is a tool; its only real requirement is that it be useful.

The outline, then, should be tailored to the job. For some kinds of writing you need elaborately worked out blueprints. For others a few lines on the back of an old envelope will do. Sometimes even the most ambitious projects begin with simple outlines, which are then expanded and filled in—the first sketch of the fabulous Crystal Palace was drawn by the Duke of Devonshire's gardener on a piece of blotting paper.

The simplest kind of outline hardly deserves the name, for it goes little beyond setting down ideas in search of a subject, as we discussed in Chapter Three. It does try roughly and skimpily to fasten a few wandering thoughts into some kind of meaningful sequence. If you intended to write a brief essay on the reasons for Macbeth's delay in murdering Duncan, you might simply jot down

Duncan had been good to him

Why risk his new-won honors?

Duncan his guest

Loyalty

Witches' promise might come true without his effort

Fear of consequences

Such a rough list might well be enough for you to think out what you wanted to say and begin to write. You would probably want to decide which of the motives were important and which were more or less rationalizations. You might conclude that fear of consequences was the determining reason, and organize your essay accordingly. If such a simple listing produces good results for you, do not bother with anything more elaborate. An outline should be a device which helps you write better essays, not unnecessary busywork.

Such a brief jotting, however, is not really an outline at all; it is the raw material for a mental outline which develops so simply and obviously that writing it down doesn't seem worthwhile. It is therefore inadequate in dealing with a long or complex subject which cannot be elaborated mentally. It is also of little use as an outline from which you expect to write an essay at some later date, because it is too brief and depends too much on information not actually on the paper. Similarly, it is of limited use to anyone else. If you are asked to turn in an outline so that your instructor can advise you on your progress and intentions, you must give him something fuller.

THE TOPIC OUTLINE

The form of outline most used is the topic outline. It is so called because each entry is a topic, a word or a phrase, not a complete sentence. But far from being simply jotted down, as in the simple listing above, these topics are carefully marshaled with parallel points in parallel positions and inferior points in subordinate positions. Suppose that we were planning to write an essay on the following thesis: "In Shakespeare's *Macbeth* the murder of Duncan cannot be blamed on either Macbeth or Lady Macbeth, but results from the interaction of his amoral ambition and her strong personality." We might make an outline such as the following:

I. Neither alone responsible for the idea of murder
  A. Macbeth hints idea initially
    1. Sees "horrid images" after Witches' prophecies begin to come true (I, iii, 135)
    2. Thinks of Prince of Cumberland as a stumbling block (I, iv, 49)
    3. Says Duncan "purposes" to leave his house (I, v, 61)
  B. Lady Macbeth has idea before Macbeth expresses it
    1. Her response to his letter (I, v, 18)
    2. Her remark on Duncan's "fatal entrance" into their house (I, v, 40)
    3. Her plea that Duncan never leave (I, v, 61–62)
II. Macbeth's primary responsibility
  A. Motive
    1. Ambition (I, vii, 27)
      a. Triggered by Witches
      b. Not conquered, only channeled (I, iii, 144)

2. No hint of Lady Macbeth's ambition—although in Shakespeare's source

B. Macbeth plans murder? (I, vii, 48)

C. Macbeth's opposition chiefly on grounds of expediency

1. Fears "judgment here" (I, vii, 8)—more certain because

a. Duncan kinsman

b. Duncan guest

c. Duncan popular

2. Fears to risk new honors (I, vii, 33)

3. Fears failure—"If we should fail" (I, vii, 59)

D. Macbeth does the deed (II, ii, 15)

III. Lady Macbeth's primary responsibility

A. Takes over leadership

1. First voices possibility (I, v, 62 ff.)

2. Offers to take over planning (I, v, 69)

3. Drugs grooms and lays out daggers (II, ii, 6, 12)

B. Browbeats Macbeth into act

1. Accuses Macbeth of cowardice (I, vii, 43)

2. Holds Macbeth to his oath (I, vii, 58)

Several things need to be said about a topic outline. First, it is usually an outline of the *body* of the essay. Any preliminaries or conclusions which seem appropriate are added when the outline is fleshed out. Second, it is—like all outlines—intended to be useful, and should be so arranged as to be as helpful as possible. Therefore one should resist a temptation which "topic" may suggest, the temptation to put down only the barest bones of ideas, often in single words. For instance, under I, *B,* 1 you might have written only "letter" and this might have been meaningful enough at the time you wrote it. But later, or to anybody else, it might not be helpful. Notice also that this outline includes act and scene references to passages which support the points. Such documentation might, of course, have been omitted: it is not logically necessary to the outline. But how helpful it is, and how much time and trouble it will save later! Always put in the outline anything that will help.

STRUCTURE OF CLASSIFICATION

Since the outline is designed to set forth the logical structure of the essay, the appropriate entries should be logically parallel. Under I the two points at issue are when Macbeth and Lady Macbeth first indicated that they were thinking of murdering Duncan. These are, therefore, points *A* and *B*. Notice that they add up to I: neither was responsible alone because each had the idea independently of the other. The points under a heading should always add up to the heading. What is an outline logically, after all?

Isn't it just a process of classification? What you are doing when you put down your capital Roman numerals is setting up the big pigeonholes in which you will file appropriate material. Obviously they must be parallel pigeonholes. You cannot alternatively file your correspondence chronologically by date of writing and alphabetically by addressee. You set up a file of dates or an alphabetical file, and stick to one or the other. And just as obviously, everything in a given pigeonhole must belong there and nowhere else. If by an auditory mistake a *B* gets into a *P* file, you remove it as soon as your eye falls upon it. The example is ridiculously evident, but the principle is exactly the same for writing, where the structure of the outline should be such as to make your eye fall upon such anomalies as, say, this:

A. Motive
  1. Ambition
  2. Fear of consequences

"Fear of consequences" is clearly not a motive, although it does act to suppress the motive: it belongs somewhere else in the outline.

Since the pigeonholes must be parallel, it is useful to make the outline entries not only logically parallel but also—where this can be done without strain—grammatically and syntactically parallel. Notice how under I, *A* all of the entries begin with a present tense verb; under I, *B* all begin with "her." This kind of parallelism is not important in itself, and it can even be forced upon material which is not logically parallel; but if used to reinforce the logical relationship, it is helpful.

For the same reasons, it is advisable to indent carefully and to stick rigorously to the labeling sequence of

I.
  A.
    1.
      a.
        (1)
          (*a*)

This system has no peculiar virtue in itself, but does have the advantage of making obvious which pigeonholes ought to match. If you have put down I. Mammals, II. Birds, III. Fishes, IV. Man, then you ought to be able to see at once that something is wrong; IV obviously belongs under I. Just as the subentries ought to add up to the heading, the various headings should be mutually exclusive: nothing should be admitted under one which belongs under another.

A basic problem in this process of classification is how many main pigeonholes to set up. As a certain biology professor used to tell his classes, "All the world is divided into splitters and lumpers." He was talking about scientists who classify living organisms; but makers of outlines must also decide whether to set up a new category or consider an idea a subspecies of an existent group. To split, or lump? If we keep refining our criteria, we can have as many classes as individuals. On the other hand, too broad categories blur vital distinctions. I would suggest, however, that most of us are in more danger of splitting than of lumping. We get so close to our point that they all seem main points. In the first rough draft of the above outline, I had *A, B, C, D* and *E* under III. Every point was shown as parallel, when they should have been logically subordinated as shown.

Not only is it implausible that we should have all main points, like an army of generals; it is also bad psychology, since the whole purpose of organizing an essay is to give it meaningful structure. Most of us have used "disorganized" as a synonym for "confusing." "Pull yourself together," we advise a flurried and incoherent friend. Well, the function of the outline is to pull ideas together in such a way as to make them easily accessible. They cannot be readily taken up unless they are presented in pieces that are a handy size. Throwing a person a whole series of points all on the same level produces the same results as throwing him a handful of salted peanuts. We should not be surprised if he catches only a few of the scattering nuts. If we put the peanuts in a cellophane bag, and the ideas in larger containing units, both can be caught. Out of a laudable zeal for perfect unity, sometimes we are tempted to the other extreme of lumping points unmanageably. Even if we are exalted by a complexly unified vision in which every idea flows out of and is connected with every other idea, we must remember that readers need to see the joints and be able to assimilate part by part: a seamless, monolithic whole can be confusing, too much to take in at once.

Usually, therefore, a short essay will have about three main points, and about three main headings under each of these points. Three is not a mystic number, although it does have behind it a great deal of authority, from the three wishes of fairy tales to the three steps of Hegelian dialectic. Longer pieces of writing can reasonably have more main points and principal subdivisions—provided they are "main," and of digestible size. Presenting only two main points, on the other hand, is not usually desirable because the essay then has a tendency to split into halves. Even in a paper organized by contrast and comparison a sort of concluding synthesis is frequently helpful to hold the two sections together.

THE SENTENCE OUTLINE

The sentence outline is no more than a logical expansion of the topic outline. For an example let's expand section II of the above outline on *Macbeth.*

II. Macbeth is himself primarily responsible for significant elements in the whole murder project.
  A. The motive seems to be Macbeth's personally.
    1. It is his ambition for kingly power.
      a. This ambition is probably triggered by the prophecy of the Witches that he will be king.
      b. He responds by saying that if chance will have him king, then chance will crown him; but he never denies the ambition.
    2. Lady Macbeth, on the other hand, is not presented as ambitious in her own right, although Shakespeare's source made her so.
  B. Macbeth apparently plans the murder, for when Lady Macbeth accuses him of breaking his oath she says that he broached the business.
  C. Macbeth's opposition to the project is on grounds of expediency, not morality.
    1. He fears the vengeance which society will demand.
      a. Retribution will be certain because he will be violating the laws of blood relation—Duncan is his kinsman.
      b. Retribution will be more certain because he will be violating the laws of hospitality—Duncan is his guest.

  c. Retribution will be heavy because Duncan is a good and popular king.
 2. He fears to risk the profit of his newly won honors.
 3. He fears failure.
D. Finally, Macbeth himself actually commits the murder.

Notice that the sentence outline is properly a genuine expansion of the topic outline, not just the minimum syntactic manipulation to turn the entries into complete sentences. Merely to change "Duncan guest," for instance, to "Duncan is his guest" does not really help very much.

The advantage of a sentence outline is principally fullness. If used honestly, it helps you find out what you intend to say on a point and whether you really have anything to say there. For a hazard of the topic outline is that an entry may be no more than a place where you have some intention of sinking an exploratory shaft. An entry ought, on the contrary, to be a certified oil producer; and the sentence outline can help you to be sure that it is. Writing out full sentences and putting subordinate elements into phrases and subordinate clauses can also help you organize your ideas and see their true relations. Of course the sentence outline, by virtue of its fullness, is the most useful to another reader; it is the best kind to submit for advance help on a piece of writing or in proposing a project in application for fellowships and grants. The chief disadvantage of a sentence outline is that it takes so much time. It is hardly worth doing for routine short essays.

A special variety of the sentence outline is the running sentence outline. This merely runs a sentence on from entry to subentries; for example, using II, *C,* 1:

1. He fears the vengeance society will exact, the more certainly because he would be
   a. violating the laws of blood relationship by killing a kinsman,
   b. violating the laws of hospitality by killing a guest,
   c. violating his vows of loyalty to a popular king.

Such run-on outlines can be used effectively when the material is amenable, and the results are briefer than a normal sentence outline. One should beware, however, of exercising strained ingenuity to tie everything together in the fewest possible sentences.

Another special outline is the paragraph outline, in which each entry is the topic sentence of a paragraph.[1] Such an outline is useful for the writer who wants to make himself particularly conscious of his paragraph structure, but is not generally economical because it almost requires that a topic outline be at least sketched out first.

AN ABSTRACT OUTLINE

All the forms of outlines we have mentioned deal in particulars. That is well, for we write about particulars. But it is difficult to see the conglomerate shape of details for the same reason that it is hard to see the forest for the trees. There are, therefore, some advantages in a kind of outline which abstracts the general from the specific. This kind of outline can be called a "method outline," because it shows the general method of the movement of thought. Let us look back at the three main points of our outline:

I. Neither alone responsible for the idea of murder
II. Macbeth's primary responsibility
III. Lady Macbeth's primary responsibility

If we stand off a little further, we can see that what this amounts to is

I. Area of joint responsibility
II. Area of Macbeth's primary responsibility
III. Area of Lady Macbeth's primary responsibility

If we look more abstractly, we can see that we could just as well substitute *A* for Macbeth and *B* for Lady Macbeth and have a formula for writing any essay concerned with apportioning blame or praise. The advantage of such information is not that we will forthwith go on writing essays to the pattern, but that we can clearly see the shape of our forest. It might be that we will then decide that it would be more logical to begin with the individual most responsible, move on to the one next responsible, and then bring all together with an analysis of their joint responsibility. This would be to use another method outline:

I. Important features
II. Secondary features
III. Whole effect

[1] See p. 122.

Other patterns of method outlines can be useful. The most fundamental is

I. Beginning
II. Middle
III. End

This formula seems quite obvious, but if we apply it rigorously we are likely to discover odd things. Samuel Johnson even complained that Milton's *Samson Agonistes* was all beginning and end with no middle. Sometimes we produce essays which are like some packaged sandwiches—almost all bread and no filling. Sometimes we have no proper ending—we just stop. Sometimes we are so slow getting started that the beginning is disproportionately long. Thus, although the beginning-middle-end pattern is empty by itself and certainly must be adjusted to suit circumstances,[2] it can help us to become aware of the structure of our essays.

Research papers in particular may fall into another general shape:

I. Problem
II. Proposed solution
III. Objections to proposed solution
IV. Improved solution

Still another pattern, some variation of which can be useful in chronological writing is the sequence I. Past, II. Present, III. Future. If we projected our essay on Macbeth a little further, the past could be concerned with the planning of the murder, the present with the execution, and the future with the aftermath. Of course the present can also be shifted to the end of the drama, since the tale is played out that far; then the future would be the reassertion of justice and the restoration of the cosmic ethic.

The method outline is inevitably too general to be of much help in the actual writing of an essay unless it is supplemented by a specific outline. The method outline may be drawn up first as a broad directive, especially for routine reports like those on chemistry experiments. Usually, however, the specific outline is done first, and the method outline is used like a template—put over the specific outline to check on its logic. The method outline can also serve to indicate whether the writer has fallen into a rut and is using

[2] See the discussion of beginning and ending paragraphs in Chapter Seven.

the same general pattern indiscriminately, whatever his individual set of particulars. Thus the method outline can both guarantee uniformity in routine reporting, where it is desirable, and help warn against monotony when variety is needed.

STRUCTURE OF THE WHOLE

Outlining, as we have suggested, is valuable as a means of splitting up the material of an essay into digestible pieces. We should keep in mind, however, that these pieces are part of a *whole*. The segmented

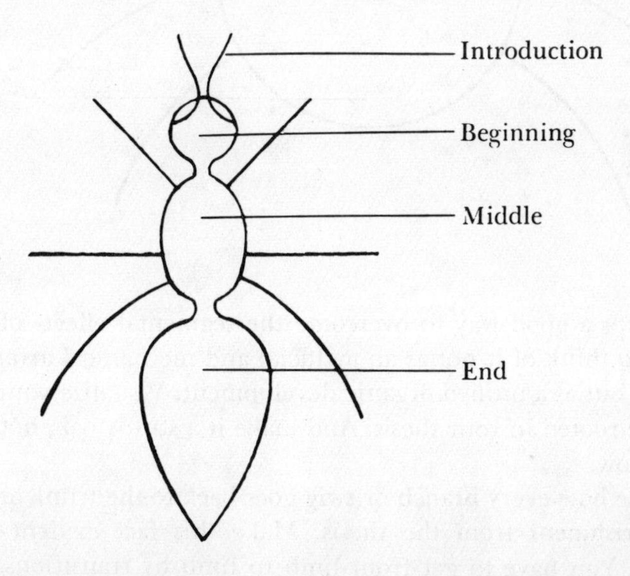

character of an outline may seduce us into forgetting that salient point. "Unity in multeity" was a favorite phrase with the poet and philosopher Coleridge. It is a good phrase for a young writer to post on his mirror. No matter how many parts there are, no matter how carefully they are distinguished, the important thing is the whole, the unity. I sometimes suggest to my students that the kind of natural structure they should admire, at least as writers, is not that of the ant or the wasp. The wasplike figure is admirable in the proper place, but not in essays. We want no heads and abdomens barely connected to the thorax by tenuous threads. We want instead the kind of solid unity that nature bestowed upon the tick. That is the figure for a writer—at any rate for his essays. A firm, rounded body, sticking tight with singleness of purpose.

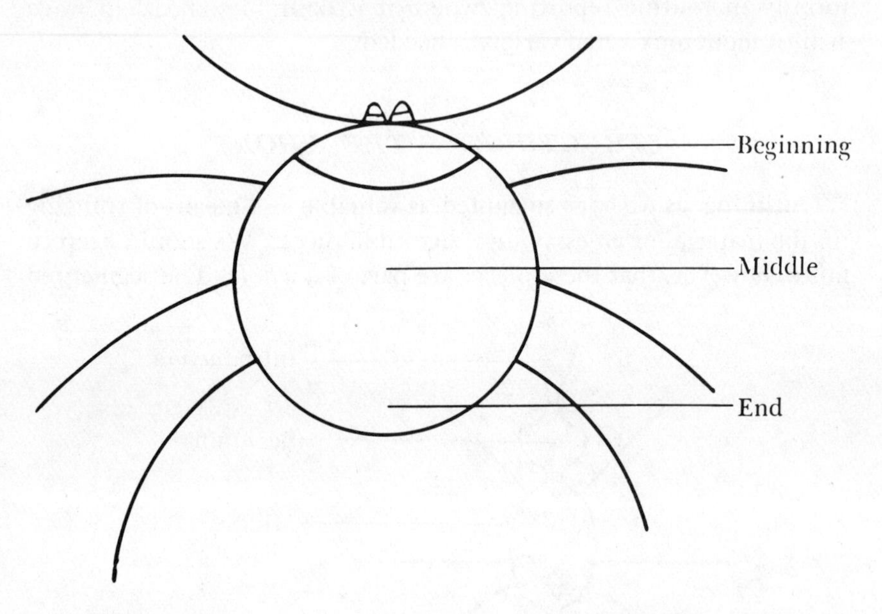

Perhaps a good way to overcome the segmental effects of an outline is to think of it not as an artificial and mechanical arrangement of ideas but as a unified organic development. Visualize your outline as a tree rooted in your thesis. And make it a sturdy oak, not a weeping willow.

Notice how every branch or twig goes back to the trunk and draws its nourishment from the thesis. Make this fact evident in your writing. You have to get from limb to limb by transitions. Do not jump; go back to the trunk or main branch and come out again. Use such devices as these: "Another reason that Macbeth must accept some responsibility for the murder of Duncan despite his wife's urgent promptings is that *he offered no real opposition on ethical grounds.*" "Lady Macbeth must also be given a large share of the blame for Duncan's murder because *she browbeat her husband into the deed.*" The sections in italics are the new points; all the rest of these sentences is made up of transitional items backwards to tie the new material solidly to the central ideas, to emphasize the unity of the essay. It is possible to overdo this kind of thing, but it is not likely—unity is too important.

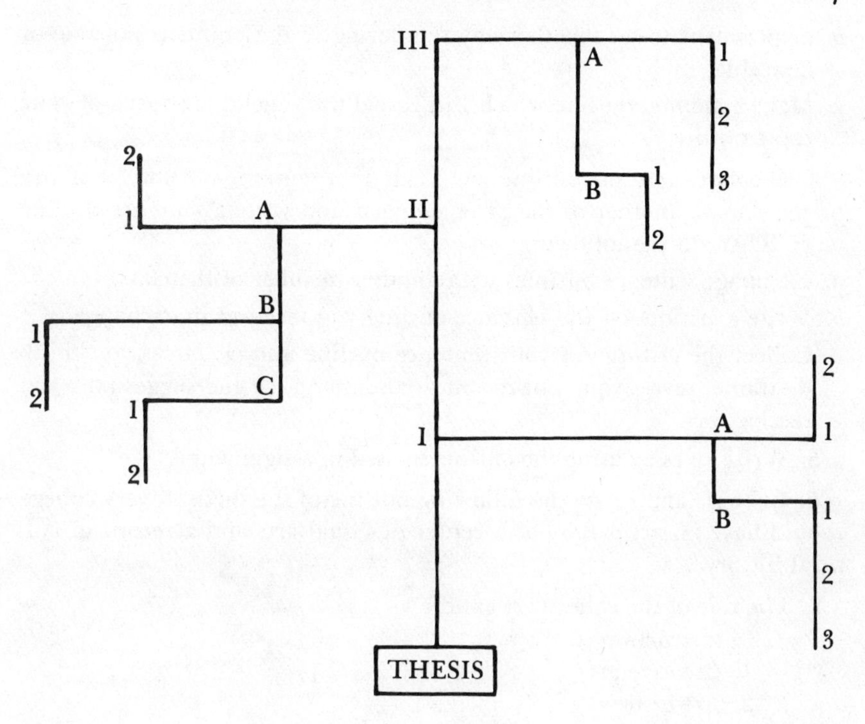

ASSIGNMENTS

1. Make a topic outline of an essay in your reading text or a magazine.

2. Make a topic outline for one of the following focused subjects:

a. A dictionary, although descriptive to its editors, inevitably takes on some prescriptive function for its users.

b. Hamlet loves Ophelia but does not believe he can confide in her and therefore breaks off their relationship as the kindest course under the circumstances.

c. Student branches of political parties provide a training ground for citizenship.

d. Student branches of political parties distract students from their proper education and encourage them to unfledged and dangerous political action.

e. College football is valuable chiefly as a means of keeping alumni interest and providing financial support for other sports.

3. Examine the topic outline you made above and do the following:

a. Explain the logical reason that point III comes after point II.

b. Experiment to see whether any reordering of the points is possible or desirable.

c. Make a method outline which will reveal the general approach of your topic outline.

4. Convert the topic outline you made to a sentence outline, or if you prefer, choose another of the given subjects and write a sentence outline on it. Then do the following:

a. Exchange sentence outlines with another member of the class.

b. Write a critique of the sentence outline you received in exchange.

c. Collect the critique of your sentence outline and, as far as you think desirable, revise your outline in accordance with the suggestions you receive.

5. Write an essay using the outline revised in assignment 4.

6. Criticize and revise the following outline of the thesis "Every college should have an art gallery as a center of visual arts and a record of cultural history."

I. The role of the college art gallery
- *A.* In instruction in the arts
  - 1. Creative art
  - 2. Art history
- *B.* In cultural studies generally
  - 1. Humanistic values
  - 2. Social and political history in representation

II. The necessity of the college art gallery
- *A.* Inadequacy of the off-campus facilities available
  - 1. Too remote from student life
  - 2. Not connected with classes
- *B.* Need for a campus center
  - 1. Students must be able to visit frequently and casually
  - 2. Visual arts can be related to other arts by tied-in concerts and dances.

III. The special character of the college art gallery
- *A.* Can draw on academic departments
- *B.* Can draw on creative-arts staff
- *C.* Can draw on collections which alumni have assembled
- *D.* Can host visiting exhibits

7. See if you can write an essay from one of the following three method outlines. Choose any subject which will fit.

I. Problem

II. Solutions previously tried

III. Solution you propose
IV. Claimed advantage

I. History of subject
II. Present situation
III. Possible future developments
IV. Recommended action to assure preferred development

I. Panoramic description
II. Close-up on selected details
III. Relation of details

8. Organize the ideas below, grouping them under main points as seems appropriate. Obviously there is no one right way to group, but be able to justify the logic and the psychological convenience of your organization:

a. Africa is shaking off colonialism.

b. Russia and China have deep conflicts.

c. Zanzibar is one of the emerging nations.

d. Nationalism is the dominant religion of our era.

e. Pan-Arabic ambitions conflict with nationalistic urges.

f. The Monroe Doctrine both fostered and insulted nationalism.

g. Monolithic Communism is cracking under nationalistic pressures.

h. The United Nations is a collection of prideful nationalisms.

i. The Soviet Union has nationalistic feelings among its Republics.

j. Nationalistic sentiments have been expressed in Puerto Rico.

CHAPTER SEVEN

Rhetoric and Relationship: The Province of the Paragraph

Writing is a synthetic process, a putting together of pieces; its basic problem is relationship: the connection between the pieces, the relation of the parts to the whole. In our discussions of finding and structuring subjects we have been trying to deal with the problems of the larger whole. But it becomes apparent that the concept of wholeness is relative, that at each level there are other wholes that have to be filled out with appropriate pieces. The organism, the cell, the molecule, the atom, the electron—each has its integrity, its own system of being. A whole elephant has more bulk but no more completeness than a whole flea. And the hierarchy goes on down, as Jonathan Swift's verse has it:

> So, naturalists observe, a flea
> Hath smaller fleas that on him prey;
> And these have smaller still to bite 'em
> And so proceed *ad infinitum.*

So it is from the essay to the paragraph to the sentence to the word —a hierarchy of wholes, all tight little systems of relationships. At each level the question remains, what is the whole? For if the whole is indeed to be greater than the sum of its parts, there must be a sort of Platonic idea of the whole. Wholes do not just happen. They are at some point a glint in somebody's eye; they are purposefully constructed. What distinguishes a whole from a conglomeration? *Unity* and *function*. A paragraph, a sentence, or a word should *be* something and *do* something.

The paragraph is the largest readily perceptible whole in a piece of writing. The complete essay may be so large that it in fact tends to break down into parts because the reader has difficulty conceiving of its wholeness. Even a section or a subdivision may extend over several pages and not be easily seen as a unit. Sentences and, more particularly, words are small enough that the reader may not be specifically aware of their parts. A paragraph, on the other hand, is obviously a whole made up of related parts. Its indentation allows the writer to say to the reader, "This much of my thought I wish you to consider separately from the rest because it seems to me to have a particular unity and to advance the idea in a peculiar way."

These indentations naturally appear at varying intervals, since any essay can be expected to be made up of points of different sizes requiring developments of different scope. Too much sameness in paragraph length is not only monotonous but also unrealistic. A preponderance of short paragraphs suggests either miniscule ideas or —more probably—painfully bare ones. A prevalence of long paragraphs suggests either indiscriminate lumping or unnecessary padding of ideas. Sometimes a one-sentence paragraph can present an idea with arresting impact; sometimes a one-page paragraph can display it in rich fullness. Most paragraphs will be variously somewhere in between, as is appropriate to their integral unity.

PARAGRAPH UNITY

Two related but separate facts must be understood about paragraph unity; the unity must be real and it must also be clearly demonstrated to the reader. Simply imposing the convention of indentation and putting in a few connective elements will not make a paragraph where no real unity of thought exists. By the same token, unity of thought, no matter how genuine, cannot be considered to be self-evident; it will not make a paragraph unless the author deliberately uses devices to underline the coherence.

Real unity is a matter of homogeneity and cohesiveness. Anyone who has ever tried sand sculpture knows the annoyance of finding bits of foreign debris and the even greater frustration of not being able to make the sand stick together. Paragraphing should be rather like clay modeling in that none of the material is foreign and everything sticks together easily. What distinguishes a paragraph from just a collection of random sentences is this: All the sentences are about the same thing and, most important, arranged in a definite order to make a point about that thing. Perhaps by wide enough circuits everything can be related to everything else and by some sort of mental gymnastics can be considered to be concerned with the same thing. Such "unity," however, is not cohesive enough; any unity that has to be defended by rationalization, that is not obvious enough to be readily apparent, is not cohesive enough.

A device for achieving real unity is the *topic sentence,* which bears the same relationship to a paragraph as a thesis does to a whole essay. It focuses the idea of the paragraph; it is the germ of the paragraph. Consider the operation of the first sentence in the following paragraph from William Hazlitt's "On Familiar Style":

> The proper force of words lies not in the words themselves, but in their application. A word may be a fine-sounding word, of an unusual length, and very imposing from its learning and novelty, and yet in the connection in which it is introduced, may be quite pointless and irrelevant. It is not pomp or pretension, but the adaptation of the expression to the idea that clinches a writer's meaning:—as it is not the size or glossiness of the materials, but their being fitted each to its place, that gives strength to the arch; or as the pegs and nails are as necessary to the support of the building as the larger timbers, and more so than the mere showy, unsubstantial ornaments. I hate anything that occupies more space than it is worth. I hate to see a load of band-boxes go along the street, and I hate to see a parcel of big words without anything in them. A person who does not deliberately dispose of all his thoughts alike in cumbrous draperies and flimsy disguises, may strike out twenty varieties of familiar everyday language, each coming somewhat nearer to the feeling he wants to convey, and at last not hit upon that particular and only one, which may be said to be identical with the exact impression in his mind. This would seem to show that Mr. Cobbett is hardly right in saying that the first word that occurs is always the best. It may be a very good one; and yet a better may present itself on reflection or from time to time. It should be suggested naturally, however, and spontaneously, from a fresh and lively conception of the subject. We seldom succeed by trying at improvement, or by merely substituting one word for another that we are not satisfied with, as we cannot recollect the name of a place or person by merely plaguing ourselves about it. We wander farther from the point by persist-

ing in a wrong scent; but it starts up accidentally in the memory when we least expected it, by touching some link in the chain of previous association.

Here the topic sentence stands first and the paragraph literally grows out of it, unfolding, spreading out as the idea develops. The second sentence uses the same contrasting structure as the first but elaborates the content. The third does the same and brings in an analogy of the positive value of effective "application." The next two sentences use another illustration to ridicule pretentious misapplication. Then the idea expands into the machinery by which the right word is chosen—a development another author might have elected to put in a new paragraph.

Paragraph Shape

The topic sentence standing first makes the simplest and most reliable kind of paragraph organization. We naturally declare what we are going to say and then say it, thus forewarning and preparing our readers. Furthermore, this paragraph structure reflects the widespread method of thought, which we saw operating in deductive logic, of moving from generalization to particulars. A generalization is made at the beginning of the paragraph, and everything in the paragraph derives from and supports that generalization. If everything cannot be derived from the topic sentence, then something is wrong with either the topic sentence or the paragraph.

Of course, the topic sentence need not stand first. One can construct a paragraph on the inductive pattern by pouring in details and concluding with a generalization contained in a topic sentence. The writer then gives the illusion of actually working out what he wants to say in the course of the paragraph, before the reader's eyes. Perhaps in his rough draft the writer actually is uncertain of what he wants to say. But by the final version this working out of material must be just an illusion designed to encourage the reader to think with the writer.

All sorts of variations on these two major arrangements are possible. Consider the following paragraph from Robert Louis Stevenson's "On Some Technical Elements of Style in Literature":

The conjuror juggles with two oranges, and our pleasure in beholding him springs from this, that neither is for an instant overlooked or sacrificed. So with the writer. His pattern, which is to please the supersensual ear, is yet addressed, throughout and first of all, to the demands of logic. Whatever be the obscurities, whatever the intricacies of the argument, the neatness of the fabric must not suffer, or the artist has proved unequal to his design. And, on the other hand, no form of words must be selected, no knot must be tied among the phrases, unless knot and word be precisely what is wanted to forward and illuminate the argument; for to fail in this is to swindle in the game. The genius of prose rejects the *cheville* no less emphatically than the laws of verse; and the *cheville,* I should perhaps explain to some of my readers, is any meaningless or very watered phrase employed to strike a balance in the sound. Pattern and argument live in each other; and it is by the brevity, clearness, charm, or emphasis of the second, that we judge the strength and fitness of the first.

Probably the last sentence in this selection is the topic sentence; but the second and third together are also close to a topic sentence. Stevenson's paragraph begins with an analogy and then draws its comparison—"So with the writer"—and sets up the parallel between the two oranges and the writer's pattern of sound and web of logic. After stressing the importance of each "orange," the paragraph then comes full circle in "Pattern and argument live in each other."

Paragraphs with more than one topic sentence are fairly frequent, particularly in the diamond-shaped design of beginning with a topic sentence and ending with a similar sentence which repeats the idea in different terms and perhaps leads into the next paragraph. This type of paragraph expands from a generalization and then narrows back into one. Thus it benefits by using both modes of thought, expanding and then narrowing, and leaves an impression of having nailed down the point. Both modes can also be combined by a sort of hourglass pattern which puts the topic sentence in the middle of the paragraph, so that some of the details add up to the generalization and some derive from it.

All these designs and the many variations on them can be used to create effective paragraphs. Although the diamond paragraph is the most foolproof, it is also the most insistent in tone and easily gets monotonous. A skilled writer will not fall into any consistent practice, but rather will develop an almost intuitive sense for the shape of his paragraphs so that they become to him plastic units for the shape of his thoughts. When you look over your next rough draft, try marking the topic sentences and drawing overlays of triangles or

PARAGRAPH SHAPES

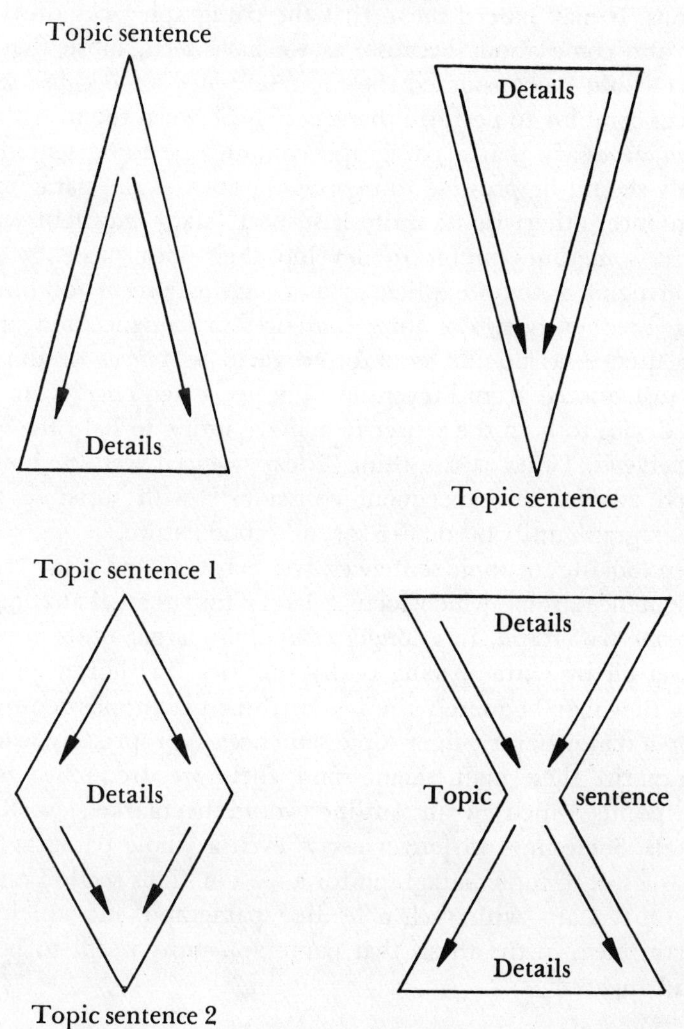

diamonds or whatever to indicate the form of your paragraphs. Read them aloud and listen to see whether they have a dying fall or come firmly to a conclusion, whether they are wobbly and digressive or stand as stalwart entities. View them as wholes and demand that they show their credentials of unity.

Probably when you set out to mark your topic sentences you will have trouble with some paragraphs which do not seem to have one sentence which is clearly the topic sentence. This is not necessarily disastrous. It may indeed mean that the paragraph lacks unity; but it may also come about because, as we have seen, more than one sentence could be considered the topic sentence, or because several sentences combine to perform the function between them. Although it is not necessary that a paragraph contain one topic sentence, it certainly should be *possible* to express the idea of the paragraph in one sentence; otherwise its unity is suspect. Many excellent writers, however, sometimes prefer to develop their idea piece by piece, never bringing it to an explicit focus which may seem too blunt or blatant. Frequently two or three sentences in sequence add up to a topic sentence, as do the second and third sentences of the paragraph just quoted from Stevenson. The topic sentence is no more than a device to help the writer to achieve unity, to help the reader to perceive it. Unity is the thing. Inexperienced writers, however, are well advised to experiment consciously with topic sentences until paragraph unity becomes a sort of second nature.

When looking for topic sentences, you may also find some "super" topic sentences, some which focus a larger unit than that contained in any one paragraph. In a longer essay these larger units are likely to be set off by extra spacing or by subtitles; in shorter pieces of writing they may be merely the two or three paragraphs required to develop a major point. Super topic sentences appropriately lead into or summarize these main themes and, therefore, frequently appear at the points which in an outline would be marked by Roman numerals. Sometimes in longer essays even a whole paragraph may stand as a sort of topic paragraph for a section. This section on paragraph unity starts with such a leading paragraph, introducing the two main ideas in the thesis that paragraph unity needs to be both real and apparent.

Connecting Devices

Other devices than the topic sentence are available for saying to the reader, in effect, "Look how this all sticks together." These devices depend mainly on *repetition,* showing the sameness of the paragraph, or on *transition,* showing the movement. Repetition of a word, pronouns which refer to it, or synonyms which stand for it weaves a unifying thread through a paragraph. Observe Charles Lamb's delicious use of repetitious elements in the playful beginning of "A Chapter on Ears":

I HAVE no ear.–

Mistake me not reader,–nor imagine that I am by nature destitute of those exterior twin appendages, hanging ornaments, and (architecturally speaking) handsome volutes to the human capital. Better my mother had never borne me. –I am, I think, rather delicately than copiously provided with those conduits; and I feel no disposition to envy the mule for his plenty, or the mole for her exactness, in those ingenious labyrinthine inlets–those indispensable side-intelligencers.

Since this is a personal subject, Lamb ties his paragraph together by repeating "I," "me" and "my." He both achieves unity and establishes his facetious tone by his series of fantastic synonyms for ears: "twin appendages," "hanging ornaments," "handsome volutes," "conduits," "labyrinthine inlets," and "side-intelligencers." Incidentally, in the fourth paragraph, he gets around to saying that he means he has no ear for music.

Devices of transition are little signs which stand around in the paragraph and say to the reader, "He went thata way." Their job is to demonstrate unity by emphasizing continuity. Every sentence in a paragraph and every paragraph in an essay should bear such a tight relationship to what comes before and after that its position could not be changed without rupturing the whole fabric. Transitional elements point up this relation, show the reader how he gets from here to there. In the manner of the fabulous goofus bird, which allegedly flew backwards because it did not care where it was going as long as it could see where it had been, transitions often look backwards, reassuring the reader that there is a connection between where he has been and where he is going. Transitions are frequently words which have antecedents, especially personal and demonstrative pronouns ("this," "that," "these," "those"), which refer back to a noun in a preceding sentence. Or they are conjunctive adverbs, which conspicuously call attention to a relation of thought:

therefore	besides	indeed	nevertheless
however	consequently	likewise	still
also	furthermore	moreover	then
accordingly	hence	namely	such as
anyhow			

Even conjunctions, once thought by some purists appropriate for making connections within sentences only, are now frequently found at the beginning of sentences. In a temporally organized paragraph words such as "when," "after," "before" preserve continuity; as do words like "behind," "here," "there," and "around" in a spatially organized paragraph. Prepositional phrases such as "on the other hand," "in contrast," "by comparison" are likewise useful in demonstrating the movement of thought through a paragraph developed by contrast and comparison.

Notice the various ways in which Matthew Arnold indicates the connections which give unity to the famous concluding paragraph of his essay "Literature and Science":

> And, therefore, to say the truth, I cannot really think that humane letters are in much actual danger of being thrust out from their leading place in education, in spite of the array of authorities against them at this moment. So long as human nature is what it is, their attractions will remain irresistible. As with Greek, so with letters generally: they will some day come, we may hope, to be studied more rationally, but they will not lose their place. What will happen will rather be that there will be crowded into education other matters besides, far too many; there will be, perhaps, a period of unsettlement and confusion and false tendency; but letters will not in the end lose their leading place. If they lose it for a time, they will get it back again. We shall be brought back to them by our wants and aspirations. And a poor humanist may possess his soul in patience, neither strive nor cry, admit the energy and brilliancy of the partisans of physical science, and their present favor with the public, to be far greater than his own, and still have a happy faith that the nature of things works silently on behalf of the studies which he loves, and that, while we shall all have to acquaint ourselves with the great results reached by modern science, and to give ourselves as much training in its disciplines as we can conveniently carry, yet the majority of men will always require humane letters; and so much the more, as they have the more and the greater results of science to relate to the need in man for conduct, and to the need in him for beauty.

The first sentence, with its "and," "therefore," "really think," and "in spite of," makes obvious allusions to what has gone before. Then the idea of "humane letters" being "thrust out of their leading place" becomes a motif for the paragraph, repeated in "letters generally," "will not lose their place," "will not in the end lose their leading place," and "if they lose it for a while," as well as in references to "human nature" and "a poor humanist." Every sentence either repeats "letters" or includes a pronoun that refers to them.

The paragraph moves from a negative statement that letters will not lose their place, to a positive assertion of their function of ministry to the human needs for conduct and beauty.

PARAGRAPH FUNCTION

Paragraphs, we said, should be something and do something. If we can keep this idea of *function* clearly in mind, most of our problems with paragraphs will be more easily solved. What does a paragraph do? To find empirical answers you might say to yourself, "I'm going to write a paragraph about. . . ." What might you fill in? ". . . the peculiar shade of yellow green in the sunset sky"; ". . . the need for tax reform"; ". . . the causes of mutation"; ". . . the sinking of the *Bismark.*" You recognize in these four possibilities the basic modes: description, argumentation, exposition, and narration.

Suppose you rephrase one of the above proposed paragraph suggestions, for example, the need for tax reform:

I'm going to write a paragraph about:

1. Examples of the need for tax reform.
2. Causes of the need for tax reform.
3. Potential results of tax reform.
4. The meaning of true tax reform.
5. Comparisons and contrasts in tax burdens.

Now you have something definite to say about the need for reform; you have the stuff of several paragraphs, the functions of which are to (1) illustrate, (2) give causes or (3) results, (4) define, and (5) compare and contrast. Let us consider briefly these particular means of development.

Examples

Paragraphs which grow by presenting examples and illustrations are hearty, ear-smacking paragraphs. They have substance and concreteness which give the ideas a "local habitation and a name." Notice how Thackeray builds up his point by an accumulation of evidence in the following paragraph from one of his essays, "On University Snobs":

HUGBY owes his eminence to patient merit and agreeable perseverance. He is a meek, mild, inoffensive creature, with just enough of scholarship to fit him to hold a lecture; or set an examination paper. *He rose by kindness to the aristocracy.* It was wonderful to see the way in which that poor creature grovelled before a nobleman or a lord's nephew, or even some noisy and disreputable commoner, the friend of a lord. He used to give the young noblemen the most painful and elaborate breakfasts, and adopt a jaunty, genteel air, and talk with them (although he was decidedly serious) about the opera, or the last run of the hounds. It was good to watch him in the midst of a circle of young tufts, with his mean, smiling, eager, uneasy familiarity. He used to write home confidential letters to their parents, and made it his duty to call upon them when in town, to condole or rejoice with them when a death, birth, or marriage took place in their family; and to feast them whenever they came to the University. I recollect a letter lying on a desk in his lecture-room for a whole term, beginning "My Lord Duke." It was to show us that he corresponded with such dignities.

I have italicized what can be considered the topic sentence, the generalization which Thackeray proceeds to support by a series of examples of the don's habitual behavior and finally to cap by one climactic illustration. Notice that although the point of view shifts somewhat awkwardly from Hugby to the observer in general and finally to the specific "I," the unity of the paragraph is preserved by the logical sequence of evidence and by such devices of continuity as the two sentences beginning "It was wonderful to" and "It was good to," interleaved by two beginning "He used to." Such a series of examples needs to be organized to build a structure, not simply placed one after another list fashion. Thus Thackeray moves from Hugby's deferential treatment of his aristocratic students to his cringing overtures to their titled parents.

A paragraph may be developed by expanding one illustration, as well as by presenting a series of examples. Thackeray might have elected to have described at length one of those "painful and elaborate breakfasts." Of course the illustration must really "illustrate," the examples must be pertinent and subordinated to the point of the paragraph. It is easy for a writer to get carried away by delight in his illustrations for their own sake and thereby to be led unconsciously off his main track into tangentially related byways. Thackeray keeps his perspective; he does not, for instance, allow himself to get off on the interesting matter of the reactions of Hugby's students to this obsequious familiarity.

Cause and Effect Paragraphs

"If reasons were as plentiful as blackberries," protests Sir John Falstaff, "I would give no man a reason upon compulsion, I." Readers, however, have a way of demanding reasons, and plentiful as blackberries or not, they make good material for filling out a paragraph. Reasons, it has been suggested, are likely to be either "good reasons" or "real reasons." Sir John's specious maneuvering falls into the former category; and most of us, likewise living in "the days of villainy," are sometimes tempted to make use of vague half-reasons and plausible pseudo-reasons. Serious writing, however, requires real reasons—solid, sound, significant reasons which stand the tests of the causal relations we discussed in Chapter Five.

A paragraph may pile up causes and conclude with the effect, or begin with the effect and then accumulate its causes. Adlai Stevenson uses the latter technique in a paragraph in the introduction to *Friends and Enemies:*[1]

> The next ten years, I would guess, will *really* prove whether this nation or any nation so conceived and so dedicated can long endure—and right now the prognosis is not good. We are losing ground nearly everywhere; we are not taking measures necessary to stop the loss; and hardly anybody seems to care. In our complacent, happy fashion, we assume that we can't lose—that if we stand firm, persevere and damn the Communists enough, Right will surely prevail in the end. Well, it didn't once before, when Athenian democracy was involved in a similar long, tiresome struggle with Spartan tyranny. On that occasion, an infinitely superior civilization went under, because it lacked the self-discipline to survive. One could cite other examples. Is it happening again, right here and right now?

The opening sentence raises a "why" in the reader's mind: why is the "prognosis . . . not good"? Stevenson devotes two sentences to specific causes and then shifts to explanation by analogy. When the emphasis is thus on the causes of some effect, the paragraph is a "reasons" paragraph, answering the question "Why?" When the emphasis is on the effects of some cause, the paragraph is a "result" paragraph, answering the question "What?" Consider how Oscar Wilde, in his amusing essay "The Decay of Lying," develops the results which he ascribes to the literalness of his age:

[1] Adlai Stevenson, *Friends and Enemies* (New York: Harper & Row, 1959).

The loss that results to literature in general from this false ideal of our time can hardly be over-estimated. People have a careless way of talking about a "born liar," just as they talk about a "born poet." But in both cases they are wrong. Lying and poetry are arts—arts, as Plato saw, not unconnected with each other—and they require the most careful study, the most disinterested devotion. Indeed, they have their technique, just as the more material arts of painting and sculpture have, their subtle secrets of form and colour, their craft-mysteries, their deliberate artistic methods. As one knows the poet by his fine music, so one can recognize the liar by his rich rythmic utterance, and in neither case will the casual inspiration of the moment suffice. Here, as elsewhere, practice must precede perfection. But in modern days while the fashion of writing poetry has become far too common, and should, if possible, be discouraged, the fashion of lying has almost fallen into disrepute. Many a young man starts in life with a natural gift for exaggeration which, if nurtured in congenial and sympathetic surroundings, or by imitation of the best models, might grow into something really great and wonderful. But, as a rule, he comes to nothing. He either falls into careless habits of accuracy, or takes to frequenting the society of the aged and the well-informed. Both things are equally fatal to his imagination, as indeed they would be fatal to the imagination of anybody, and in a short time he develops a morbid and unhealthy faculty of truth-telling, begins to verify all statements made in his presence, has no hesitation in contradicting people who are much younger than himself, and often ends by writing novels which are so like life that no one can possibly believe in their probability. This is no isolated instance that we are giving. It is simply one example out of many; and if something cannot be done to check, or at least to modify, our monstrous worship of facts, Art will become sterile, and Beauty will pass away from the land.

Defining Paragraphs

Writers sometimes lean upon that tempting crutch, "according to Webster," usually to the irritation of their readers. For readers can look up words in a dictionary themselves; even when they are actually too lazy to do so, they may resent so obvious an implication. If a writer thinks that he must define some of the words he is using, he should consider whether his level of diction is wrong for his audience. When his subject and his purpose—possibly he wants to educate his readers and improve their vocabularies—make some definition necessary, quoting the dictionary is not likely to be the solution. For relatively simple and unimportant terms, unobtrusive parenthetical definition is sufficient: "the didi, a fabulous South American ape." For central and difficult ideas, a full-scale, custom-tailored definition needs to be worked out in a defining paragraph. About the only justification for a writer's quoting a dictionary is his intention to amplify, qualify, or take exception to the definition given there, or perhaps to cite the *Oxford English Dictionary* for an archaic meaning.[2]

Defining paragraphs are necessary whenever a writer uses a significant term or concept his readers may not understand. This situation can arise either because the term is new to the readers and has for them no meaning, or because it is too familiar to the readers and its meaning is fuzzy.[3] It is at least as necessary to define "liberal" or "democracy" as it is to explain the meaning of "cybernetics" or "serendipity." In fact, words whose meaning every one knows are likely to be particularly in need of specific definition in at least one carefully worked-out paragraph.

Defining is logically a matter of placing something in a class to which it belongs, and then pointing out how it differs from other members of the class. A definition is helpful if the class is one that suits the purposes of the writer, and the differentia are significant. Most things can be put into several classes, depending upon the point of view or the purpose of the definition. A diamond, for instance, can be classified chemically as a form of carbon, distinguished by its isometric crystalline structure. Or it can be classified artistically or economically, distinguished by its brilliancy or value. This purposeful element in definition is most important: beginning writers should try to free themselves of the notion that things have only one uniquely "true" definition. Although theoretically there may be an exhaustive definition, it is seldom contemplated and not ordinarily appropriate; a number of different definitions can be true in the contexts chosen. Any practical definition has an arbitrary element because the writer selects the relationship he wishes to emphasize by choosing the class into which he puts whatever he is defining. His intention is to explain not so much what the term means as what *he means* by it. Thus he can define school spirit as either a kind of self-cultured group dynamics or a kind of subtle administrative control exercised through pressures of tradition—provided his

[2] See Chapter Twelve, p. 239.
[3] See Chapter Nine.

readers are prepared to understand these classes. For certainly the class chosen will not suit the purposes of the writer unless it is known to the reader. The information that a manatee is a sirenian, although quite correct, will not help the nonspecialist reader. The class must also be a real class, not just a synonym or different verbalization, e.g., "A star is a stellar body."

Once a writer decides upon the class he is going to use, he then procedes to elaborate the differentia which are important to his purpose. Almost anything can be distinguished from other members of the same class by a variety of means. Consider two famous definitions of man: "Man is a two-legged animal without feathers." "Man is a reasoning animal." Both of these definitions assign man to the class animal, but they choose opposite differentia. The first is a fairly accurate external discrimination—especially when one remembers that the ancient Greeks who produced it had never seen a kangaroo or a gorilla. But the differentia two-legged and without feathers do not seem as fundamental as that of the second definition, for we men are pleased to think that our power of reason is what really distinguishes us from the lower creation. It is possible to play upon these differentia, depending upon the author's purpose. Swift, for instance, insisted that man is not a reasoning animal but an animal capable of reason.

When the class is very broad—as often happens with concepts which require defining paragraphs—the point of the definition resides in the differentia. In his famous definition of a gentleman John Henry Cardinal Newman chooses as the class "one"—anyone who fits the differentia:

Hence it is that it is almost a definition of gentleman to say he is one who never inflicts pain. This description is both refined and, as far as it goes, accurate. He is mainly occupied in merely removing the obstacles which hinder the free and unembarrassed action of those about him; and he concurs with their movements rather than takes the initiative himself. His benefits may be considered as parallel to what are called comforts or conveniences in arrangements of a personal nature: like an easy chair or a good fire, which do their part in dispelling cold and fatigue, though nature provides both means of rest and animal heat without them. The true gentleman in like manner carefully avoids whatever may cause a jar or a jolt in the minds of those with whom he is cast;—all clashing of opinion, or all collision of feeling, all restraint, or suspicion, or gloom, or resentment; his great concern being to make every one at their ease and at home. He has his eyes on all his company; he is tender towards the bashful, gentle toward the distant, and merciful towards the absurd; he can recollect to whom he is speaking; he guards against unseasonable allusions, or topics which may irritate; he is seldom prominent in conversation, and never wearisome. He makes light of favours while he does them, and seems to be receiving when he is conferring. He never speaks of himself except when compelled, never defends himself by a mere retort, he has no ears for slander or gossip, is scrupulous in imputing motives to those who interfere with him, and interprets everything for the best.

"Knowledge Viewed in Relation to Religious Duty," Sect. 10
The Idea of a University

Newman's paragraph goes on even longer. It defines largely by giving examples of the differentia, the various ways in which a gentleman seeks to avoid inflicting pain. Newman also employs, however, one analogy: "like an easy chair or a good fire." Analogies are useful in defining because they can explain a concept not familiar to the reader by relating it to one that is well known to him. The grounds of the analogy must be made clear, as Newman makes clear that the similarity between a gentleman and a chair resides in the convenience: we can get along without either, but life is much more pleasant as a result of the presence of both. The analogy is not trite; it is indeed rather startling. We are not accustomed to think of gentlemen as being like chairs or fires; and the effort forces us to recognize that gentlemanliness is something contrived, something added to the human condition, but still not something sophisticated and luxurious—rather among the simple comforts which make life tolerable.

A defining paragraph often needs to point out what is not meant. This is particularly true of abstract terms which have a long history. Matthew Arnold obviously has to clear away unacceptable definitions in order to advance his view of culture:

If culture, then, is a study of perfection, and of harmonious perfection, general perfection, and perfection which consists in becoming something rather than in having something, an inward condition of the mind and spirit, not in an outward set of circumstances,—it is clear that culture, instead of the frivolous and useless thing which Mr. Bright, and Mr. Frederic Harrison, and many other Liberals are apt to call it, has a very important function to fulfill for mankind. And this function is particularly important in our modern world, of which the whole civilization is, to a much greater degree than the civilization of Greece and Rome, mechanical and external, and tends constantly to become more so.

"Sweetness and Light," *Culture and Anarchy*

After emphasizing that he does not mean by culture merely a vain acquisition of classical polish, Arnold goes on to develop his defining paragraph by demonstrating how the concept of culture as function is at variance with the English temper. This kind of negative definition is but a variety of contrast, just as defining by analogy is but a species of comparison—two more generally useful paragraph functions.

Contrast and Comparison

Every student recognizes "compare and contrast . . ." as a favorite formula for examination essay questions: "Compare and contrast Macbeth with a modern dictator." In any comparison or contrast—which is no more than a negative comparison—there must be at least two terms. One is given in the context of the subject, the others must be more or less selected. Since a number of second terms are possible, more than one may be used, but singly or together they are likely to be paired with the first term. In this particular question the examiner undoubtedly wants to test the student's knowledge of *Macbeth,* and within limits leaves the choice of the other term to the writer. After the second term has been selected, or even when both terms are given, the writer still has to choose the grounds for the comparison. The grounds may be any similarity or dissimilarity—in appearance, in essence, in background, in location, in origin—in almost anything, as long as it is (1) real, (2) significant, (3) accessible to the reader.

Nothing is gained by virtuoso efforts to compare or contrast two things which actually have nothing in common. That is not to say that the elements of a comparison should be customarily linked. Comparisons may be unusual, as was Newman's comparing a gentleman to a chair; but they must not seem far-fetched. Once the two terms are brought together, the reader should sense a peculiar appropriateness in the juxtaposition, even though he never saw it before, and the result should be some kind of illumination.

It is not enough, however, for a comparison or contrast to fit: it must also be meaningful. Macbeth was a Scot, Hitler an Austrian—but what is the value of such a contrast? That Macbeth had a strong wife who spurred on his ambition, while Hitler belatedly married a submissive mistress may, however, be made to tell something about character. That both men were superstitious is significant, although it says more about the twentieth-century Fuehrer than about the eleventh-century chieftain.

Finally, no matter how potentially instructive a comparison may be, it will remain futile unless the reader knows and is able to use the yardstick chosen. He must, for instance, be able to draw inferences from the fact that a man is superstitious. He need not, however, be familiar with either of the subjects of comparison. For comparisons can be used in two quite different ways. When the intent is to illuminate one term, obviously the second term should be one known to the reader. Although in your more abused moods you may think your father the greatest tyrant since Macbeth, such a comparison would be of limited value in characterizing Macbeth to the average reader. You might indeed construct a parallel by describing your father and then assigning the same traits to Macbeth, but this description would be double labor with few of the advantages of comparison. The intent may, however, be to expound both terms; for it is possible to compare and contrast fruitfully two unknowns, making the similarities and distinctions illuminate each other. In such cases the second term is chosen, not because it is for the reader the easiest approach to the first term, but because it has some natural affinities with the first term and enlarges the area of knowledge. Thus readers innocent of cetology can profit from a comparison of the sperm whale and the right whale, provided the comparison is on such accessible grounds as length, weight, and habitat. A comparison of vertebral conformation or tooth configuration, however, would be of little help except to the specialist.

The contrast and/or comparison paragraph moves by turning the reader's attention back and forth, so that he becomes like a spectator watching an exciting tennis match. Here, as well as in whole essays developed by the contrast/comparison technique, rarely does it work to try to present to the reader first all aspects of one term and then all of the other. Keep comparing and contrasting different facets, one at a time or in convenient groupings, by such transitional devices as the following:

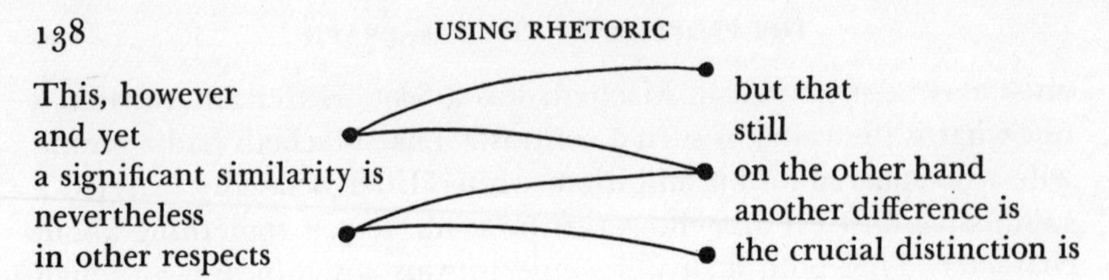

E. B. White manages this back-and-forth motion easily:[4]

Kenneth Roberts' working methods and ours differ so widely it is hard to realize we are in the same line of business. We've just been looking through his book "I Wanted to Write" and marvelling at his stamina and his discipline. The thought of writing apparently stimulates Roberts and causes him to sit upright at a desk, put in requests to libraries, write friends, examine sources, and generally raise hell throughout the daylight hours and far into the night. He works at home (where his privacy is guarded), writes in longhand, counts the words, keeps a record of moneys received, and gets a great deal done. Now turn for a moment to your correspondent. The thought of writing hangs over our mind like an ugly cloud, making us apprehensive and depressed, as before a summer storm, so that we begin the day by subsiding after breakfast, or by going away, often to seedy and inconclusive destinations; the nearest zoo, or a branch post office to buy a few stamped envelopes. Our professional life has been a long, shameless exercise in avoidance. Our home is designed for the maximum of interruption, our office is the place where we never are. From his remarks, we gather that Roberts is contemptuous of this temperament and setup, regards it as largely a pose and certainly as a deficiency in blood. It has occurred to us that perhaps we are not a writer at all but merely a bright clerk who persists in crowding his destiny. Yet the record is there. Not even lying down and closing the blinds stops us from writing; not even our family, and our preoccupation with same, stops us. We have never counted the words, but we estimated them once and the estimate was staggering. The only conclusion we can draw is that there is no such thing as "the writing man," and that after you have waded through a book like "I Wanted to Write" you still don't know the half of it, and would be a fool to try and find out.

The contrast, set up in the first sentence by "differ so widely," is established on a pattern of "we," "ours" versus "he," "his" by the second sentence. The first main shift is "Now turn for a moment," which emphasizes the parallelism between "The thought of writing apparently stimulates . . ." and "The thought of writing hangs

[4] E. B. White, "Writers at Work," *The Second Tree from the Corner* (New York: Harper & Row, 1954), pp. 162–163.

over . . ." and prepares for the two contrasting sentences beginning with "our." Then White looks again at Roberts in "From his remarks" and notes another difference by "It has occurred to us . . . Yet. . . ." White's attitude toward counting words harks back to Roberts' mentioned in the fourth sentence; and the reference to *I Wanted to Write* recalls the second sentence, bringing the paragraph neatly full circle.

Beginning Paragraphs

Of all the paragraphs in a paper the first is probably the most important. In the first paragraph the writer makes his initial impression on the reader, attracts his attention or bores him, pleases him or disgusts him, leads him on into the essay or drives him away. The average reader picks up a piece of writing in a more or less receptive, more or less critical mood, and reacts strongly to the opening section. The writer, then, must in his beginning paragraph pay particular heed to matters of address, be sure that from the outset he is using the style which will seem appropriate to his intended readers. Here he should set the tone of the paper and indicate the direction it is to take.[5] All of this is to deal honestly with friend reader, to attract him, but not on false pretenses. A humorous beginning to a solemn paper would perhaps entice some readers, but unless handled most carefully it would be off key, misleading, and ultimately disgusting. By the conventions of the genre, an after-dinner speech may begin with a funny story, no matter what the subject. In cold print an essay should be consistent from the start.

This consistency is often threatened by the explicit or implicit notion that the beginning is something apart, that it is perhaps an "introduction" standing before the paper proper rather than an integral part of it. Some elaborate pieces of writing do benefit from frankly introductory material, a preface or a foreword. Most essays are better for jumping into their subjects. A good trick is to try cutting off the first paragraph of a draft to see if the paper cannot get along without it. An editor once surprised me by writing, "I hope you will understand why I have cut out your first paragraph . . . it just doesn't sock as hard as the second paragraph as an opening." Introductions, after all, are generally dull and delaying—even at parties. Writers' introductions sometimes bear an unfortunate re-

[5] See pp. 61–62.

semblance to a baseball pitcher's windup—gyrations by means of which he tries to put all of his power behind the pitch and disturb and confuse the batter. Obviously a writer does not want to disturb and confuse his reader, and it behooves him to develop his momentum privately.

The writer's cue is to remember always that the beginning that stands first on the paper is the *reader's* beginning, not his; that its function is to get the reader into the subject, not necessarily to rehearse the way in which the author got into it. If the writer can keep this point in mind, he will be leery of beginnings that go too far back into the history of the writing project. He may find fascinating the fact that this subject first attracted his attention when he was a child visiting on his uncle's farm in Oklahoma; the reader probably will not. Writers should be cautious about any beginning which makes some kind of personal appeal to the reader which is not consonant with the rest of the essay. One of the most dampening is the opening apology: "I am no authority on the subject, but to the best of my limited ability. . . ." If you don't have anything to say, don't write; if you do, don't apologize—your reader can decide for himself how much of an authority you are.

Beginning paragraphs are not different in kind; any of the paragraph developments we have just discussed can be used at the beginning. Since special attention is required for the opening, however, we might survey some of the devices that have worked well. Suppose we see how we might start an essay on the following subject: "John Donne's poetry uses awkwardness deliberately and effectively."

We might simply begin with the thesis, perhaps doctoring it up a little: "John Donne's poetry is characterized by a deliberate awkwardness used to surprisingly good effect." A trenchantly phrased statement of the thesis might stand arrestingly as a one-sentence paragraph, or as the topic sentence of a paragraph developed by restatement, that is, by judicious repetition of the theme in slightly different forms:

> John Donne was rough and crusty in his verse because he wanted to be and because he could get away with it. His deliberate awkwardness allowed him to achieve effects that would have been impossible in a neat and classical vein. Much of his strength, his vigor, and his power comes from intentional bluffness and incongruity. He does not sing smoothly, because he wants to shout or argue or quibble.

This beginning with the thesis accomplishes more smoothly the intention of the unnecessarily blunt, "The purpose of this essay is to discuss the ways in which John Donne deliberately uses awkwardness to achieve his poetic ends." The motive of telling the reader exactly what we propose to do is admirable, but we can do it a little more subtly.

To move to the other extreme from the sober statement of purpose, we might look for a striking epigrammatical formulation which can tease the reader into attention, perhaps something paradoxical like, "The charm of Donne's poetry lies in its deliberate disdain of charm." This kind of opening is dangerous, however, and must be handled with a sensitive feeling for its appropriateness to the subject and the audience.

A question can be a good beginning, since it invites reader participation. Rhetorical questions, the answers to which are obvious, are sometimes effective; but real questions which the writer intends to try to answer are better:

> Why is John Donne's verse rough and tongue-twisting? Is it because he lacked an ear? Because, as De Quincey remarked, his sensitivity had been perverted by the cacophonous collocation of "his own baptismal name, when harnessed to his own surname—*John Donne* . . . hideous jingle"?

The quotation from De Quincey reminds us that a quotation is a possible way to begin, but De Quincey himself also warns us that the habit of sprinkling one's writing with quotations is a sort of "mouth diarrhea." We must be most careful that the quotation is really apt —not something we dragged in with only a tortuous application. We must be certain that it is from someone who has some claims to be an authority on the subject, and that it says whatever we want to say effectively and arrestingly enough to be allowed to stand in the strategic opening position. Lines from the poet and critic S. T. Coleridge might qualify for a beginning such as the following:

> With Donne, whose muse on dromedary trots,
> Wreathe iron pokers into true-love knots.
>
> Thus Samuel Taylor Coleridge put his finger on one of John Donne's most interesting traits. This humpy uncouthness and perverse use of intractable materials is characteristic of his verse. It is a part of a deliberate awkwardness which Donne twists to his poetic purpose.

An illustration is another effective way to capture the reader's attention, provided that the illustration is brief, apt, and interesting. We might try something like this:

For God's sake hold your tongue, and let me love . . .

So begins John Donne's poem "The Canonization." Did a love poem ever begin more unorthodoxly, or a lyric poem less euphoniously? This awkwardness, however, is characteristic of Donne, part of a game he plays with his readers. He is intentionally crude in style because he wants the shock effects.

We might, of course, start at the logical or chronological beginning of the subject, or at the logical or chronological end of it. Logically this usually means beginning with the cause or the effect. We might start with an explanation of Donne's intention to break away from the smooth neoclassical or sugary Elizabethan verse into a more conversational and rational mode, and then show how this resulted in a deliberate roughness of style—thus moving from cause to effect. Or we might start with a description of his awkwardness and show how it derived from his desire to move away from conventional "dainty devices" and shock his readers into thinking. We might even open with a revealing contrast and comparison by putting side by side typical verses from Ben Jonson and Donne, and thus lead into our thesis about the latter's awkwardness.

Whatever we do, we will want to be sure that the opening paragraph can stand firmly on its own, that it does not lean upon the title of the essay. The first sentence should never refer back to the title in this fashion:

DONNE'S SKILLFUL AWKWARDNESS

Skillful truly it is, for his is a deliberate awkwardness, cleverly designed to achieve . . .

If for no other reason, this is a bad practice because titles are usually set in a different kind of type in a different process, and may well get separated from the body of the text. It should not then be left with a decapitated air.

Ending Paragraphs

Endings are also of great strategic importance. Our recognition of this fact may be blunted by our daily experience with news stories, which taper off into trivial and repetitious last paragraphs designed to be dropped in make-up if necessary. Essays, we remember, are tick-like wholes and they should be rounded off. Endings should not be some ritual "in conclusion"—a phrase better banned—but an inevitable completion. The last paragraph is crucial because it leaves the last taste in the reader's mouth, sends him away convinced or dubious, pleased or queasy.

A reader wants to feel that the essay has come to a fulfilled end, not just stopped. We should therefore be careful of abrupt endings, using them only when we intend a specially calculated effect. We should also avoid any sudden introduction of new material for which the reader is unprepared, and which gives him a sense that we were just about to start over again when we collapsed. Since our reader should have the impression that we end strongly, not sort of fade out, we should resist the tendency to sweep together an assortment of minor points missed elsewhere into a catch-all ending. And we should eliminate any weak afternotes, such as apologies for inadequacies of the paper or vague references to points that could have been covered but were not. If the reader is going to be satisfied, the aims of the paper will have to be made clear to him long before the end—probably toward the beginning—and he will have to be made to believe that the writer deliberately left out the areas uncovered, for good reasons, not because he ran out of time, energy or knowledge.

This test of the satisfied reader will determine whether the essay ought to end with that old standby, the summary. Does the reader need a summary? Or will it seem unnecessary and repetitious? If the paper is a fairly short one, he might resent the summary as almost implying that he is not capable of knowing for himself what has been said. In such cases it is usually better to work the summary in more subtly, perhaps through an incremental introduction to the last point by appropriate variations of the formula: "Besides point one and point two, there is also point three," like this:

> Shifting the presidential line of succession from cabinet officers to the speaker of the House and the president pro tempore of the Senate does, then, have the advantages of placing the responsibility upon elected rather than appointed officials [*point one summarized*], and on men of long governmental experience instead of men often recently drafted from business, industry, or education [*point two summarized*]. But there is also a significant disadvantage to be considered [*point three introduced*].

The presiding officers of the House and Senate usually reach their elevated positions by reason of great seniority. They are frequently elder statesmen, full of years and wisdom, but relatively low on vigor and vitality. They are comfortably set in the patterns of their legislative routines. It is doubtful whether many men in these positions would have the energy, the versatility, or even the desire to take on the heavy administrative burdens of the presidency. In a time of crisis we might find our country in the reluctant and unsteady hands of an octogenarian—a respected man and an elected man, but not elected to be president. Before this happens is the time to re-examine our succession rules.

For long papers the reader may appreciate a more formal summary. He will then usually prefer main points to be woven into an interesting and logical paragraph, not more or less listed. At any rate, a summary is not the only defensible ending—as students sometimes seem to believe. Most of the devices we just looked at as possible beginnings can also be adapted to the ending: an apt quotation, a clincher illustration, a question left in the reader's mind. If the thesis encourages a look into the future, suggests a practical application of the theory advanced or an action in view of the position reached, then the paper might end strongly on such a point. The important thing is that the essay end strongly, with all the pieces put into place.

ASSIGNMENTS

1. Write paragraphs on the following topic sentences:

a. A paragraph need not have a topic sentence.

b. To a college student grades are money.

c. To be useful, a definition must be purposeful.

d. Beginning paragraphs are more important than ending paragraphs. (or vice versa)

2. All the sentences in the following paragraph have been rearranged except the last. Try to put them in the most logical and effective order. If you want to compare your result with the original, it can be found in chapter XII of Anthony Trollope's *Autobiography*.

> The reading of a volume of history or on science may represent itself as a duty; and though the duty may by a bad style be made very disagreeable, the conscientious reader will perhaps perform it. The language in which the novelist is to put forth his story, the

colours with which he is to paint his picture, must of course be to him matter of much consideration. If he be confused, tedious, harsh, or unharmonious, readers will certainly reject him. It is the first necessity of his position that he make himself pleasant. Let him have all other possible gifts—imagination, observation, erudition, and industry,—they will avail him nothing for his purpose, unless he can put forth his work in pleasant words. To do this, much more is necessary than to write correctly. But the novelist will be assisted by no such feeling. He may indeed be pleasant without being correct,—as I think can be proved by the works of more than one distinguished novelist. Any reader may reject his work without the burden of a sin. But he must be intelligible,—intelligible without trouble; and he must be harmonious.

3. Write a paragraph incorporating the following points:

a. If man reaches the moon he will have problems of moving around there.

b. The moon has no atmosphere.

c. The surface of the moon may be like wet firm sand or crunchy snow.

d. Observations of lunar eclipses show that the shaded area cools off very rapidly.

e. Rapid cooling suggests an exceedingly porous surface.

f. Vehicles with broad tracks or large soft tires will be required.

g. New photographs dispute the theory that the moon is covered by 100 feet of dust.

4. Examine the following paragraph:

Writing can be fun. Of course it can also be work, but it need not be all work. Its being fun depends upon the writer's attitude and the pressures pushing upon him. He must be relaxed and able to take an interest in writing for its own sake, and as an activity, not as a required means toward some end. Anything that is done simply because it is necessary to the acquisition of something else becomes a task. Anything, on the other hand, which requires a technical proficiency that can produce the thrill of achievement and perfection of style can give pleasure—whether or not it is also a livelihood. The professional writer, then, as well as the amateur, can enjoy his craft.

a. Mark what seems to you closest to a topic sentence.

b. Try to rewrite the paragraph putting the topic sentence in two other positions.

c. Mark the transitional devices.

5. Write a paragraph developed primarily by each of the following methods as discussed in this chapter:

a. Examples
b. Cause and effect
c. Definition
d. Comparison and/or contrast

6. Mark the transitions in the paragraphs you have written in assignment 5. Do you have enough transition? Is it smooth, logical, and helpful to the reader? If you see the need of any improvement, revise accordingly.

7. Choose an essay from a reading text or periodical and analyze its paragraph construction. Does it regularly present topic sentences? Where in the paragraph does it most often put them? What different devices for paragraph unity does it use?

8. Analyze the beginnings and the endings of five essays in your reading text or periodicals. Write a paragraph describing the beginning you think best and explaining why. Do the same for the ending you prefer.

9. Write an essay on one of the following subjects:

a. The Theater of the Absurd makes special demands upon the audience.
b. College students today are more concerned about off-campus issues than students were a generation ago.
c. When superior novels are made into moving pictures they usually lose much of the quality that distinguished them from ordinary novels.
d. The return of the paperback book has some disadvantages.
e. The age of the lone explorer is past: today's frontiers require massive cooperative effort.

10. Look at the essay you wrote for assignment 9 and analyze what made you use the beginning and ending you did. Are they well suited to the subject and the audience? Write two alternative beginnings and try them out on a representative audience.

CHAPTER EIGHT

Rhetoric and Emphasis: Differences in Sentences

> There are nine and twenty ways
> Of writing tribal lays
> And every single one of them is right.

The key to writing is the recognition and exploitation of differences. No two formulations of words are quite the same, each may be right in its place, and for any specific purpose one is never just as good as another. The differences are likely to be matters of emphasis—a little more weight here, a shading of color there. Although these differences are cumulative and ultimately make themselves felt—like everything else in the writing process—in the shape of the whole, they operate most fundamentally and conspicuously in the arena of the sentence. Three concepts are necessary to an understanding of the character of sentences: the principle of separation, the principle of relationship, and the principle of emphasis. Emphasis partly subsumes the others, for separation produces emphasis, and relationships control emphasis. Let us, however, look at them one at a time.

THE PRINCIPLE OF SEPARATION

Few activities are as hazardous as attempting to define a sentence. Consider, for example, the conventional formulation: "A sentence is a group of words which conveys a complete thought and has a subject and predicate." Obviously, a sentence does *not* have to be a group of words, or have a subject and predicate:

Fire!
Coming?
Yes.

And if "He fell down" is a complete thought, what is, "He fell down and hurt himself"? A more complete thought? Putting aside the metaphysical question of whether there is such a thing as a complete thought, it is doubtful whether a sentence can hold one. About the only thing that can be asserted positively about a sentence is its separateness. It is a segment of human discourse capable of standing alone. It makes sense by itself. In spoken utterances it is set off by pauses more marked and of longer duration than normally occur elsewhere—called open junctures—and by terminal intonation patterns—a falling inflection for statements and a rising inflection for questions. When we learn our language we learn the meanings of these pauses and inflections, for they are suprasegmental phonemes, signs of meaning added to the grosser phonemic pattern. We learn to know by these signs that the speaker is intentionally separating an element of his thought, that he wants us to receive it as a unit. If these signs set off elements which are not capable of standing alone because they do not make sense by themselves, we are confused, or we think the speaker is.

In written discourse the same situation obtains, except that the signs are visual instead of audible. We start a sentence with a capital letter and end it with a mark of terminal punctuation: a period, a question mark, or an exclamation point. If we find these signs separating material which does not make sense by itself, which is left up in the air and does not come to the kind of conclusion we expect from a terminal mark of punctuation, we are puzzled and dissatisfied.

Here, then, are two important aspects of the concept of separateness. It depends upon both the intention of the writer and the acceptance of the reader. The writer intends to cut out a piece of his thought, but he must cut a piece that his reader can perceive as having a kind of wholeness. He must present a unit, not a fragment. That is why a real "sentence fragment" is a criminal offence. A real sentence fragment is one that leaves the reader dissatisfied, not one that merely lacks a complete subject or predicate. Objectionable fragments usually, indeed, violate both requirements of separateness: they are not a result of the writer's deliberate intention; they are careless lapses which are the more insulting because they seem to overlook the reader's needs. They generally result from a writer's losing control of an ambitious sentence, forgetting where he is in it, and producing something like this: "Although Shakespeare's imagery is characteristically profuse and various, when an image cluster strikes a symbolic note, as often happens." The following passage also contains three constructions which could be considered sentence fragments. See whether you would defend them.

A man's home may be his castle. If he can meet the monthly payments. Moats have gone out of style, however, and wire-tapping has come in. You have to be careful with sunbathing in the back yard if there are neighbors with second-story windows and twenty-twenty curiosity. Laws prescribe how high your ceiling may be, how many windows, how much floor space, what kind of plumbing you can have. But you can still lock the front door, take off your shoes, and yell at the children. Provided you don't violate the anti-noise ordinance. Yes, a castle all right, a real stronghold.

The author of this passage is affecting a "double-take" style, and for that reason has separated two elements which are not logically separable: "If he can meet the monthly payments" and "Provided you don't violate the anti-noise ordinance." Since they follow elements which they qualify, they do not really bother the reader a great deal. But the punctuation is unconventional; these elements might better be connected to the preceding sentences by dashes. The last sentence, however, while technically a fragment, is entirely acceptable and more effective than it would have been had it been cast in conventional form.

These references to unconventional punctuation and conventional form remind us of something else important about the sentence. It is the ground on which rhetoric and grammar meet.[1] In most of our discussion so far we have been able to think in terms of the unique demands of a particular situation, to consider what structure of ideas and forms best suits our potentialities and our readers' needs and interests. We can arrange sentences into a paragraph in any way that

[1] See Chapter One.

seems to us most effective; conceivably we can construct a paragraph fundamentally different from any other ever written. With sentences, however, we cannot be so original because part of the pattern of relationships of words in a sentence is determined by the grammar of our language.

THE PRINCIPLE OF RELATIONSHIP

In Latin, *Canis puerum mordet* is translated "The dog bit the boy," no matter in what order the words are arranged. *Canis* is in the nominative case, and must be the subject; *puerum* is in the accusative case, and must be the object. Such certainty is one of the advantages of an inflected language. English, of course, has by now lost most of its inflections, a condition which also has its advantages, but which imposes a relatively strict word order. Obviously we cannot say "Bit the boy the dog"; our meaning would also not be clear if we said, "The boy the dog bit," or "The dog the boy bit"; and it makes a great deal of difference whether we say "The dog bit the boy" or "The boy bit the dog." Thus part of the pattern of relationship in sentence structure is grammatical. It also makes considerable difference whether we say "Money is the root of all evil" or "Money is of all evil the root." But the difference is rhetorical, not grammatical. Most of our concern as writers is with the finer nuances of rhetoric, but these in turn depend upon a knowledge of what is grammatically possible in the language and what can be accomplished by variations on it.

The normal word order in declarative sentences is:

Subject	*Verb*	*Object*	*or*	*Complement*
I	saw	him.		
I	came			home.

We have to be careful about sentence order, or we have the boy biting the dog. Neither can the verb stand at the beginning of the sentence except in questions or commands. In older English this pattern was common:

Verb	*Subject*
Came	he?
Come	ye.

Now it is almost restricted to the verbs "will," "shall," "can," "need," "must," "may," and split formulations with "do":

Will you? Do you know the answer?

By putting other elements into the simple pattern, however, we can shift the order considerably without changing the basic relationship. A verb may come before the subject in a declarative sentence, provided it is initially modified:

Finally came the order to retreat.
After an overwhelming series of preliminary delicacies appeared the main course.

An emphatic object may come before the subject:

That aspect she refused to discuss.

Obviously the force of an inversion depends upon the recognized normalcy of the standard word order. Rhetoric is partly a structure of controlled violence against routine grammatical patterns; it has to operate, however, within grammatical limits, or it ceases to be language. The inversion above does not affect the fundamental relationship of the grammatical pattern: "aspect" is still the object. The subtler relationships are, nevertheless, modified: "aspect," although grammatically the object, is rhetorically the subject of the sentence —it is the most important element.

It appears, then, that there are two kinds of relationships which a sentence must handle: grammatical and rhetorical. The first kind puts some restraints upon the writer, yet at the same time offers patterns which are both conveniences and opportunities for significant variation.

Our considerations might, therefore, lead to a definition of a sentence something like the one below. It will certainly not suit formal grammarians, but it might be helpful in suggesting to the writer the requirements and potentialities of the sentence. Here, then, is a writer's definition:

A sentence is a grammatical and rhetorical device for expressing relationships among the elements of that segment of an idea which the writer wants to separate and present as a unit and which the reader can accept as capable of standing alone.

This definition makes explicit in the primary constructs of writing those principles we have held out from the beginning of this book: the choice of the writer to fit the demands of the reader. It emphasizes that a sentence is both a collection of parts and a whole, and is essentially a device for shaping and showing the complex relationships among these. The concept of a "device" may seem demeaning. We may feel that our sentences are organic structures, that if we cut them they will bleed. Granted a great sentence takes on life, but it does so, I suspect, because the writer knew very well what he wanted to do with it. If we think of our sentences as devices we can tinker with, we are less likely to become infatuated with premature formulations. For only by persistent tinkering are we likely to express precisely the intended relationship among the elements of the sentence.

THE PRINCIPLE OF EMPHASIS

The principle of emphasis does not amount to an injunction to strain and intensity, any more than yelling is the only way of being emphatic. The point is that *some* emphasis is inevitable. A perfectly level human utterance is impossible, because we have at least to put our words in some sequence, and this order is inescapably meaningful. It is not a question of whether or not to have emphasis, but of what emphasis to have. Control of emphasis is simply the means by which we make a group of words say what we want them to say. Emphasis does not merely enhance or underline meaning, it defines meaning. Much inept writing results from writers' insensitivity to the devices of emphasis. Not having worked out precisely what they want to say, and not knowing how to say it precisely, they produce a rough approximation—often without realizing how far off they are.

Emphasis, of course, is a way of calling attention to something. We pay attention to whatever "sticks out," whatever is conspicuous because of a difference in appearance or location. Difference, it is important to recognize, is highly relative. In a context of great variety, where no two structures are alike, any pattern of repetition stands out. In a context of similarity, where everything fits and balances, any discordant uniqueness is conspicuous. Difference for its own sake has value: "variety is the spice of life." Meaningless variety, however, soon ceases to be spicy. It becomes irritating, frustrating, and frenetic. Since the point of difference is the point of emphasis, it should be meaningful.

A difference may be blatant or subtle, it may be on the surface or profoundly essential, it may be external or internal. Just as in spoken language the signs of emphasis may be volume, pitch, or gesture—the lift of an eyebrow, the purse of a lip, or any of the supplementary devices of meaning called kinesics—so in written discourse the signs may also be external, something added to the flow of words.

External Devices of Emphasis

External emphasis is like a woman's make-up, which when applied with discretion can be effective but cannot work wonders and is easily overdone. Too much superficial emphasis marks a "school girl" style, where we find a theatrical gush of superfluous and self-defeating underlining, double underlining, wavy underlining, small capitals, gothic script and combinations thereof, sprinkled with exclamation points, singly, in pairs, or in battalions.

Such physical features have a legitimate but limited place. Exclamation points are proper to mark a real exclamation—and then generally one is sufficient. Underlining, or italics in print, can be used to call attention to a word that would be stressed in oral discourse, particularly to distinguish between possible degrees of emphasis without revising the simple and straightforward utterance. Consider for example the sentence

I never said that.

Any of the four words might be stressed, and at least one probably would be in spoken language. The above written form, however, is so flat, so normal, that one cannot be sure of the emphasis. Alternative versions could make the emphatic element quite clear:

I, of all persons, never said that.
Never did I say that.
I never made the statement.
I never said such a ridiculous thing.

All of these would go fairly well in informal English except the second. If "never" is the point of emphasis, the more natural sentence would probably be the original with an underscore:

I *never* said that.

Italics can also be used effectively to point up parallel relationships, especially when the key words are prepositions or are otherwise inconspicuous; but they should be used sparsely:

> It is not that Blake's Prophetic Books are impenetrable: the difficulty is not so much how to get *in* them as how to bring something *out*.

The more clamorous devices, such as small caps, can sometimes be used in newspaper columns to break up expanses of gray type, or in headings to mark sections and subdivisions in long essays and chapters; they have no place as designators of emphasis in serious writing. Such writing depends chiefly on the more basic internal emphasis.

Internal Devices of Emphasis

Internal emphasis, ultimately, is the result of a pattern produced by the writer's shuffling words around. For all we do when we write is to arrange words in patterns of relationships which give pre-eminence to certain elements. A sentence is a sort of verbal kaleidoscope. Turn it and watch the words fall into different patterns. Some of them will be ungrammatical, outside of the language, or on those fringes occupied by writers like James Joyce, Gertrude Stein and E. E. Cummings. Many—and their number and variety are amazing—will be beautifully and richly meaningful. The patterns are wrought by such concrete and manipulable things as coordination, subordination, predication, intensification, qualification, repetition, parallelism, position, length, rhythm, and euphony.

COORDINATION

Coordination is a means of putting equal elements side by side in such a way as to emphasize their equality. The most natural way to do this is by using coordinating conjunctions:

and   but   for   nor   or   yet

An especially obvious kind of coordination can be produced by pairs of correlative conjunctions:

both . . . and
either . . . or
neither . . . nor
not only . . . but also
whether . . . or

The coordinated elements may be words, phrases, or clauses; they may be in pairs, triplets, or greater numbers; they must, however, be rhetorically and grammatically equal. Coordination is easy and natural: The preceding sentence, for example, contains two sets of coordinated nouns ("words, phrases, . . . clauses"; "pairs, triplets, . . . numbers"), one set of coordinated adverbs ("rhetorically . . . grammatically"), and a set of coordinated clauses ("the coordinated elements may be . . . ; they may be . . . ; they must . . . be").

One of the most comforting of logical exercises is finding similarities. The mind rejoices in the process of pairing things off—like the animals entering the Ark. Coordination is the structural device for emphasizing similarity, and it is important for the writer to recognize that the element of *parity* is essential in the coordinating process. Even when the relationship is one of opposition or contrast, the items must be on the same level so that they can be contrasted. You can write,

> I got up early, but I missed the train.

You cannot say,

> Getting up early, but I missed the train.

The coordinating conjunction *but* is improper because the ideas are not put on the same plane or in the same grammatical form. You could conceivably say,

> Getting up early, I still missed the train.

But now the elements are not expressed coordinately. The idea of "getting up early" has been reduced from the status of a separate clause with an independent verb to that of a participial phrase; the two actions are not considered as equal and sequential, but are more intimately and subtly related.

Since coordination is so natural and consoling, we tend to overdo it. You probably remember a childhood experience of giving a report in class and stringing everything together with "and" 's. A more sophisticated awareness recognizes that everything is not logically parallel, that some things are more important than others, and that a variety of complicated relationships exists between ideas. A more sophisticated syntax copes with various emphases by different patterns of subordination.

Let us take a pair of ideas and consider some of the changes that can be rung upon them.

> Life is a struggle.
> Life is worthwhile.

When these ideas are put as above in parallel, similar, yet grammatically discrete units, they are coordinated, but in such a way as to emphasize their separateness. The impression this presentation creates is that here are two distinct ideas which have been manhandled together by rhetorical parallels. This form says to the reader, "Look, here are two ideas which may seem entirely unrelated, but which can be put side by side. What do you make of this relationship?" Other kinds of coordination say more to the reader about the character of the relationship:

> Life is a struggle; life is worthwhile.

By putting the two ideas in one sentence the writer implies that there is an intimate connection between them. He does not yet say what he thinks that connection to be. The absence of any conjunction stresses abruptly the back to back relationship. Less terse and more natural is

> Life is a struggle, and life is worthwhile.

The conjunction "and" puts ideas together on a dead level. Since no reason for the relationship is advanced, there is a vague implication of "that's the way it is." Still coordinated, but with a clear expression of one aspect of the character of the relationship is

> Life is a struggle, but it is worthwhile.

Up until now the writer had allowed the paradoxical nature of the juxtaposition of the two ideas to stand without comment; the "but" emphasizes it, although simply and easily. More pointed, and more formal, are

> Life is a struggle, but it is nonetheless worthwhile.
> Life is a struggle; nevertheless it is worthwhile.

Since the version using the conjunctive adverb "nevertheless" requires a semicolon, it does not make as smooth a coordination; the reader is hauled up abruptly and the paradox exploded at him.

SUBORDINATION

A writer may not be content simply to place these ideas side by side in a compound sentence. He may wish to subordinate one to another in any of a number of different ways. The most emphatic is by a subordinate clause in a complex sentence. Suppose that the relationship between these ideas is considered to be causal:

Because life is a struggle, life is worthwhile.

This same basic relationship may be implied by an overtly temporal or spatial formulation which invites the reader to draw the cause and effect conclusion from experience:

When life becomes a struggle, it becomes worthwhile.
Where (wherever) life is a struggle, it is worthwhile.

Or the connection between the ideas may be concessive:

Although life is a struggle, it is worthwhile.

This relationship may be made somewhat stronger if expressed negatively:

Unless life is a struggle, it is not worthwhile.

Or it may be put in correlative form:

Either life is a struggle, or it is not worthwhile.

It is worth noting that the concept of subordination here is primarily grammatical: the dependent clause cannot stand alone; it needs to be completed by the attached independent clause, and in that sense it is subordinate. Rhetorically, however, the subordinate clause may contain the most important ideas. In the following sentence other devices of emphasis overrule rhetorically the grammatical subordination and place the stress upon the first clause:

Just because life *is* a struggle, it is worthwhile.

All of the above versions of our chameleon sentence have two complete predicates, two finite verbs and their complements. A possible modification which will change the emphasis is to reduce the predication. One of the clauses can easily be turned into a phrase:

Life is a struggle, but worthwhile.
Although a struggle, life is worthwhile.
Being a struggle, life is worthwhile.

Reduced predication usually results in less elaborate, less formal syntax and in further subordination of the elements deprived of their full verbs. It also brings brevity and economy and sometimes produces a neatly emphatic formulation:

> Life is a struggle worth making.

This version is probably better than the full relative clause:

> Life is a struggle which is worth making.

Possibly the most effective way of stating this idea is the simple construction,

> Life is a worthwhile struggle.

Here the content of what could be an independent clause has been reduced to one word, "worthwhile." But the very fact that this idea is reduced grammatically to an adjective and made to qualify ironically the other pole of the complex points up the basic incongruity of the concept. The tensions are made immediate and intimate, as in St. Chrysostom's famous dictum on the same pattern:

> Woman is a desirable calamity.

INTENSIFICATION

Most blatant of the internal means of emphasis is intensification. This is produced by the use of superlative adjectives and adverbs, compounds of "-self," and words like "very" and "remarkably." Because intensification is obvious, and because it is easy, it is easily overdone:

> Life itself is the bitterest of struggles, but it is nonetheless very much worthwhile.

The trouble with such lavish use of intensives is that it defeats itself because it arouses the reader's incredulity. His reaction is likely to be, "It isn't so," followed by anger or contempt or laughter, depending upon how seriously he takes the whole thing. That life is a struggle most people will admit; that it is a bitter struggle some may concede; that it is the bitterest of struggles raises the question of from where outside of life the standards for comparison are coming.

The stripped, bare statement is sometimes the strongest—"bare, as the mountains are bare," said Hazlitt of Wordsworth's poetry. Yet the bareness of a mountain is a relative thing: it may be intensified by rocks, or snow, or even a cloud cap. Used judiciously, devices of intensity give color and texture to style. Some words, however, designed as intensives, are actually weakening, either because they are so much used as to have become routine or because they are ambiguous. "Measurably," "significantly," "considerably," and "appreciably" are often used as if they meant "importantly," yet they carry a connotation, and often clearly mean, "just enough to measure or signify or consider or appreciate." Overused intensives include "colossal," "stupendous," "tremendous"–adjectives of Hollywood press agents, and "super," "neat," "keen," and "tight"–vocabulary of teen-age slang. "Very" can be considered in the overused category. A well-known story has a distinguished city editor exorcising the word from his paper by telling his reporters to use "damn" instead of "very," and instructing his copy editors to cut out all profanity. Personally, I think that is going a little far: "very" does very well when a moderate and comfortable degree of intensification is desired. The use of "perfectly" as in "perfectly acceptable," is a cliché of intensity that is weakening, partly because it is routine, partly because it is not supportable, perfection usually being out of range.

Intensives, we should make clear, emphasize certain aspects of a statement; they do not, therefore, necessarily strengthen the whole statement, since the aspect selected may be weakening. Take the sentence in the above paragraph, for instance: "Personally, I think that is going a little far. . . ." "Personally" intensifies "I," and is actually depreciatory in effect, for it suggests possible differences of opinion. The selective character of intensification is apparent in the following alternatives; each is acceptable, but where the intensive is put makes a big difference:

Life is certainly a struggle, but it is worthwhile.
Life is a struggle, but it is certainly worthwhile.

QUALIFICATION

Most of the techniques of intensification discussed are methods of qualification. Qualification is a device of emphasis which depends upon giving the reader something and then taking part of it back. The writer qualifies the simple statement by limiting or elaborating it. He tells the reader a dog is red, and then adds "a sort of reddish brown with a high gloss." The psychological effect of this process is to make the statement more complicated and, therefore, to attract attention to it. This system works quite well, enhancing the precision, clarity, and effectiveness of the statement—provided the complexity does not get too involved. If it does, the process is self-defeating, for the qualification takes away so much that the reader is frustrated and confused. Try to test any qualification to see whether it does make for precision and clarity by adding something valid and important. Qualification is bad when it is no more than a sort of decoration, a product of that impulse which makes some writers act as if a noun without an adjective were indecently exposed.

In the previous section we were dubious about the intensive qualifier "bitterest" in "Life itself is the bitterest of struggles. . . ." What sort of qualification would be helpful? In the two basic predications, that life is a struggle and life is worthwhile, the concept "worthwhile" is logically close to an absolute. We may feel that life is *sometimes* worthwhile, but we cannot turn it off and on. We have to strike a balance and conclude that on the whole it either is or isn't. All we can do is indicate our sense of the preponderance in that balance:

> Life is overwhelmingly worthwhile.
>
> Life is by and large worthwhile.

Our previous sentences have treated "life" as if it also were an absolute, taking it to be synonymous with all human life. It can, of course, be qualified temporally, geographically, and socially:

> Life in the twentieth century is a struggle.
>
> Life in the desert is a struggle.
>
> A share-cropper's life is a struggle.

Notice that these qualifications change the meaning of the statement much more fundamentally than do most of the alternative forms we have considered: the difference is a matter of substance as well as emphasis. The limitations provide more precision and clarity, but at the cost of making the utterance less proverbial, less gnomic. If the broader scope is desired, no limitation is appropriate. Indeed, the qualifier may emphasize the inclusiveness:

> All life is a struggle.

Although one could imagine a context in which the "all" might seem natural, it does not appear to contribute much here; it seems redundant—"life" includes "all life," and the simpler statement is more effective. Never embroider when the plain stitch will serve the purpose better.

A case can be made, then, for the simplest form, which carries a connotation of flat inevitability: "Life is a struggle." Most minds, however, will resist the general proposition that life is always and only a struggle; and that fact accounts for the successful combination of "worthwhile struggle." A skillful and accurate writer might anticipate this union by the right qualification of the "life is a struggle" part of the combination. What can we try?

Life is partly a struggle.

Life is more or less a struggle.

These are accurate, but rather dull. Perhaps, exploiting an echo from Shakespeare, "Life is a fitful struggle."

REPETITION

Even as the patterns of a kaleidoscope rely for their effects upon repetition produced by mirrors, so sentence patterns can use repetition of form and diction for emphasis. Verbal repetition, as we have seen, is more likely to be employed to tie a paragraph together. Compare, however, these two versions:

Although life is a struggle, life is still worthwhile.

Although life is a struggle, it still seems worthwhile.

Much of the strength of the first sentence results from the repetition of "life" and "is."

Repetition is, however, like most rhetorical instruments, double-edged. It should never be allowed to result in redundance or to suggest a poverty of vocabulary. "Beauty is as beauty does" is a deliberate and effective use of patterned repetition. "A beautiful girl is beautiful not so much because of her physical beauty as because of the beauty of her conduct" is an inept and probably unintentional use of repetition that actually appears repetitious, which the proverbial version does not.

Does the duplication make the first of the following versions better than the second?

Life is a struggle, but it is a worthwhile struggle.

Life is a struggle but worthwhile.

Probably not, but the line is a narrow one. Change the rhythm slightly and the same device takes on power:

Life is a struggle—a worthwhile struggle.

The only safe way with verbal repetition is to read the sentence aloud, hear how it sounds, and try to analyze its effects. Unconscious repetition is likely to be bad, at least until the writer's intuitive ear has been well trained.

PARALLELISM

Repetition of form is generally called parallelism, and is in fact only a detailed sort of coordination. Parallelism is a mark of an organized style; it imparts to a sentence an ordered solidity and achieves an emphasis through deliberate statements, as in the prelude to the Declaration of Independence:

When, in the course of human events, it becomes necessary for one people
| to dissolve the political bands which have connected them with
| another, and
| to assume, among the powers of the earth,
        the | separate and
            | equal station to which
                    the laws of | nature and
                                | nature's God entitle them,
a decent respect to the opinions of mankind requires that they should declare the causes which impel them to the separation.

Notice, incidentally, how the interpolated phrases "in the course of human events" and "among the powers of the earth" loosen the rhythm and moderate the pace of the parallelism.

Parallelism does the same thing in writing that repetition of forms does in a painting—calls attention to the blocking. Items which are paralleled should, therefore, have some structural importance. In the above example "to dissolve" and "to assume," "separate" and "equal," "the laws of nature" and "nature's God" are crucial. Parallelism need not, however, be elaborate, or reserved for such important occasions as the Declaration of Independence. It can be used simply and naturally in the kind of writing college students do. Several of the versions of our "Life is a struggle" sentence employ simple parallelism. If the device is used excessively, it produces a mannered style, which can even become cloying and unclear when the patterns pile up. Ruskin sometimes overdoes it, as in this passage from his famous description of St. Mark's in *The Stones of Venice:*

And so, taking care not to tread on the grass, we will
go along the straight walk to the west front, and there
stand for a time, looking up at its
deep-pointed porches and
the dark places between their pillars
where there were statues once, and
where the fragments,
here and
there of a stately figure are still left, which has in it the
likeness of
a king, perhaps indeed
a king on earth, perhaps
a saintly king long ago in heaven;
and so
higher and
higher up to the great mouldering wall of
rugged sculpture and
confused arcades,
shattered, and
grey, and
grisly with heads of
dragons and
mocking fiends,
worn by the rain and
swirling winds into unseemlier shape, and
coloured on their stony scales by the deep russet-orange
lichen, melancholy gold;
and so,
higher still, to the bleak towers, so far above that the eye
loses itself among the bosses of their traceries, though they are
rude and
strong, and only
sees like a drift of eddying black points,
now closing,
now scattering, and
now settling suddenly into invisible places among the
bosses and
flowers,
the crowd of restless birds that fill the whole square
with that strange clangour of theirs,
so harsh and yet
so soothing, like the cries of birds on a
solitary coast between the cliffs and
sea.

Few writers are now tempted to try anything as elaborate as this. College writers are likely, however, to have two sorts of difficulty with parallelism. First, they may fail to complete a parallelism which they have promised the reader. Note in the example below, borrowed from Ruskin, how the parallelism is broken by the word "scattered."

> Thousands of birds eddied about, now closing, now scattered, and now settling suddenly into invisible places among the bosses and flowers.

The other difficulty, which plagues particularly the writer who lacks a sensuous awareness of the patterns of his words, comes from suggesting to the reader unintended and false parallels. This is especially likely to happen with homonyms:

> *As* the meeting was important, and *as* I was late, I drove *as* fast *as* I could.

Much better here to use "because" in the first two clauses.

POSITION

Parallelism is partly a matter of the physical relationships between the parallel elements in a piece of writing, including their position within the sentence. The physical position of words in the sentence, as we have already noted, is in our uninflected language important in establishing basic relationships of subject and object. That it is likewise important in determining lesser shifts of meaning is sometimes overlooked by writers who are careless with the location of their words. Try moving "only" from position to position in the following variation on Robert Browning's "Ah, did you once see Shelley plain" (*Memorabilia*):

He claimed that he saw Shelley plain.
Only he claimed that he saw Shelley plain.
(He alone made the claim.)
He only claimed that he saw Shelley plain.
(He claimed, but could be mistaken.)
He claimed only that he saw Shelley plain.
(That was all he claimed.)
He claimed that only he saw Shelley plain.
(He claimed no one else saw.)

He claimed that he only saw Shelley plain.
(He didn't hear him speak.)
He claimed that he saw only Shelley plain.
(He saw no one else.)

In more subtle ways the relative position of elements within a sentence also controls emphasis. From one point of view a sentence is a display case, in which some items are prominently exhibited and others inconspicuously tucked away. What are the emphatic positions? The most prominent positions in a sentence are normally the beginning and the end. Another way of looking at these strategic points, however, is as opening and closing curtains. Since the dramatic moment of the dimming of the houselights and the raising of the curtain is likely to be marred by noisy late comers, playwrights sometimes count on repeating anything important that is said in the first five minutes. Similarly, anticipatory constructions like "there is" and "it is" are frequent enough in English that we do not always expect something important at the outset.

The beginning of a sentence is nonetheless of potential strategic value: it is set off from the preceding sentence by a pause, so that the reader's attention is drawn anew; and the very fact that our syntactical patterns permit weak beginnings makes a bold start more prominent. By avoiding anticipatory constructions and using devices to dramatize the first words, we can make the opening strong when we want to. Always to do so would make for a monotonous and wearing style. Compare the following:

There is conclusive evidence that life is a struggle.
Conclusive evidence proves that life is a struggle.
Life, conclusive evidence proves, is a struggle.

The second sentence would be generally preferable to the first, except perhaps in response to a sceptic who had denied the existence of such evidence. Between the second and the third sentences the choice would depend upon the context and the author's intentions. Unless these made an emphasis upon "conclusive evidence" appropriate (e.g., if it had been charged that the evidence were weak) the last version would be better. Its punctuation and rhythm set off "Life" in such a way as to give it particular emphasis and focus attention upon the central assertion.

The end of the sentence is naturally the strongest position. If readers are conditioned to accept a slow beginning, they usually expect a climactic ending, and they are likely to be impressed by what comes last. It is recognition of this principle that prompts women in their traditional insistence upon "having the last word." Notice the difference between

> Life is a struggle, but worthwhile.
>
> Life is worthwhile, but a struggle.

The two sentences add up to about the same thing, but each carries a peculiar emphasis because of the climactic power of the last word.

By the same principle, the last word or phrase before a semicolon or other strong stop within a sentence is in a potentially emphatic position. If these terminal positions are not used for key words, the effect is weakening. Unintentional weak use of strong points produces the flabbiness and ambiguity of an uncontrolled style. Purposeful failure to put the expected words in the terminal spots may, however, result in an ironic undercutting of the primary statement. Out of context it is hard to tell which this is:

> Life is a struggle more or less; but it is worthwhile generally.

PERIODIC AND LOOSE SENTENCES

A special exploitation of the value of the final word is the periodic sentence, which cannot be grammatically satisfying until the period. It is like the trajectory of a projectile, a sustained flight of words with the bang at the end. A loose sentence, on the other hand, contains at least one independent unit with which the sense could stop before the period, for example:

> In fact, a loose sentence is so constructed that it can be brought to an earlier end simply by moving up the period, sometimes to any one of several possible terminations, each of which would make different but satisfying sense.

The preceding loose sentence could have stopped at "end," "period," or "terminations." Rephrase it as follows, and it becomes a periodic sentence:

> In fact, a loose sentence is so constructed that simply by moving up the period, sometimes to any one of several possible terminations, each of which would make different but satisfying sense, it can be brought to an earlier end.

In the above construction the meaning does not come to any resolution until the last word, which thereby takes on a special importance. This effect is achieved here, however, at the cost of moving "it" far from its referent.

Loose sentences and all but the simplest periodic sentences are *cumulative*. They grow by accretions similar in kind but placed at different points in the sentence. If we suppose that a primitive core sentence generates additions of complicating and qualifying elements, as shown in the diagrams, we can see easily the distinction between these two kinds of sentences. The additions to a periodic sentence are syntactical elements less complete than an independent clause which *precede* and look forward to or *intrude in* and expand the core sentence. Clauses, noun clusters, verb clusters, adjectives, and adverbs can be prefaced or interpolated to produce a great variety of periodic effects. Try experimenting with what other elements you can add to the core sentence in the diagram.

PERIODIC SENTENCES

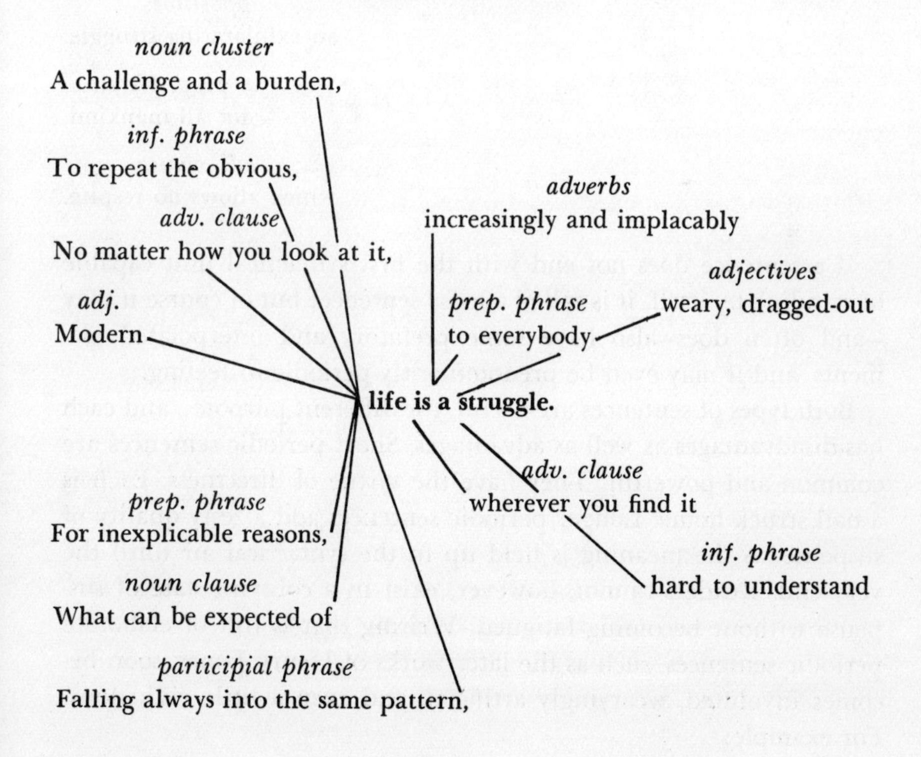

Loose sentences, on the other hand, are generated by the additions of *independent clauses before* the core sentences, or *any attachable elements after* the grammatically complete core and looking back at it.

LOOSE SENTENCES

part. phrase
demanding our best.

adv. clause
whatever else it may be.

ind. clause
Still, time drags on, and

ind. clause
and man has to conquer it.

life is a struggle

adv.
unceasingly.

appositive
an exhilarating struggle.

prep. phrase
for all mankind.

adj. clause
which allows no respite.

If a sentence does not end with the first syntactical unit capable of standing by itself, it is called a loose sentence; but of course it may —and often does—also have some prefatory and interpolated elements, and it may even be predominantly periodic in feeling.

Both types of sentences are useful, for different purposes, and each has disadvantages as well as advantages. Short periodic sentences are common and powerful. They have the virtue of directness. Each is a nail struck home. Longer periodic sentences add a zesty quality of suspense, as the meaning is held up in the syntactical air until the very end. Readers cannot, however, exist in a constant state of suspense without becoming fatigued. Writing that is full of elaborate periodic sentences, such as the later works of Henry James, soon becomes involuted, wearyingly artificial, and even a little ridiculous. For example:

The periodic sentence, whatever its qualities, and these are indubitably manifold and admirable, nevertheless, especially in the hands of the inexperienced and syntactically unsophisticated, or perhaps oversophisticated, writer, can be, for a number of reasons, exceedingly dangerous.

A style characterized by periodic sentences, or by long sentences which are periodic until the last few words, is as formal as a Mozart quartet. The reader cannot relax, but must sustain his attention to the end of the sentence. He feels a certain deliberation and premeditation on the part of the writer who can hardly ever indulge in afterthoughts or tack on anything, but must give each utterance a precious orbicularity.

Loose sentences are easy and natural. They are like wandering paths provided with a number of comfortable seats where the traveler may stop, rest, and survey the vista. They have the virtues of apparent intimacy and sincerity, for they suggest that the writer is working out his idea, piece by piece, before the reader's eyes. The cumulative effect can even give a special power to the end of the sentence, different from that of the periodic sentence, yet emphatic in its way. But wandering paths are not the shortest distances between two points, and a style made up exclusively of loose sentences may seem lax, uncontrolled, and indecisive.

A good writer inserts periodic elements in loose sentences and mixes up loose and periodic sentences, just as a good quarterback mixes up plays, to provide variety and surprise and thereby make points. He is not trying to trick his reader, but neither does he want him to know always what to expect. The writer, like the quarterback, selects plays not just because they are different but because he hopes they will gain ground. In a context of loose sentences, one conspicuous periodic sentence will break through. Such a periodic sentence should, of course, be used to carry an important idea.

SENTENCE LENGTH

Another syntactic variation which controls emphasis is the length of sentences. A sentence may be almost any length, from one word up; the only criterion for any particular sentence is its function in its context. The general limitations on sentence length in any piece of writing depend, as does everything else, on the subject, the reader, and the writer. Seventeenth-century writers, such as Milton, sometimes constructed sentences over a hundred words long, partly because they used semicolons where we would use periods. Nineteenth-century writers, such as Ruskin, sometimes built elaborate long sentences for the musical effect. Twentieth-century writers, such as Joyce and Faulkner, sometimes string sentences out to produce the quality of stream of consciousness: the last chapter of *Ulysses,* some forty-five pages, is all one sentence. Such "sentences," however, are somewhat difficult to read because they violate the "principle of separation" which we saw to be fundamental to the sentence. Perhaps they ought not to be called "sentences."

On directions for lighting hot water heaters and in textbooks, newspaper stories, and most informal writing, propriety requires predominantly short sentences. In more formal writing, lofty in subject and pretentious in style, propriety allows longer and more complex sentences; ultimately the boundary is the reader's endurance. Few writers nowadays, however, are willing to push that very far in any kind of expository writing. The first six sentences of a lead article in yesterday's newspaper had this pattern of sentence length based on number of words: 21, 51, 27, 44, 20, 10. The opening of an essay in the last issue of *The Saturday Review* runs 43, 17, 5, 6, 10, 7, 14, 29, 9, 31, 30, 37. The first paragraph of a recent book on Moliere's comedy is more even: 24, 34, 25, 22, 23, 22, 19, 32, 31. A paragraph from the work of a contemporary historian runs 22, 11, 17, 17, 13, 22, 24, 25, 59, 36, 36; one from a philosophizing modern scientist, 52, 20, 54, 25, 33, 34, 25, 12, 25, 23, 12.

Short sentences are strong sentences. They are crisp and clear. They hit hard. Long sentences wind their way "in linked sweetness long drawn out" around and about a subject, wrapping "the concernancy," as Hamlet says, in a rich cocoon of words, and sometimes pleasing the reader with their all-inclusiveness, sometimes losing him hopelessly in the intricacies of their endless coils. But absolute sentence length is of little importance. "No absolute," said D. H. Lawrence, "is going to make the lion lie down with the lamb." Relative length is what matters. In a context of sixty-word sentences, one of twenty-five words will appear powerfully laconic. Among sentences of six to ten words, the same twenty-five word sentence will seem elaborately long. A writer must tune his eye and his ear to the patterns of sentences, and use the difference of length—as he does every other difference—to mark emphasis and define meaning.

RHYTHM AND EUPHONY

Length is but one element in the vastly complex business of sentence rhythm and euphony. Listen to this passage from Thomas De Quincey's "Levana and Our Ladies of Sorrow":

> The second sister is called *Mater Suspiriorum*—Our Lady of Sighs. She never scales the clouds, nor walks abroad upon the winds. She wears no diadem. And her eyes, if they were ever seen, would be neither sweet nor subtle; no man could read their story; they would be found filled with perishing dreams, and with wrecks of forgotten delirium. But she raises not her eyes; her head, on which sits a dilapidated turban, droops for ever, for ever fastens on the dust. She weeps not. She groans not. But she sighs inaudibly at intervals. Her sister, Madonna, is oftentimes stormy and frantic, raging in the highest against heaven, and demanding back her darlings. But Our Lady of Sighs never clamours, never defies, dreams not of rebellious aspirations. She is humble to abjectness. Hers is the meekness that belongs to the hopeless. Murmur she may, but it is in her sleep. Whisper she may, but it is to herself in the twilight. Mutter she does at times, but it is in solitary places that are desolate as she is desolate, in ruined cities, and when the sun has gone down to his rest.

Here is skillful variation of sentence length: 11, 11, 4, 34, 23, 3, 3, 6, 19, 14, 5, 9, 9, 11, 31. Notice the impact of the short sentences in their context. Observe the build-up to the climactic last sentence, which trails off in a manner appropriate to the sense. Listen to the effect of the turns like "droops *for ever, for ever* fastens" and "never clamours, never defies, dreams not," when the expectation of a third "never" is surprised. Hear the incremental parallelism of the end: "Murmur she may, but" followed by 5 words, "Whisper she may, but" followed by 7 words, "Mutter she does at times, but" followed by 25 words. Note the alliteration patterns in "*f*ound *f*illed with perishing *d*reams, and with wrecks of *f*orgotten *d*elirium."

Such skillful manipulation of sound requires an ear more delicate than most of us possess. It requires an ear like that of De Quincey, who could not abide to have on his shelf a book cacophonously entitled "Burke's Works." His compulsion to perfect sentence rhythms is apparent in his quotation, in a letter to the Wordsworths, of a remark an Oxford acquaintance made about Coleridge's periodical, *The Friend:*

"He" (i.e. Mr. Coleridge) "will have to repel equally the arrow of criticism—the dagger of envy—the bludgeon of calumny—and the (broad-)—sword of literary persecution." I confess to have added the word *broad;* as it seemed to be necessary to the climax—and the music; but the rest is correct. (Oct. 9, 1809)

If you, reader, can see why he thought "broad" was necessary, there is some hope for your ear. Still, the writer who has not felt on the pulse many and many a sentence had better not strive for the finer effects of euphony, but simply content himself with attempting to avoid cacophony. Sentence music is the last and the highest of the devices of emphasis.

ASSIGNMENTS

1. Here are two related ideas:

    Love is blind.

    All the world loves a lover.

Put these ideas into one sentence in as many different ways as you can. Decide which you think is the best version and why.

2. Look back at one of your recent themes and do the following:

a. Count the number of loose sentences. Do any of them have long periodic elements?

b. Count the number of periodic sentences. Are they mostly short?

c. Count the number of simple sentences. What proportion is this?

d. Count the number of compound sentences (those with two or more independent clauses).

e. Count the number of complex sentences (those with at least one dependent clause).

f. Make a tabulation of the length of the sentences.

g. As a result of this analysis do you conclude anything about your usual sentence structure?

3. Do the following sentence exercises:

a. Write two sentences using parallelism. Choose the one you like best and write a paragraph analyzing the effects of the parallelism.

b. Write two periodic sentences. Change them into loose sentences.

c. Write two sentences using intensives. Experiment with substituting different intensives. Pick the combination you prefer and write a paragraph explaining why you think it is most satisfactory.

4. Rewrite the following sentences in different ways, experimenting particularly with the effects of putting different elements at the beginning and the end.

a. There are many reasons to believe that in human relations the easiest distance between two points is not a straight line.

b. It is a mistake to equate deviousness with dishonesty and to suppose that only the forthright man has a heart of gold.

c. Most of the time a man quite properly does not say all that he thinks, and frankness is a virtue which can be of dubious value.

d. That lubrication of society which is sometimes known as "social grace" often takes the form of keeping your mouth shut.

e. My father used to tell me that it was better to keep my mouth shut and be thought a fool than to open it and remove all doubt.

5. Rewrite the sentences in assignment 4, reducing the predication to a minimum.

6. Read through an essay in your text or in a periodical and make a list of five sentences you would have liked to have written. Write a paragraph in which you try to discover what, if anything, these five sentences have in common and what you can deduce from them about your taste in sentences.

7. Consider the following passage from Swinburne's answer to critics of his *Poems and Ballads* and be prepared to discuss the devices by which he obtains balance and variety:

> To all this, however, there is a grave side. The question at issue is wider than any between a single writer and his critics, or it might well be allowed to drop. It is this: whether or not the first and last requisite of art is to give no offense; whether or not all that cannot be lisped in the nursery or fingered in the schoolroom is therefore to be cast out of the library; whether or not the domestic circle is to be for all men and writers the outer limit and extreme horizon of their world of work. For to this we have come; and all students of art must face the matter as it stands. Who has not heard it asked, in a final and triumphant tone, whether this book or that can be read aloud by her mother to a young girl? Whether such and such a picture can properly be exposed to the eyes of young persons? If you reply that this is nothing to the point, you fall at once into the ranks of the immoral.
>
> "Notes on Poems and Reviews"

8. Experiment with all the most varied qualifications you can insert in the following sentence, and then decide which version you think best:

The boy stood on the deck of the ship while the wind howled and the sea roared.

9. From your reading bring in examples of fragmentary sentences and be prepared to discuss their propriety and effectiveness.

10. John Ruskin put all the following ideas in one sentence in the *Stones of Venice*. Trying to see how much you can get into a sentence is not generally to be recommended, but just as an exercise in the relation of ideas, see if you can duplicate Ruskin's feat:

a. Tortuous channels cut the salt and sombre plain.
b. The gondola and the fishing-boat advance through these channels.
c. The channels are seldom more than four or five feet deep.
d. They are often choked with slime.
e. The sea water is clear.
f. The heavier keels furrow the bottom.
g. The crossing tracks look like ruts upon a wintry road.
h. The oar leaves blue gashes upon the ground at every stroke.
i. Thick weed fringes the banks.
j. The weed is a heavy weight of sullen waves.
k. It leans to and fro on the slack tide.
l. Oars get entangled in the weed.

If you are curious, you can find Ruskin's sentence in "The Throne."

CHAPTER NINE

Rhetoric and Diction: Meaning Through Words

When Polonius asked Hamlet what he was reading, the Prince replied, "Words, words, words." This unexpected answer was, of course, part of his feigning insanity; but, as Polonius observed, there was "reason in his madness." What else do we read, but words? What else do we have to work with as writers—a few punctuation marks and words! Rhetoric is ultimately the art of the right words in the right places.

This is well enough. Other modes of language are possible, but none is as convenient, flexible, and reliable as words. Mathematics is a language of sorts: the proud mother was not far wrong when she bragged, "My Johnny is studying algebra—Johnny, speak to the lady in algebra!" This language, however, is largely limited to the convertible and the measurable. Words have a wider domain. In the other direction from mathematics are the languages of the dance, ritual, and love. A stylized movement, a melting look can be richly meaningful—perhaps even beyond the power of words. They are not, however, as portable, as transferable, as preservable. The convenience of words is ironically demonstrated by Jonathan Swift in the third voyage of *Gulliver's Travels:*

> The other project was a scheme for entirely abolishing all words whatsoever; and this was urged as a great advantage in point of health as well as brevity. For it is plain, that every word we speak is in some degree a

diminution of our lungs by corrosion, and consequently contributes to the shortening of our lives. An expedient was therefore offered, that since words are only names for *things,* it would be more convenient for all men to carry about them such *things* as were necessary to express the particular business they are to discourse on. And this invention would certainly have taken place, to the great ease as well as health of the subject, if the women in conjunction with the vulgar and illiterate had not threatened to raise a rebellion, unless they might be allowed the liberty to speak with their tongues, after the manner of their ancestors; such constant irreconcilable enemies to science are the common people. However, many of the most learned and wise adhere to the new scheme of expressing themselves by *things,* which hath only this inconvenience attending it, that if a man's business be very great, and of various kinds, he must be obliged in proportion to carry a great bundle of *things* upon his back, unless he can afford one or two strong servants to attend him. I have often beheld two of those sages almost sinking under the weight of their packs, like peddlers among us; who when they met in the streets would lay down their loads, open their sacks and hold conversation for an hour together; then put up their implements, help each other to resume their burthens, and take their leave.

Words are not only more convenient than things, they are also more powerful. The old Navy expression "to get the word" means to know and understand the latest order, to be prepared to act. Our culture is marked by the power of words: we are inspired by watchwords, cajoled by catchwords, and admitted by passwords. The "word" is the truth, the creative reason, the *logos:* "In the beginning was the word."

The power of words makes them dangerous in unscrupulous or incautious hands; their convenience, accessibility, versatility, and mutability increase the hazard. If words are not as cumbersome as a sack full of things, neither are they so unequivocably specific. A word is already an abstraction from nonverbal reality, a generalization, an approximation, a variable in an association pattern. For words are not so simply names for things as Swift suggests. They enter into meaning in a complicated way: they do not just mean. Although it is convenient to speak of them as doing so, words actually mean nothing by themselves. Out of context you cannot even tell, for instance, whether "rank" is a German or an English word. What does "turn" mean? You cannot be sure, for it may be used as several different nouns and verbs:

Whose turn is next?
Make a right turn.
Turn right.
To turn a phrase.
We turn the chair legs on a lathe.
Turn the crank.
Turn the pancake.
Let's make a turn of fudge.
Take a turn through the park.

Is "nut" something that you eat, or screw on, or commit to an insane asylum? These difficulties do not always result from homonyms, either. Even a relatively single word like "mother" has surprising variations on the female parent theme:

The Mother Superior made a moving plea.
The mother was a cloudy blur in the bottom of the vinegar bottle.
Virginia is the Mother of Presidents.
English is his mother tongue.

A word has meaning not only in the context of other words, but also in the context of who is using it to whom. That is, a word does not just mean; it means *for* and *to*. Meaning, as Susanne Langer put it, is *"a function, not a property, of terms."*[1] Five terms usually enter in: (1) A *writer* may actually begin with (2) an *idea* (concept), (3) a *thing* (referent), or (4) a *name* (word), but he must make relationships between them which are mirrored for (5) the *reader*. Since the name or word is what the writer has to present to the reader, it serves as a starting point in the communication—something like what we have diagrammed below.

The kind of meaning which emphasizes the relationship between the writer-reader, the word and the referent is called *denotation*. The word *denotes* or points to the referent; the relationship is fairly specific. A "bomb" is—that is, means denotatively—an explosive weapon capable of destruction dependent upon its size. But, at least since Hiroshima, "bomb" suggests violent horrors and sweeping destruction. The word does not so much point to something specific as it triggers reactions because of ideas associated with it. This kind of meaning dependent upon the relationship between the writer-reader, the word and the ideas clustered around the concept is called *connotation*. Many words are richly connotative. Like flies swarming over a slice of watermelon at a picnic, the connotation may have no necessary connection with the word, but is almost always inevitable and has to be reckoned with. Connotation is tricky because it changes

[1] *Philosophy in a New Key* (New York: New American Library, 1942), p. 45.

from context to context and from reader to reader. To some readers "automation" suggests lower costs, increased production, greater leisure; to others it implies lost jobs, readjustments, labor problems.

The writer's job is the complicated one of choosing just the words which in context carry the proper denotation and connotation to induce in the reader he is addressing exactly the concept he intends. To change any one of these variables is to influence the others and alter the entire complex. Since the tolerances are liberal in day to

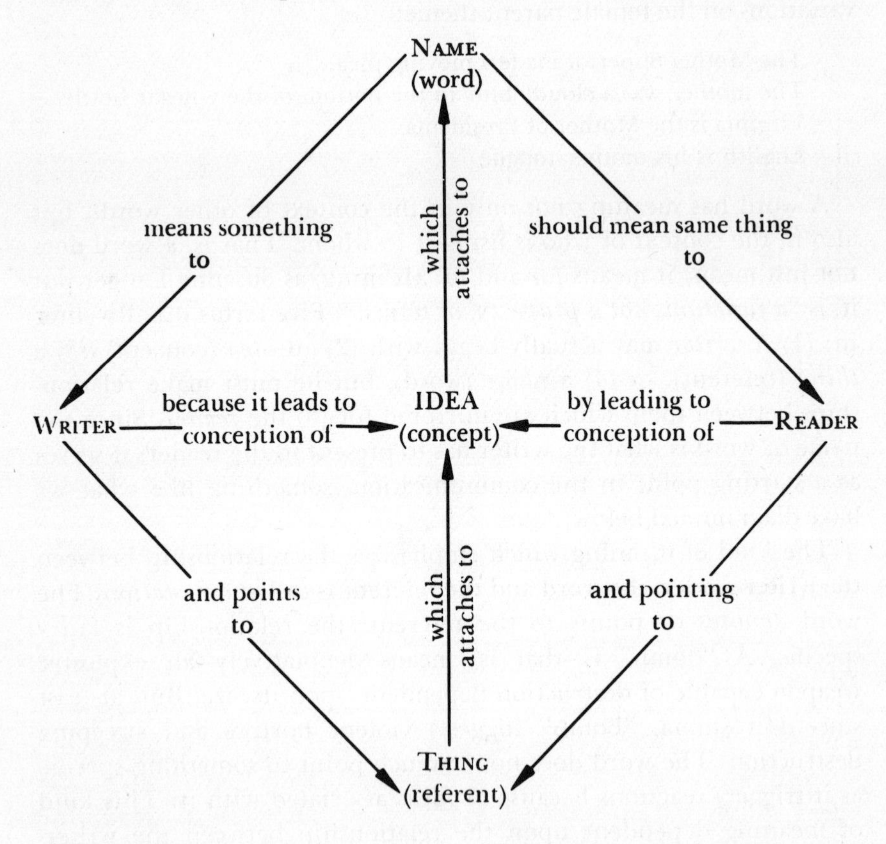

day talking and writing, most of us manage to blunder along, communicating approximately what we intend, without paying attention to all of the elements involved in getting precisely the right word. Slang, in particular, is full of more or less all-purpose words: at the moment my three sons call almost everything a "dealy." Good writing, however, requires accurate selection; the best writing—

beyond most of us—demands the meticulous care which the French novelist Gustave Flaubert spent in his arduous search for the "right word":

> Possessed of an absolute belief that there exists but one way of expressing one thing, one word to call it by, one adjective to qualify, one verb to animate it, he gave himself to superhuman labour for the discovery, in every phrase, of that word, that verb, that epithet. In this way, he believed in some mysterious harmony of expression, and when a true word seemed to him to lack euphony still went on seeking another, with invincible patience, certain that he had not yet got hold of the *unique* word.[2]

Most of us do not have such "invincible patience" or so much time, but we can make more effort than we usually do to get the right word. We need to sharpen our word sense so that we recognize distinctions among words—realize that one word is usually better than another, always slightly different from another. We need especially to value the ultimate precision that is attainable with words. Science majors condescendingly in freshman English are sometimes wearisomely puffed-up over their "precise science": the English language is also an instrument capable of exactness for those who care enough to use it precisely.

SYNONYMS

The choice of the *unique* word demands consideration of alternative possibilities. English is such a rich language that usually several alternatives are available to express any concept. Very few words, however, mean the same thing. Because of its remarkable capacity for assimilation, English has brought into its vocabulary words from many sources and on many levels. The Germanic stock of the Anglo-Saxon early picked up bits of Celtic, Latin, and Scandinavian and added substantial increments from French after the Norman invasion. Sometimes the borrowed word drove out the old—as the Scandinavian "take" replaced the Old English *niman*—but often the two forms lived side by side and took on differences of meaning. A particularly interesting example of specialization of doublets is "shirt" (from Old English) and "skirt" (the Scandinavian form of the

[2] Quoted by Walter Pater, "Style," *Appreciations* (New York: Macmillan, 1902), p. 26.

same word). The Saxon herdsmen raised the *hogg* (cf. Welsh *hwch*) or *swin* (cf. German *Schwein*) which on the tables of their Norman masters became the Old French *porc*. Thus English evolved not only "hog" and "swine" and "pork," but went on to coin "porker" also. The classical revival of the Renaissance produced more "ink-horn" Latinate words: "esteem" was put beside the older "value" (itself from the Old French), and "describe" and "delineate" added dimension to "draw" (cf. Icelandic *draga*) and "sketch" (from the Dutch *schets*). While the sun was never setting on the British flag, the language was making such conquests as adding the Hindu "jungle" to the Old French "forest," the Spanish "ranch" to the French "farm," the Caribbean "canoe" to the Old English "boat" and "punt," the Middle English "wherry," and the French "skiff" (taken from the Italian *schifo,* from the Old High German *scif*). Scientific discoveries, industrial progress, and modern slang are continuing to expand the language, usually by new words for new concepts, but sometimes by words which also supplement an already existent term: "patter" says something like the older "talk," but with significant qualification. Thus the language acquires its stock of useful synonyms.

Synonyms usually carry significantly different shades of meaning in this way: they have approximately the same referent, but subtly modify the concept; they have nearly the same denotation, but a different coloration of connotation. The distinction may be in level of usage,[3] each variant appropriate to different categories of readers who can be expected to respond to it in the desired way. The difference may be in implications of value or attitudes of judgment: a concept may be presented solemnly, objectively, or flippantly. Consider the synonyms in the diagram, all of which will convey the concept and invoke in a responsive reader a recognition of the physical symptoms. But each does so in a slightly different way, suggesting a different attitude toward the concept and a different relationship with the reader. "Drunk" is relatively flat and uncolored, a statement of fact; it could be used under most circumstances. "Intoxicated" has a more legal flavor—it can be defined in terms of the amount of alcohol in the blood—and for that very reason is somewhat less blunt and earthy than "drunk." "Inebriated" is on a level of diction which seems to remove the fact further from the realm of

[3] See pp. 59–62.

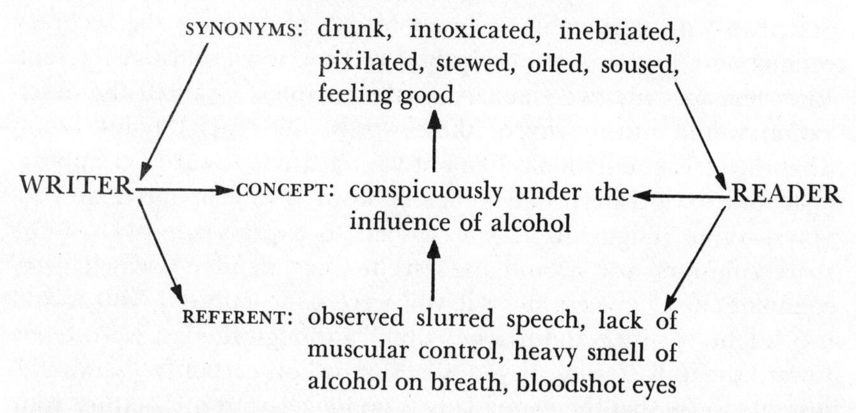

reality; unless the whole context were on a similar level, it would appear cute or strained. The other terms convey the idea more indirectly. "Stewed," "oiled," and "soused" are all slang words that do not literally mean drunk, but which have been accepted in some societies and periods as carrying that meaning. They both suggest an excessive degree of intoxication and partly qualify it by a jocular tone. "Pixilated" (which literally means amusingly eccentric, acting like a pixy) and "feeling good" are, on different levels, euphemisms: they seek to mollify any adverse judgment by putting the best face on the concept.

TONE

Selecting among synonyms is the process of getting the right word to say to the chosen reader what the writer wants to say. Accuracy, then, is purposive and pragmatic: the right word is the word that works. It works because it strikes the right tone. Consider the situation in the diagram.

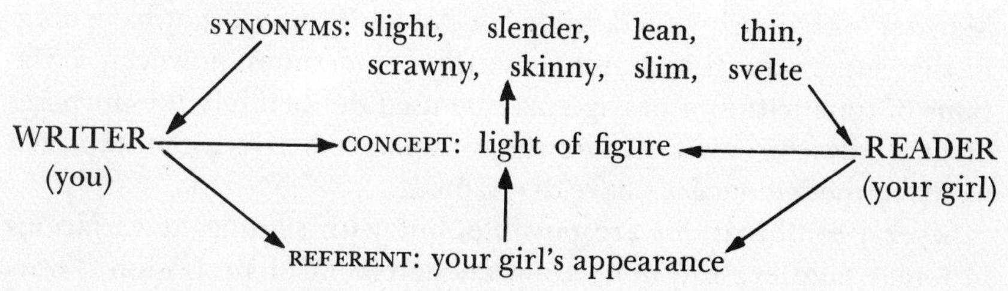

Which of the synonyms would you use? All of them denote approximately the same thing. The girl's physique, we'll suppose, could be described with reasonable accuracy by any of them—*if* the accuracy resided only in the relationship between the word and the referent. But these are only two elements in the complex. Granted the observation would justify any of these words, the crucial point is not what the girl actually looks like but your attitude toward her appearance and toward her. The choice of word is interpretative and involves value judgment. If you wished to express approval of the spare contours, you would use "svelte" or "slender," which carry connotations of gracefulness; if you were noncommittal, you would use "slight," "slim," and maybe "thin," although the last word tends toward the unflattering. If you use "skinny" or, certainly, "scrawny," it is safe to say that the young lady is no longer your girl—either your deliberate choice indicates that fact or your blundering produces that effect. Although the terms can be called synonymous in that they have nearly the same referent, they are significantly different in that they come at different points in the concept spectrum:

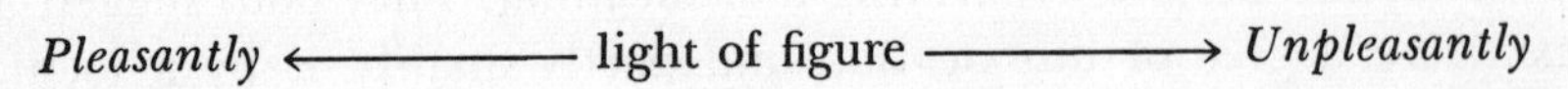

Most words carry these overtones of attitude. Sensitivity to such shades of value and responsible employment of the distinctions make the difference between getting the right word or just one that comes close. Sometimes *close* is a long way off: it makes a tremendous difference, for instance, whether you use "mannish" or "manly," "religion" or "religiosity," "aged," or "antique."

Since words have meaning in context, tone is an aura around a whole sentence or passage, and part of the problem in selecting among synonyms is that of *maintaining the tone.* Words which might in other respects serve the writer's purpose may be unacceptable because they are off key, they clash with the environment. Coleridge called his famous poem "The Rime of the Ancient Mariner": obviously "aged sailor" or "old salt" would not have done in that supernatural and archaic setting. Sometimes, however, variations of tone within a passage may be used deliberately for purposes of emphasis or irony. Consider the consonance between the italicized words in the sentence we have diagramed.

Several combinations are possible, but with significant variations in tone. "Soldier" is a noncommittal statement of profession; "warrior" and "conqueror" are more honorific and should be followed by nondepreciatory terms unless the intention is to be critical or

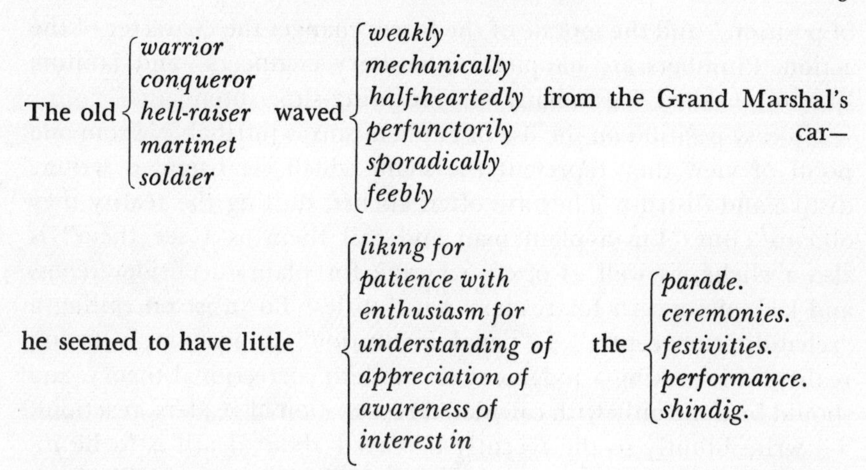

ironic. "Martinet" and "hell-raiser" carry overtones of the soldier's character: "martinet" has an unfavorable connotation of an inflexible disciplinarian; "hell-raiser," in a less formal key, might be affectionate, jocular or pejorative. "Martinet" would be appropriate with "mechanically." "Conqueror," "perfunctorily," "patience with" and "performance" could go together to suggest the veteran's contempt for the civilian show. "Conqueror" with "irresolutely" would emphasize an ironic contrast in character which might be supported by "awareness of"; "warrior" and "feebly" would rather point up a pathetic physical deterioration. "Parade" is the most specific and flattest of the final terms; "festivities" lightens and "ceremonies" solemnizes the occasion. "Shindig" is slang, out of key with everything else except possibly "hell-raiser": it should be used in this context only when the soldier or the author is scoffing at the event.

EUPHEMISMS

Euphemisms are an order of synonyms which try to adjust the facts of life to writers and readers. They are a commentary on the Pollyannaism of mankind. Some realities are hard to face, and words can appear to, indeed sometimes actually can, change them. A rose by another name would *not* smell as sweet; garbage under the name of "refuse" smells sweeter. Call a "depression" a "recession," and the changed attitude of the public may make it less serious. Call a "penal institution" a "rehabilitation center," and the atmosphere and results are different. Call a "retreat" a "withdrawal" or an "adjustment of position," and the morale of the forces changes the character of the action. Plumbers are happier as "sanitary engineers" and janitors like to be called "custodians" or "building superintendents."

No easy position on the use of euphemisms is justifiable. From one point of view they represent the sham which clear-sighted writers dislike and distrust. They are often clichés, dulling the reality they obscure. But "I'm a plain man and call them as I see them" is also a cliché, as well as often a façade for plain inconsiderateness and lack of concern for readers' sensibilities. To insist on calling a "rehabilitation center" a "penal institution" is not simply facing reality; it is making a judgment on modern correctional theory, and should be done only with calculated recognition of readers' reactions. To write bluntly to the recently bereaved about death is to be inconsiderate. To be unnecessarily explicit about certain bodily functions is bad manners. When euphemisms have the sanction of usage, the writer who is more forthright risks offending his readers.

Writers should, however, avoid using trite euphemisms just because they are readily available. Most readers are willing enough to accept an objectively realistic statement. Usually it is better to write "died" then to take refuge in "passed away," "went to his reward," "cashed in his chips" or "shuffled off this mortal coil." If a writer wants to force his readers to look clearly at subjects they are accustomed to screen behind obliquities, then he should spurn euphemisms, with full recognition of what he is doing. On this basis he makes a decision among, for instance: "puked," "vomited," "was nauseated," "had an upset stomach," "was not feeling well," "was indisposed." Notice that as the readers' sensibilities are considered the information gets less precise, the image less vivid.

USING WORDS RESPONSIBLY

Getting the "right word" is, finally, not just a matter of aesthetics, propriety, or efficiency—it is also a matter of ethics. Some kinds of writing are designedly irresponsible. Propaganda and advertising often fall into this category. The label which says boldly, "Fully guaranteed!" is exploiting the prestige value of the word "guaranteed." What does it mean on a catsup bottle? Guaranteed to be red, to contain tomatoes? The trusting purchaser, perhaps unconsciously, takes it to mean "guaranteed to satisfy." That is probably what the labelers intended him to think; maybe it is what they mean themselves, but they cannot be pinned down. Such deliberate ambiguity may be an unethical and reprehensible misuse of the power of words. Or it may be the relatively innocent sort of deception Lamb describes in his friend Captain Jackson:

> He was a juggler, who threw mists before your eyes—you had no time to detect his fallacies. He would say, "Hand me the *silver* sugar tongs"; and before you could discover it was a single spoon, and that *plated,* he would disturb and captivate your imagination by a misnomer of "the urn" for a tea-kettle; or by calling a homely bench a sofa.

Most of us hide behind such deceptions from time to time. If we are late, we declare we "were delayed"; if we fail a course, we "lost interest" in it; if we do not want to go somewhere, we "have a previous engagement."

Irresponsibility, however, is more likely to be simply the result of ignorance and carelessness. Most of us handle language irresponsibly a good deal of the time—just as, if we will admit it, we handle an automobile irresponsibly or neglect our health. The results can nevertheless be serious in each case; and in life, as in law, "ignorance is no excuse."

To take a practical example, suppose you were a business executive and a client wrote that he would like to see you to discuss a "proposition which should prove of mutual benefit." Which of these sentences would you incorporate in your answer?

> I shall arrange to grant you an interview.
>
> I shall be glad to talk the matter over with you.
>
> I am delighted by your proposal.

Obviously these sentences all agree to a discussion of the client's idea, but they do not "say the same thing." If you are using language responsibly, your choice of alternatives will depend on your opinion of this client and your judgment of whether his "proposition" is likely to be worth your time. The first version would be appropriate only if you did not wish to turn him down flat, but did not want to give him any encouragement either. The second is polite and noncommittal and leaves the way open for you to accept or reject gracefully. The third is effusive and should mean that this is a highly valued client whose offer you are certain you will want to accept. To interchange these formulations and attitudes would be to mislead, perhaps disastrously. Yet such mistakes have been made by writers insensitive to differences like the mechanical implications of "arrange" and the suggested hauteur of "grant."

Such mistakes come from difficulties in connotation, as a result of fuzzy or misunderstood concepts. The *wrong* word, the lapse in communication, may come also from the reader's not attaching the

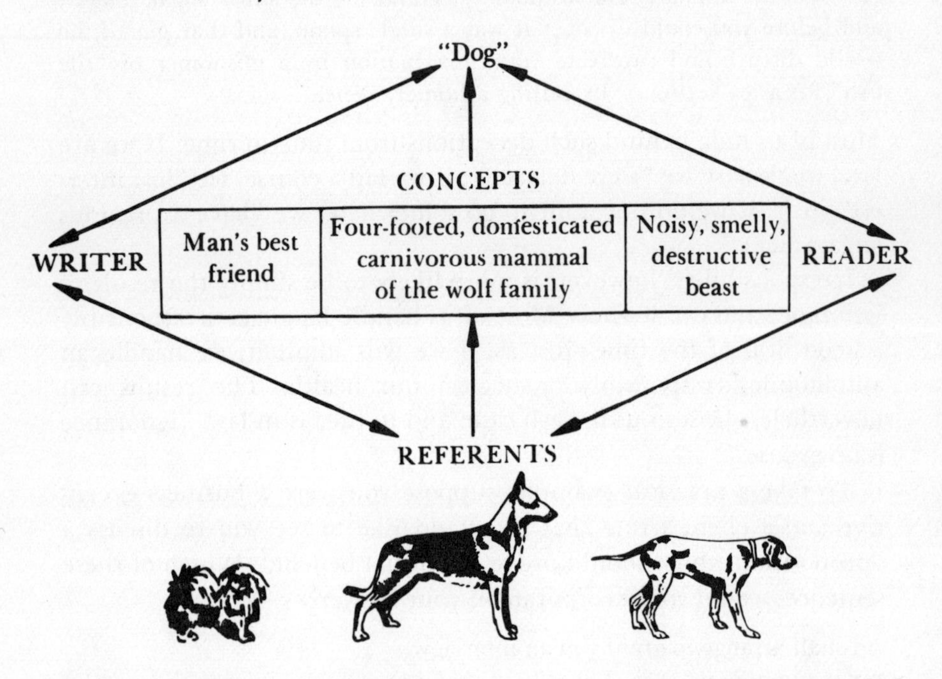

referent which the author intends. Some unfamiliar terms may have almost no connotation at all, so that communication depends upon accurate identification of the referent. If a reader thinks an aardvark is a Swedish automobile, intelligible exchange is impossible. To guard against such a possibility, a foresighted writer might include the parenthetical information that it is a species of anteater. Trouble is more likely to come, however, from relatively common words with multiple referents. For example, in the diagram above the word "dog" is inevitably ambiguous. It can point to a number of similar but different referents and evoke several interconnected but quite dissimilar concepts. The responsible writer recognizes that dogs are not all alike—just as all Scots are not tightfisted, all professors are not absent-minded, all actors do not lead Bohemian lives, and all politicians are not smooth-talking baby-kissers.

No stereotype is reliable. Even if all dogs were identical, all people would not have the same attitudes toward them. The writer has to realize, then, that he cannot put his dependence on the word "dog" by itself. He cannot expect the reader to average the referents and attached concepts and come up with some universal notion of the dogness of dog. If such an expectation were reasonable, the result would not be likely to answer the writer's purpose anyway, because he usually has in mind a specific dog or breed or character of dog, and at any rate intends a certain attitude toward the concept. He must, therefore, put "dog" in a context of qualification—"a friendly flop-eared dog," "a frisky nervous dog"—or use a synonym. Actually "hound" would fit better in the first example, "terrier" in the second. "Puppy" puts "dog" in its most ingratiating and yet unreliable form; "cur" (probably a Middle English imitation of a snarling dog) suggests the less attractive aspects of the canine family.

With most words the danger is that the writer will carelessly overlook the range of possible interpretations open to the reader. The more engrossed the writer is himself in the subject, the more likely this is to happen. Just as the dedicated dog-lover may act as if he believed the whole world would react warmly to "dog," we may all unthinkingly expect a stereotyped response to words and phrases which are weighted for us—for instance, "peace," "sport," "book," "civil rights." Such writing is irresponsible.

Remember Cassim in the story of "Ali Baba and the Forty Thieves," desperately shouting at the magic doors of the treasure cave: "Open barley!" "Open wheat!" "Open rye!"? But the doors would respond only to "Open sesame!" Writers who command words know that they do not simply *mean;* they open doors—when they fit the situation, when they are the right words.

ASSIGNMENTS

1. Here is a list of approximate synonyms. Describe the situation in which each word might be used and for what effect.

a. intellectual, intelligent, brilliant, bright, smart, clever, brainy

b. tremendous, gigantic, huge, large, big, oversized

c. obese, stout, fat, plump, rolly-polly, *embonpoint*

d. wealth, money, cash, dough, capital, resources

e. clothes, clothing, garb, dress, apparel, garments, threads, attire

2. List euphemisms for the following words and consider under what circumstances, if any, they might appropriately be used:

a. stink
b. poor
c. fail
d. success
e. undertaker's place of business

3. Without using a dictionary, see how many different meanings you can think of for each of the following words:

a. rat
b. bob
c. well
d. dress
e. pipe
f. wash

Now look them up in the Oxford Dictionary (see Chapter Twelve) and find out if you missed any meanings.

4. Be prepared to discuss the connotations of the following words:

a. administration
b. betrothed
c. gridiron
d. guts
e. politics
f. space
g. stiletto

5. Be prepared to discuss the differences between the denotations and connotations of each of the following words:

a. country
b. yacht
c. virtue
d. pledge
e. concern

6. Examine the following sentences and consider whether you could substitute synonyms for the underlined words. If you changed some of the words, would you have to change others to keep the tone constant? For what readers would the different versions be appropriate?

a. The *grandfather clock struck* every hour as though time could not go on without its *authoritative pronouncement.*

b. *Under the guise of extending gracious hospitality,* the Mayor was *mending political fences* and *undercutting* the *opposition.*

c. Whatever she had *expected*—and she was not *really sure* what this was —she was *still somehow disappointed.*

d. *No sooner had* the *bell rung* than students began to *pour* out of the *various buildings,* first *trickles,* then *streams,* and finally *floods.*

7. Here are some famous expressions. Do you think their fame derives chiefly from their ideas or their happy choice of words? Be prepared to discuss and defend your view.

a. "The quality of mercy is not strain'd."

b. "Poets are the unacknowledged legislators of the world."

c. "The better part of valour is discretion."

d. "True wit is Nature to advantage dress'd,
What oft was thought, but ne'er so well express'd."

e. "God's in his heaven:
All's right with the world."

f. "Give me liberty, or give me death."

g. "I have not yet begun to fight."

h. "In the spring a young man's fancy lightly turns to thoughts of love."

i. " 'Tis better to have loved and lost
Than never to have loved at all."

j. "Trust thyself: every heart vibrates to that iron string."

If you do not recognize some of these and would like to know the source, use a dictionary of quotations (see Chapter Twelve).

8. Here is a list of concepts concerning which it is possible to hold a variety of attitudes ranging from unreservedly favorable to vigorously unfavorable. For each write out as many synonyms as you can, arranging them in order of the connotations from favorable to unfavorable.

a. Tending to scrutinize established procedures.

b. Tending to make one's own decisions.

c. Tending to spend money cautiously.

d. Tending to face dangers.

e. Tending to show feelings.

9. Knowledge of etymology can help a writer (e.g., "lacrymal") or confuse him (e.g., "stark"). Leaf through your dictionary and find ten interesting examples each of helping and hindering etymologies.

10. Thomas Huxley recommended that one should write as if he had to stand an examination on each word. Look over a recent paper of yours and pick out a key sentence. Copy it over at the top of a sheet of paper, allowing plenty of room for alternative versions. Are you willing to justify the choice of each word? If not, suggest changes. Be prepared to write your final version on the blackboard and defend it.

CHAPTER TEN

Rhetoric and Diction: Qualities of Words

Nobody can tell a writer what are the right words for him. He must find them out himself and bend them to his purposes—big words, little words, hard words, easy words, new words, old words, general words, abstract words, concrete words, relative words, specific words, figurative words. If he is to choose wisely he must make himself conscious of the qualities of words, turning them over and over like a coin collector fingering his hoard, getting to know the characteristics and worth of each.

SOLID WORDS

Some words are more solid than others, because they have clearer and more definite referents. You can pin them down, in context. Since man is a creature whose aspirations exceed his grasp, he also needs some words for general, relative, abstract things that cannot be pinned down readily. Such words and such ideas, however, are hard to deal with and offer a special temptation to irresponsibility. It behooves most of us to keep on as firm ground as we can and make our diction as solid as possible.

Solid words are *specific* words:

Shoes and ships and sealing wax, and cabbages and kings.

Not:

> Footwear and transport and closing material and vegetables and rulers.

Action as well as things can be specified. Consider what specific verbs can do to this sentence:

> The man *went* out of the room.

Instead of "went" try each of the following:

ran	sailed	bounded	wheeled
walked	jerked	hopped	ducked
shuffled	oozed	lolled	stomped
tottered	sauntered	spun	stormed
wobbled	strolled	whipped	tip-toed
tripped	backed	whirled	dashed
skipped	hurried	teetered	danced
crawled	galloped	slithered	stumbled
inched	ambled	dove	pranced
waddled	trotted	jolted	writhed
wriggled	stepped	vaulted	hobbled
jumped	slid	eased	cavorted
rolled	slipped	glided	waltzed
strode	squirmed		

Some of these terms are metaphorical, some a little strained; they will not all do in any kind of writing, and a style in which people always "wriggled," or "teetered," or "vaulted" would be tiring, if not ridiculous. But a style in which they always just "went" or "moved" would be flat and dull. Specific words are more colorful, more interesting, more accurate.

General words also have their place—in some ages and aesthetic theories a large place. Samuel Johnson set forth the standard of the general in Imlac's famous definition of a poet in chapter 10 of *The History of Rasselas:*

> "The business of a poet," said Imlac, "is to examine, not the individual, but the species; to remark general properties and large appearances. He does not number the streaks of the tulip, or describe the different shades in the verdure of the forest: he is to exhibit in his portraits of nature such prominent and striking features, as recall the original to every mind; and must neglect the minuter discriminations, which one may have remarked, and another neglected, for those characteristics which are alike obvious to vigilance and carelessness."

Many writers think otherwise, and set themselves to numbering the streaks of the tulip, believing it to be their peculiar business to preserve all the discriminations which carelessness overlooks. There is a danger, however, of counting so many streaks that one does not see the tulips, or seeing so many tulips that one misses the garden. General words are a good protection against myopia, and a convenience for summing up.

Suppose a large van loaded with clothing were wrecked, strewing the contents all over the highway. You could write:

> Garments of every description were scattered about in every direction.

Or

> Pants, shirts, sweaters, blouses, dresses, socks, suits, underwear, overalls, skirts, slips, ties, hats and handkerchiefs were spread all over the road.

Although the second sentence is vividly specific, it is too much of a good thing. It would be improved if changed to

> Pants, shirts, sweaters, blouses and a variety of other clothing were spread all over the road.

General words are necessary. They must, however, have substance behind them. That's why the third version of the sentence is the best of the three: "clothing" here is not an empty generalization; its solid content has been demonstrated.

If a writer forgets that generalities are convenient summations for a series of actualities, he is likely to be in trouble. "Army" is a fine general term, but an army will not get very far if its leader forgets that it is a group of men who must be fed—"An army marches on its stomach," said Napoleon. "Science" is a shibboleth of our time, but anyone who would use the word responsibly must be able to put behind it a definite methodology and a body of practice. "Faculty" has a dignified and learned sound, but it is no better than the "teachers" who compose it. In some quarters it is fashionable to think of "corporations" as soulless entities, but there is truth in a recent advertisement: "General Motors is people." Furthermore, "people" are men and women, husbands and wives, veterans and neophytes, welders and stenographers, and—to use a cliché which indicates the drive we all have toward the specific—"the man next door."

Solid words are *concrete* words. Their substance resides in the fact that one can point to a definite referent. The writer or the reader may never have seen it or heard about it—but it actually exists; and once it has been identified there is no doubt what it is. Concrete words attach to identifiable acts and things, and in this realm the writer is most secure. He can confidently write:

The book lay on the shelf.

But he has introduced uncertainties as soon as he feels moved to write:

The large red book lay on the high narrow shelf.

How large is large? What shade is red? How high is high and how narrow narrow? These terms are *relative* terms; they deal with degrees and relations which are not inherent but are projected by the describer; they are "projectile" words which presuppose judgment. That these are all common enough words indicates how often we are called upon to make relative judgments. Still, we need to recognize that they are vague words, and that if we want to sharpen and clarify the picture, we need to write something like

The dark red folio lay precariously on a shelf not so wide as the book and just out of reach.

Of course it would be possible to be even more specific: to give the exact measurements of the book and shelf and the height from the floor. Such detail might be desirable, but it would more probably be destructively irrelevant. The version above puts enough solidity into the description to allow the reader to gauge the relatives for himself and suggests the desired quality of the scene. The relative "large book" can be translated into the concrete "folio," but not all projectile words are amenable to such conversion. What about "beautiful book"? *Abstract* words like "beauty" pose special problems suggested by the diagram on the next page.

The "referents" in the diagram are all different, and that quality which we think of as "beauty" in each is different. Furthermore, different individuals and different cultures have different standards for what constitutes beauty. Some African tribesmen like their belles as plump as possible, and Chinese music seems unlovely to many Western ears. It would be practically impossible for a writer to count on a definite referent for the word "beauty." The same is true of many abstract words, and the result for the reader may be vagueness or confusion, unless the writer finds some means of clarification.

Abstract words are, of course, general words of sorts. They do not, however, add up to the total of their parts in the same way that an "army" is a group of soldiers and a "faculty" is a group of teachers.

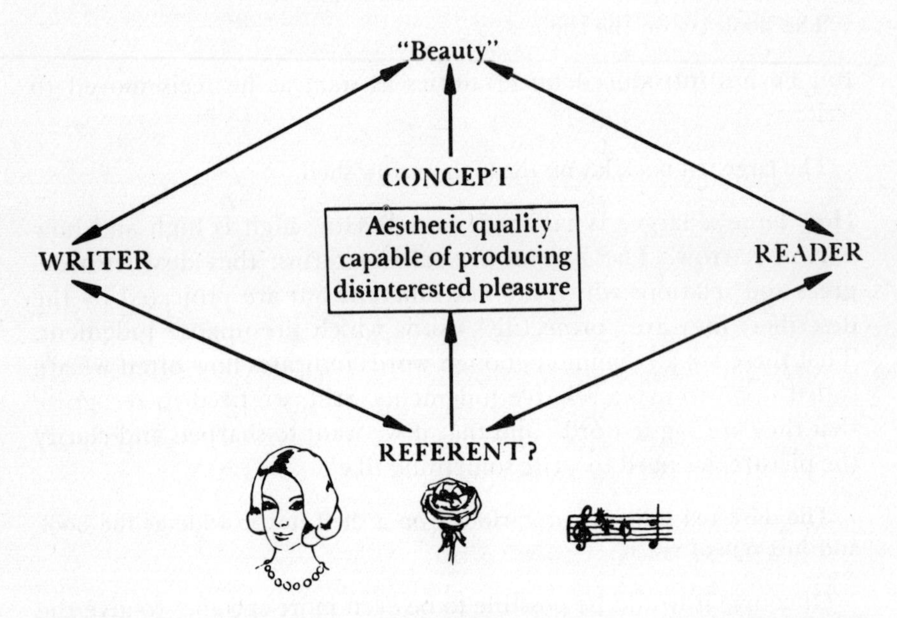

Abstract words deal with ideas; they are words for which the concept is more important than the referent. Because abstract words have indistinct, relative, and more or less detached referents, their meaning is more connotative than denotative. They are evocative and provocative; they can generate more heat than light. They are words of controversy, sometimes meaning one thing to the "good guys" and another thing to the "bad guys." Often they are words not to reason with but to hit over the head with. "Patriotism," said Samuel Johnson, "is the last refuge of a scoundrel." But he also said, "That man is little to be envied whose patriotism would not gain force upon the plain of Marathon." Obviously the patriotic feeling aroused by thoughts of the gallant stand at Marathon is to him real; the other "patriotism" is a pose, a word used defensively, self-seekingly, irresponsibly. By not making his meaning clear, not qualifying his flat condemnation, he is himself irresponsible. Writers exploit unfairly many other abstract words such as "liberty," "capitalism," "socialism," "communism," "romanticism," "classicism," "modernism," "automation." These terms are neither badges nor anathemas; they ought to be used rationally in rational communication.

Shakespeare points out some complexities of abstractions when he makes Sir John Falstaff declare on the battlefield:

> What is honor? A word. What is in that word honor? What
> is that honor? Air. A trim reckoning! Who hath it? He
> that died o' Wednesday. Doth he feel it? No. Doth he hear
> it? No. 'Tis insensible, then? Yea, to the dead. But will
> it not live with the living? No. Why? Detraction will not
> suffer it. Therefore I'll none of it; Honor is a mere scutcheon.
>
> *Henry the Fourth, Part I,* V, i, 133–140

Pope is more subtle in *The Rape of the Lock.* Thalestris cries:

> Honor forbid! at whose unrival'd shrine
> Ease, pleasure, virtue, all our sex resign.
> Methinks already I your tears survey,
> Already hear the horrid things they say,
> Already see you a degraded toast,
> And all your honour in a whisper lost!
>
> Canto IV, 105–110

What kind of "honor" overrides virtue and can be lost in a whisper? What do we mean by "honor among thieves"? This is not to say that there is no such thing as honor or that the word "honor" is meaningless. Alfred Noyes, in the process of trying to define poetry, told this child's riddle:

> What's the difference between a loaf of bread and an elephant?
>
> I don't know.
>
> Well, you'd be a heck of a person to send to the store after a loaf of bread!

We may not be able to define abstract words with exhaustive precision, but we can tell them from elephants. We can use their connotative power responsibly and avoid their potential vagueness and confusion if we are careful to put them in a context of qualification which makes our meaning clear. "Democracy," for instance, obviously means something different to the Western world from what it does to the "democratic peoples' governments" of the Communist countries. To communicate we must define our terms workably, make clear that "democracy" is government by the will of the majority expressed through free elections. Thus even abstractions can be given a sort of solidity.

STRONG WORDS

Under the influence of misunderstood propaganda on how to build a vocabulary, some students busy themselves with thesauri and act as if they think good writing requires ornate, elaborate, and sesquipedalian language. Of course a writer should have as rich a vocabulary as possible, for the more tools he owns, the more likely he is to have the right one to do the job. But words *are* tools; and a three-quarter horsepower precision-geared, rubber-mounted, shock-proof plastic-cased, dynamic-balanced electric drill will not do you much good if you need a hammer. As we saw when we considered connotations of synonyms, the word with the most syllables is not necessarily the best word to use for a given purpose. The choice rests on a number of factors: propriety to the subject, the writer, the reader; whether or not the word has been used in preceding sentences; the needs of euphony and rhythm. The prevalent freshman presupposition that the best words are big words leads to "fancy writing"—that strained and preposterous mongrel style we warned against in Chapter Two. The following passage is a *tour de force* of a kind not recommended, but it does suggest what can be done with only monosyllables:

> The best words may not be big words. Might can come in small chunks, and short words can be strong words. They can pack a good punch, if they are sound, if each is right in its place. For strength means great force at a point, and short words can hit hard, since their might is in one piece—bang! Short words make sense; they strike home. The fool yearns for pomp, and lards his style with big words, long words, fine words. How much has he said? Does his point stick? Short words are firm, hard, sharp, quick to be seen and to be heard. They ring in the mind like the true coin they are.

Exotic Latinate diction, what Thomas De Quincey called "long-tailed words in -osity and -ation," may be out of place for two main reasons. First, these words simply may not communicate. There is a story that a do-it-yourselfer wrote to a federal bureau to share his discovery that hydrochloric acid would clean out drain pipes. The bureau, it is said, wrote back solemnly to the effect that his method was "of dubious merit since it was incompatible with metallic durability." Only after he had written again to say he was glad they liked his idea did they come out and tell him, "Don't use hydrochloric acid; it eats hell out of the pipes!" A recent news story tells of a Marine Corps doctor's writing to the mother of a recruit that her son's trouble was only "an acute attack of nostalgia." The irate mother complained to her senator that her boy was never bothered with "nostalgia" before and she thought the Secretary of Defense should check up on the the medical facilities.

More probably, inflated diction will communicate, but will also communicate something about the writer's insecurity and insensitivity. It may suggest a six-year-old girl, proudly playing dress-up in her mother's high heels, with hiked-up frock, last year's hat, and too much lipstick. For elaborate language can be ridiculous. Try converting any well-known passage into the most high-flown diction you can muster, such as in the version of "Twinkle, twinkle little star" which begins "Scintillate, coruscate stellar miniscule" or in this corrupted classic:

Mary possessed, in fee simple, an *ovis aries* diminutive,
Whose filamentous covering was blanched as crystalline aqueous flakes;
And through all Mary's multifarious peregrinations attentive
Her faithful ovine companion an inevitable second makes.

Since this language is obviously inappropriate for a nursery rhyme, the effect is ludicrous. It is worth noting, however, that this version contains a good deal more information and is much more specific than the child's version. Where they are appropriate, in serious writing on complicated subjects to sophisticated audiences, big words can be strong words, because of their precision and convenience. "Condensation," "transubstantiation," "mitosis," and "entropy" express concepts which it is difficult to put into short words without awkward circumlocution. The monosyllabic passage above shows as much strain, of a different kind, as the ornate version of "Mary had a little lamb." Good writing is easy reading, and the strong words are those which contribute to that end, be they long or short. Still, a good rule for inexperienced writers is never use a long unusual word where a short common word will *in every respect* do the job as well. For if it will do it as well, it will do it better.

FRESH WORDS

Words can go stale. Plain straightforward words with denotative emphasis rarely become trite, but words in set formulas and words which exploit modish or sentimental connotations can turn into clichés. "House" and "hat" remain generally useful; "home" and "chapeau" may in some contexts become hackneyed. What makes words wear out is constant, and often inappropriate, repetition of what might once have been an arresting expression. William Wordsworth, in a famous plea for naturalness, deplores such repetition in poetic diction, a set of clichés used by some poets:

> The earliest poets of all nations generally wrote from passion excited by real events; they wrote naturally, and as men: feeling powerfully as they did, their language was daring, and figurative. In succeeding times, Poets, and Men ambitious to the fame of Poets, perceiving the influence of such language, and desirous of producing the same effect without being animated by the same passion, set themselves to a mechanical adoption of these figures of speech, and made use of them, sometimes with propriety, but much more frequently applied them to feelings and thoughts with which they had no natural connection whatsoever.
>
> Appendix to "Preface" to *Lyrical Ballads*

The first writers to call a nurse a "ministering angel," bread "the staff of life," and money "filthy lucre" were imaginatively creative. Some of their early imitators perhaps used the same phrases effectively, but now anyone "desirous of the fame" of a writer cannot use them seriously.

A problem with trite phrases is that a certain amount of experience is required to recognize them. Anything is new and fresh to the individual who discovers it for himself, no matter how hackneyed it may be to the rest of the world. In a way this is fortunate, for thus youth rejuvenates a jaded culture: there is always the exciting chance that the "discovery" will take a twist and become really new. Most trite writing, however, comes not from inexperienced writers who by accident hit upon a cliché, but from those who have heard one used, been struck by it, and think it is pretty good because they do not realize how overworked it is. They are usually disposed to defend their triteness, even belligerently—sometimes actually on the grounds of currency: a student once protested to me, "I know it's good; I've heard it a hundred times!" Exactly, and that is part of the reason it is bad. Everybody has heard it a hundred times, and either become sick of it or so accustomed to it that it is bland, ineffective, almost meaningless.

Not every much-used phrase, however, becomes an objectionable cliché. Some formulas have so struck the imagination of English speakers and writers, seemed so right and so convenient, that they have been sanctioned by usage and converted into idioms. Most readers will consider still useful such familiar phrases as "strike the imagination," "stand on ceremony," "brook interference," "chain of events," "the world of . . . ," "lost opportunity," "dead center," "critical mass," "class struggle," and "iron curtain." It may be difficult "to draw the line" (an acceptable idiom) between the faded and weary and "the tried and true" (a cliché). The only way a writer can learn to distinguish is by getting experience and developing his ear. Generally, however, he can be suspicious of phrases which, although much-used, still have a cute, strained, or slick quality. He may be able to trust those which sound natural and which convey his ideas in convenient and economical form.

Trite expressions range from the wheezing "unaccustomed as I am to put pen to paper" to the superfluous or misleading "in conclusion." Cliché users "view with alarm," "point with pride" and "dare to aver without fear of successful contradiction." They have a "will of iron," or a "vein of whimsy," and "hopefully," a "touch of genius." To them things are always "light as a feather," "broad as the ocean," "hard as nails," "soft as a cloud," and incomprehensibly, "brown as a berry." Have you ever noticed that on sunny days people never go to the beaches—they always "flock to the beaches"? Once they get there they become a "mass of humanity." Or if they head the other way, they "trek to the mountains," where they become "intrepid individualists" or "pioneer spirits."

Members of certain trades and professions (that is, "walks of life") have their own pet collections of clichés known as jargon. Politicians, for instance, are fond of "the rock-bound coast of Maine," "that dedicated public servant," "that distinguished son of the state of" (supply any state), "that humble man of the people," "unalterably opposed," "irrevocably committed," and "the sun-kissed shores of California."

Scientists slip easily into "of the order of," "rigid control," "along fundamental lines," and "characterized by." Educationists talk about "peer groups," "curriculum articulation," "learning motivation," and "group dynamics." Sports writers have "grid clashes," "net tilts," "diamond contests" in which players "battle it out," "show class," or "come from behind," in a "stunning upset" because of "brilliant coaching" by their "mentors" and the combination of their "superb condition," "do-or-die spirit," and "spunk," "grit," or "heart."

Jargon shades off into shoptalk and becomes the language of the initiates, which under some circumstances may be acceptable and convenient, particularly in spoken discourse. A careful writer, however, should avoid "little gems" of clichés "like the plague," unless he consciously uses them for some special effect. He may maneuver his devices of emphasis in such a way as virtually to say to the reader, "You and I know this is a cliché: I am not presenting it to you as something original but as a deliberate bit of stylization, because I think there is significance in the fact that this idea is expressed in this way, or because I expect you to enjoy this particular turn of phrase." Thus a speaker introducing Mary McCarthy remarked that she had "a *stubborn streak* of scholarship." She herself deliberately used trite language to characterize Henry Mulcahy's mind at the beginning of *The Groves of Academe.* Unless a writer has such control over clichés, he had better leave them alone.

FIGURATIVE LANGUAGE

The fact that some of the clichés and idioms we have mentioned are similes and metaphors suggests how popular, how natural figurative language is. English is full of "dead" figures, expressions which were once original figurative conceptions, perhaps passed through a trite stage, and have now become so much accepted that we use them without much consciousness of their figurative character. We speak easily of the "head" of a corporation, the "leg" of a journey, the "hand" of a clock, and the "foot" of a bed. (The "arm of the law" and the "finger of fate" are still clichés, and the "heel of Achilles" is a trite allusion.) The "foot" of the bed is especially interesting, because the bed has "legs" which have "feet," but it also has a "foot." The "feet" come from the figure of comparison; the "foot" is a figure of association—that is, the end at which the sleeper puts his feet.

To speculate upon these assimilated figures, however, is to "consider too curiously." The writer does not expect it; it would disrupt the tenor of his thought. Thurber, in his amusing essay "The Secret Life of James Thurber," points out the consequences of suddenly becoming alert to such figures: a "skeleton key" conjures up frightening spectres, a husband who "never puts his foot down" must be forever standing on one leg, and a little boy looks all over the house for the missing organ when he is told that a girl "cried her heart out." These unconscious figures in our everyday speech have little of the figurative power.

Figures used consciously for a deliberate effect are something else again. They provide the writer multiple opportunities to be original, and invite the reader to extend his horizons through new combinations of words and ideas. They are particularly congenial to the poet; and an elaborate accumulation and manipulation of figures is more appropriate to poetry than to prose. A highly figurative prose style is at best ornate, mannered, "poetic"; at worst it becomes intolerable "fancy writing." A judicious sprinkling of figures, however, adds variety, color and depth to any prose and is quite in the province of rhetoric. For good figures provide not only a means, but sometimes the most natural, economical, and only feasible means of conveying an idea. How can you get across to the average reader the concept of softness except by some kind of comparison? Can you expect him to react to a statement of specific density or surface resistance in pounds per square inch? What more literal formulation can say as effectively, "This was one of those games when the whole team blocked like Whistler's Mother"?

Older handbooks of rhetoric concerned themselves largely with burnishing an arsenal of figures, distinguishing as many as 250 kinds. Such discrimination is a work of technical virtuosity comparable to an advanced analysis of possible moves in chess; given the major types of figures, a writer can develop his own variations. A rough division can be made between figures of sense and figures of sound, the first concerned primarily with the manipulation of ideas, the second with the patterning of sounds, although possibly including a semantic function. Figures of sense are based on comparison or similarity and contiguity.

Figures of Similarity

Comparisons are of two basic sorts: comparisons expressed or implied of something with *something else,* by simile, metaphor and allusion; and comparisons of something with *some other form of itself,* by exaggeration, understatement, and irony. As speakers and writers we use them all more than we perhaps recognize.

The *simile,* expressing comparisons overtly with "like" or "as," is the most obvious of the figures of similarity. This is perhaps the reason that the Beatnicks have distorted it—"like crazy, man!" In similes, as in all kinds of comparisons, the writer needs to be concerned that the comparison is apt, fresh, and meaningful to the reader. Not "soft as a cloud" (trite); not "soft as a wombat's fur" (won't mean anything specific to most readers); probably not "soft as tar in the sunshine" (this is soft all right, but is more likely to suggest stickiness). If the implications are favorable, perhaps "soft as a Persian kitten"; if dubious, perhaps "soft as an overripe banana."

The *metaphor* assimilates the comparison and declares an identity —instead of saying a man "eats like a hog" (simile), it says he "is a hog." The identity, however, is never literal, and it is enough for the identification to operate on one significant level. A man may have hoggish characteristics in appearance, appetite, or table manners or a preference for wallowing in filth. The more facets of similarity that are relevant, however, the richer the figure.

A metaphor, like other figures, may be merely suggested, many of its implications left submerged in the text; or it may be elaborated and extended:

> A flick of his wife's tongue could disrupt his peace, and her daily tirades of sarcasm and criticism were almost too much for his uneasy conscience.

The "flick" here clearly suggests the cut of a whip, but does not push the idea. Compare:

> A flick of his wife's tongue could cut him smartingly, and every day she laid on almost more stripes of sarcasm and criticism than his raw conscience could bear.

Now the "whip" figure is brought out sharply and carried through. Done with discrimination and precision, such development can be effective; but it can be easily overdone, and is particularly susceptible to the chief danger of figurative language—mixing figures. For example:

A flick of his wife's tongue was a wearisome burden to him, and she constantly rubbed him the wrong way with her chatter.

Here the notion of a stinging cut in "flick" is abruptly blurred by the incompatible sense of dull weight in "burden" and the again inconsistent image of stroking an animal against the fur. Furthermore, "chatter" suggests desultory and inconsequential speech rather than the deliberate hurt of "flick."

Complete consistency, however, is a "hobgoblin of little minds," and a writer can sometimes manage striking effects by deliberately mixing figures:

She left the room like an ocean liner setting out to sea, her lapdog husband bobbing in her wake.

The metaphoric "lapdog" does not really fit into the ship simile; but since its implications suit the image of the *grande dame,* its very incongruity reinforces the figure.

A special kind of comparison is the *allusion,* which invites the reader to bring into the context of the discussion something from his experience. This may be done by quoting, imitating, or referring to some familiar person, object, or event. It is a valuable labor-saving device which, if properly used, has the effect of pushing a button that gives the writer the benefit of an area of reference without his having to spell it out. Allusions also have the advantage of strengthening the rapport between the writer and the reader, since they imply a shared experience. The danger, of course, is that the writer will miscalculate what is in the reader's experience. Skillful use of this figure demands that the author pay particular attention to the address of his writing, to try to be sure that his allusions are ones the reader will recognize, or at least accept and be able to decipher. I feel fairly confident about the accessibility of the above allusion to Whistler's Mother. I am less sure about that to Emerson's dictum: "A foolish consistency is the hobgoblin of little minds, adored by little statesmen and philosophers and divines"; therefore, I have tried to use it in such a way as to make the meaning clear to those who do not recognize the quotation.

Freshman writers, understandably, are tempted to draw allusions from their high school literature texts, the Bible, and proverbial sayings. Some of these may fit their subjects and stir warm recognition in student readers. But after a while one gets a little tired of variations on "to be or not to be," "all the world's a stage," "spare the rod," "my brother's keeper," "a stitch in time," or "a watched pot." Students have a reservoir of fresher and currently more acceptable references in *topical allusions*—what is happening around them to them and their contemporaries on and off campus. If a Dean greets everyone with "Hi, neighbor," the word "neighbor" is charged in that setting. If there is a building of notable character, a professor of predictable behavior, or an "activity" of recognized asininity—and where is there not?—they are all ready at hand for allusive purposes. So are well-known events and people anywhere—from Civil Rights to Elizabeth Taylor.

A disadvantage of local and topical references is that their impact is limited in place and time. They localize and date a piece of writing—in fact, scholars find them very useful in placing and dating older works of uncertain origin. Campus allusions can fall flat among nonstudents—one reason college humor magazines usually seem just mildly funny to outsiders. Freshmen in the sixties will connect with John F. Kennedy a reference to "moving ahead with vigor," but will they relate "fireside chats" to Franklin D. Roosevelt and "I do not choose to run" to Calvin Coolidge? As Lillian Gish is, so Elizabeth Taylor will be. Still, college students rarely write for eternity, and their most useful allusions are from the world they know.

Allusions are useful but beguiling. They can turn a writer into a window-dresser, and make the reader suspicious. Learned allusions can look like an attempt to show off one's reading, and topical allusions may seem an effort to demonstrate how up-to-date one is. The writer, of course, must be not only innocent but above suspicion. He ought to employ allusions to make his points and should not even *appear* to be dragging them in to ornament his prose.

Hyperbole, Litotes, and Irony

The more subtle figures for implying comparison of two versions of the same thing are hyperbole, litotes, and irony. We all indulge in *hyperbole,* or exaggeration, occasionally—perhaps sometimes subconsciously, sometimes defensively, with intent to deceive ourselves or others. The rhetorical figure of hyperbole, however, involves no substantial deceit; instead it requires that the reader recognize some discrepancy between the real situation and the version presented to him. A skillful writer can then by his tone and emphasis simply invite the reader to enjoy the virtuosity of the heightening, good-humoredly suggest that he accept some of the intensification, or satirically bring him to realize how different the reality is.

In this passage from *Heart of Darkness* Joseph Conrad is deliberately overwriting to capture the intensity of Marlowe's feeling and suggest the unreality of the situation:[1]

> What I really wanted was rivets, by Heaven! Rivets. To get on with the work—to stop the hole. Rivets I wanted. There were cases of them down at the coast—cases—piled up—burst—split! You kicked a loose rivet at every second step in that station yard on the hillside. Rivets had rolled into the grove of death. You could fill your pockets with rivets for the trouble of stooping down—and there wasn't one rivet to be found where it was wanted. We had plates that would do, but nothing to fasten them with. And every week the messenger, a lone negro, letter-bag on shoulder and staff in hand, left our station for the coast. And several times a week a coast caravan came in with trade goods—ghastly glazed calico that made you shudder only to look at it, glass beads value about a penny a quart, confounded spotted cotton handkerchiefs. And no rivets.

A man under less pressure would admit that rivets were not quite so plentiful down the river, that the calico did not literally make one shudder, and that the beads were probably worth a little more than a penny a quart. The reader recognizes this exaggeration and senses the ridiculous hysteria of the scene.

Litotes, negative contrast or understatement, is just the other side of exaggeration's coin and can be used in the same ways. It is perhaps more congenial to the Anglo-Saxon temperament than exaggeration and appears frequently in such phrases as "not bad at all." A famous example of restrained understatement is Admiral Nelson's message of inspiration at Trafalgar: "England expects every man to do his duty."

Irony is usually a more sustained counterpoint between appearance and reality, available to wit and satire, and requiring a steady hand to bring off. Verbal irony is the simplest kind: the statement which really says the opposite of what it appears to say. Swift is a master of the technique, as shown in "A Modest Proposal for Preventing the Children of Poor People in Ireland from being a Burden to their Parents or Country, and for Making them Beneficial to the Public":

[1] Joseph Conrad, *Heart of Darkness* (New York: Norton, 1963), p. 28.

> I do therefore humbly offer it to public consideration, that of the hundred and twenty thousand children, already computed, twenty thousand may be reserved for breed, whereof only one fourth part to be males, which is more than we allow to sheep, black-cattle, or swine, and my reason is that the children are seldom the fruits of marriage, a circumstance not much regarded by our savages, therefore one male will be sufficient to serve four females. That the remaining hundred thousand may at a year old be offered in sale to the persons of quality, and fortune, through the kingdom, always advising the mother to let them suck plentifully in the last month, so as to render them plump, and fat for a good table. A child will make two dishes alone, the fore or hind quarter will make a reasonable dish, and seasoned with a little pepper or salt will be very good boiled on the fourth day, especially in winter.

This "modest proposal" is really an immoderate indictment of English rule of Ireland: Swift is suggesting that children ought to be cherished, not relished.

Another sort of irony is situational irony, in which the twist comes not in the contrast between what is said and what is meant but in the incongruity between what is said and what is expected:

> With the silent ease of controlled power, the immaculate limousine pulled up before the sedate mansion. A uniformed chauffeur, displaying just the right combination of dignity and smartness, came around deferentially to open the door. The important personage inside, impeccably attired in evening dress, stepped gracefully forth, and with a lightning movement stooped to scoop a cigarette butt from the gutter.

Dramatic irony is that which results in drama or narrative from a character's taking some action or attitude because he lacks knowledge which is in the possession of the reader, as when Claudius is delighted that Hamlet is taking an interest in the Players, unaware that the play is to be the thing to catch the conscience of the king.

Figures of Contiguity

The two most common figures of contiguity are *metonymy* and *synecdoche*. Metonymy is a kind of substitution in which something closely associated with something else comes to stand for it. It may be some accoutrement or accessory, as "the crown" is the king, "the bench" the jurist, "the cloth" the clergy. It may be a material of which something is or has been made, as "silver" is eating utensils—even when they are not actually silver—and "linen" is bedclothes—even when they are of cotton. A synecdoche is a special variant in which some part stands for the whole: a fleet of fifty *sail,* a choir of thirty *voices,* a factory *hand.* This figure is fairly common in slang: "threads" means clothes, "wheels" means an automobile, and a "smoke" means a cigarette.

Accepted figures in this area become in fact additions to the language; they can often be used without taint of triteness and they retain some of their figurative force. They may take on the status of *symbols.* "Wall Street" is useful shorthand for the financial empire of the United States and "the Cross" a convenient symbol for Christianity. But there are logical traps here for the unwary writer who acts as if Wall Street were the total of American business and the Cross subsumed all of Christianity.

Figures of Sound

The Duchess in *Alice's Adventures in Wonderland* announced as one of the morals she was fond of finding in everything, "Take care of the sense, and the sounds will take care of themselves." The saying is false, because one cannot really separate sound and sense; but its emphasis is valid for the inexperienced writer of prose. Concentrate on the sense, on getting across what you want to get across, and at the beginning let your concern with sound be largely negative: read your work aloud and listen to how it sounds, and try to avoid cacophonies and awkwardness in rhythm. As your ear develops you will come to recognize that the figures of sound have a role in prose as well as in verse, although a more subtle and delicate role.

Any organizing pattern of rhyme is, of course, out of place in prose; but phrases tied together by rhyme can be used effectively—as advertising men have discovered. We all rejoice in formulations like "ants in the pants." A near rhyme can be used to reinforce contrast, as in the sentence above: "Swift is suggesting that children ought to be *cherished,* not *relished.*" Beware, however, of jangling unintentional rhymes, which can make ridiculous what was intended as a serious sentence:

After a pause the Senator discussed the last clause of the road load laws.

Alliteration, repetition of initial sounds, can also serve to emphasize relationships. Given the choice between "stateliness and decorum" and "dignity and decorum," most of us would prefer the latter because of the attraction of alliteration. This siren call, however, sometimes needs to be resisted. Excessive alliteration can be absurdly reminiscent of "Peter Piper picked a peck of pickled peppers," and the alliterative pull can persuade us into phrases which we do not actually mean. I once tried to give a paper on "Wordsworth's Wit," and got into trouble because I really meant "humor."

Prose can also weave patterns of vowel sounds (*assonance*) and consonant sounds (*consonance*). Robert Louis Stevenson remarks on the almost too obtrusive play of "s" and "r" in Milton's well-known sentence in *Areopagitica:*

> I cannot praise a fugitive and cloistered virtue, unexercised and unbreathed, that never sallies out and sees her adversary, but slinks out of the race where that immortal garland is to be run for, not without dust and heat.

And, of course, the prose writer as well as the poet can make use of *onomatopoeia* when he wants imitative words that snap, crackle, pop, rustle, or clank. For it is characteristic of words that they can go out with both a bang and a whimper.

ASSIGNMENTS

1. Rewrite these sentences, putting in as many specific terms as possible:

a. A large crowd came to the event.

b. All the new models are on display at the Automobile Show.

c. The counters were covered with merchandise.

d. The President made his usual speech, and not many students paid attention.

e. The value of literature lies in its peculiar combination of the objective and the subjective.

2. The verb "to be" is indispensable, but it often can be replaced by a more vivid and accurate verb. See what you can do in these sentences:

a. All through the voyage the Captain was on the bridge.

b. At nightfall the lights of New York were just on the horizon.

c. Sick and unhappy, I was in my cabin when we docked.

d. The rest of my family were on the deck.

e. Behind the dock railings were the customs officials.

3. The following terms are general and abstract. For each construct two sentences: one in which the general term is appropriate, and one in which a more specific word recognizing the content of the abstraction would be desirable.

a. transportation
b. prosperity
c. labor
d. democracy
e. education

4. Each of the following sentences contains relative terms. Rewrite them clarifying the relatives as desirable for specific purposes and audiences.

a. A tiny swaying footbridge spanned the deep canyon.
b. The old man stooped to go under the low tent flap.
c. The cost of education is high for the underprivileged.
d. Since *Hamlet* is a long play, it is often cut for contemporary productions.
e. Burns was born in a small thatched cottage near Ayr.

If you believe that any of the sentences can stand without revision, show what elements in the sentences operate to give the relatives a defining context.

5. Read an essay in your reading text or a periodical and make a list of ten words that you like. Analyze the list and write a paragraph on the criteria for your selection. Did you choose the words because of their effectiveness in context or some inherent attractiveness? Are they long words, vivid words, active words? Are they the kind of words you use—or wish you used?

6. Just for the fun of it, see what your first reaction suggests to fill out the following:

a. Quick as . . .
b. Rich as . . .
c. Smooth as . . .
d. Round as . . .
e. Slow as . . .

Then see what improvements you can make upon reflection.

7. Write a paragraph in which you deliberately use as much figurative language as you can use effectively. Then write a paragraph in which you analyze the kinds of figures you employed and say why you think they are effective.

8. Read an essay in your reading text or a periodical and mark all the figures. Pay particular attention to the allusions. Are they effective? Try to substitute other allusions appropriate for other audiences.

9. The following paragraph shows an insensitivity to sound patterns. See if you can improve it:

> The *Way of the World* is perhaps the best known, and maybe the best, and at any rate certainly notably typical of Renaissance plays. Renaissance plays, Lamb has claimed, are amoral. Their characters exist in a highly artificial world and engage in a wryly social game. There is no real flesh and blood there. To Macaulay and the Victorians, however, they were immoral, definitely reprehensible. Sex reared its ugly head. The Victorians were suspicious of these things, and not to be put off by Congreve's witty dialogue, brilliant and sophisticated characters, and complicated plot.

10. Choose a word which interests you because of its meaning, history, or associations and write an essay on that word. You may find it helpful to look into the section on dictionaries in the next chapter.

CHAPTER ELEVEN

Rhetoric at College: Writing Examinations and Themes

Animals survive if they can adapt to their environments. The giraffe stretched his neck and is still around; the stegosaurus was too set in his ways. Man as a writing animal has exhibited amazing adaptability. The physician scribbles a prescription in minimal Latin abbreviations to save his time and discourage the patient from practicing pharmacy; the safety engineer prints a sign in colors, letters, and words scientifically selected to attract attention and communicate as widely as possible. Thus each flourishes in his place. If the college student is to flourish in his, he must adapt his writing to the demands of the classroom. What has been said in the preceding chapters of this book about the principles of writing is generally applicable to college situations, but there are also a few special tricks for special cases.

HOW TO WRITE AN EXAMINATION

The best advice for writing examinations is in the Book of Proverbs: "Get wisdom, get understanding." There is no satisfactory substitute for knowledge. Seasoned students—and frank professors—will admit, however, that the students who get the best grades on examinations and midterms are not always those who know the most about the subject on which they are being questioned. For it is not enough to have factual knowledge; one must also know how to display it effectively. Sometimes even a little knowledge can be made to go a long way! At least, a student who understands the techniques of examination writing can put his best academic foot forward—provided he has a leg to stand on.

What distinguishes examination writing from other kinds of writing? The greater restrictions on the writer: his range of selection is markedly limited. All writing, as we have seen, is made to fit into the subject-reader-writer-purpose box. Usually, however, the writer has some control over three sides of that box. When he sits down with a blue book he has no choice of audience—he must address his professors and readers. He has little choice of mode. He may use elements of narration, description, and argumentation, but his mainstay will be straightforward exposition; he can rarely go far on the paths of irony, satire, humor, or pathos. He has relatively little choice of subject: the question is set for him, and he must treat it, not freely as his own fancy or interests might suggest, but as the context of the course dictates. The important criteria are not whatever he might select, but accuracy and fullness—"the truth, the whole truth, and nothing but the truth." It is an unimaginative formula and one not all writers—as Plato pointed out—find congenial. Still, within the limits of time and human ability it is the law of the witness stand and the blue book.

Proportion Your Time

Time is one of the most important, and most artificial, restrictions on the examination writer. If an instructor says, "Write a thirty-minute essay on . . . ," it matters not that books could be written on the subject. Don't panic, don't fume that the instructor is an unreasonable fool; give him credit for wanting a half-hour's cream off the top, and set to skimming. Don't give him the ripe fullness of your knowledge in an hour's essay, at the expense of leaving undone the last question. He cannot allow you more credit for the complete hour answer than he could for a perfect half-hour answer, and he may give you less for not sticking to the terms of the question; in any event, he will have to take off for the unanswered last question. The writer must accept the instructor's time scale, whether this is indicated by assignment to the various questions of specific time limits or of credit points. In a fifty-minute test an identification question worth two points ought to be answered in one minute. To lavish ten minutes on it is profitless folly. On such a question the instructor expects hard quick facts. Yet students sometimes even reverse the order of an examination to answer the identification questions first, with the illusion that they are thus getting the "shotguns" out of the way so that they can concentrate on the essay questions, when in fact they are often giving more information on the identifications than is desired or than they can get credit for, and are robbing their essays, which carry the most point value.

All these restrictions may be mortifying. Some writers, including some good writers, chafe under them, and grumble about the academic system's favoring parroting and regurgitation, conformity and mediocrity. This complaint may contain some truth; but plenty of opportunity for originality exists within the rules of the game, and it takes a better man to go around the course brilliantly than to cut across the track with a flair. Part of any examination is the discipline of answering the question precisely, of knowing the subject well enough to be able to gauge accurately the detail appropriate to a fifteen-minute answer or an hour answer. Furthermore, restrictions are assets in that they reduce the number of decisions the writer normally has to make and thereby save his most precious commodity on an exam—time. View every limitation put into a question as cutting off something you do not have to worry about, and concentrate on the area of your control.

Analyze the Question

The first requirement, then, is to find out just what is wanted. The Bunker Hill advice is still sound: "Don't shoot until you see the whites of their eyes." How often students waste their ammunition on a wild, scattering shot. How often do blue books come in with the first page of an answer scratched over or torn out. This practice of meandering around on paper until the question really comes into focus is a way of writing quite out of place in the examination room. Better take a few minutes to crank in all the ballistic data, maybe by means of jottings or a rough outline, and lock on target before you fire.

First scrutinize the question. If necessary, rephrase it. Instructors sometimes phrase a question generally because they want the student to find his own handle, to choose his own emphasis. But the student cannot answer it generally; he must convert it to specific terms. Questions which start out "discuss," "examine," "consider," or "describe" usually need such translation. For example: "Discuss the relation of Lemuel Gulliver to Jonathan Swift." This question is not a license to pour out everything that you might know about Gulliver and Swift. Even if you are well prepared on, for instance, the devices of verisimilitude by which Swift makes real the world of Gulliver's travels, and hate to waste such material, don't be tempted to drag it kicking and screaming into the answer. Pay yourself the compliment of supposing that you know a little something about the subject that is not relevant to the question.

Part of knowing what *is* relevant is knowing where the answer should begin, how far back to go, how much to take for granted. Implicit in the limitations an instructor incorporates in a question are some "givens." Learn to look for them and build on them. "Discuss the relation of Lemuel Gulliver to Jonathan Swift" asks for nothing except how the two men relate to each other. The question assumes that you know Swift wrote *Gulliver's Travels*—when, where, and how need not enter into this answer. Although to show the changing Gulliver-Swift relationship you will touch upon some aspects of structure and plot, you need not include all the details. Students are prone to tell "what happens"—such facts are relatively accessible and fill up pages comfortably. Instructors usually are more interest in why it happened and what it means: they may assume all of the story except so much as is necessary to make clear your interpretation. This question supposes that there is a relationship between Gulliver and Swift worth talking about; it does not, however, assume anything about the character or significance of that relationship. Within the framework of the question it is possible to hold that the relationship is confused or undeveloped. Similarly, a question on the unity of a novel, for instance, assumes that the issue is valid. Students often begin answering such a question with a needless introduction about how the matter of the unity of the work is indeed worthy of consideration, because unity is a significant aesthetic quality, and so on. All this the reader recognizes as padding, for such points the question grants. It does not, however, assume that the work *is* unified. A good answer might point out disruptive as well as connective elements, and conclude that the novel lacks sufficient unity.

To cope with the Gulliver query you need to see the underlying specific question:

> Is Gulliver to be identified with Swift?

This, however, is not the whole question. The rephrasing ought also to elaborate the question and break it down into its component parts:

> Does Gulliver express Swift's point of view? What evidence is there?
> What are the techniques of differentiation, if any?
> What are the effects on the style and tone of the work?
> What is the resultant theme or thesis?

Once you have broken the question down into its component parts, you can determine which are the most important and which deserve most emphasis. This process should not be confused with determining the things in which you are most interested or about which you happen to be able to write the most. Where there is legitimate choice, of course pick the aspect about which you have the most information; but except in dire emergencies—for it is always better to write something than nothing—let your emphasis be dictated by the values of the subject rather than by your personal predilections. Since Gulliver is the narrator, if Swift disassociates himself from Gulliver's point of view he has to do it by implication. The important thing is to show how and why this is done, to demonstrate its ironic patterns and its satiric purpose.

Organize Your Answer

If you know "how" and "why," you have reached a decision regarding the core of your answer. It is a good idea to formulate in your mind a focus which sums up the answers to the component questions:

> Swift begins by appearing to identify himself with Gulliver; but gradually he makes Gulliver unwittingly reveal his own ridiculousness, thus adding his own irony to Gulliver's intended irony and furthering his purpose to show the pride and folly of mankind.

You are now ready to write, and the transition to paper can be easy, for usually you will want to begin with a general statement something like the focus. It need not be so blunt, but may be decked out in the best style you can summon quickly, perhaps as follows:

Jonathan Swift and Lemuel Gulliver were roughly contemporaries; they were both educated middle-class Englishmen; but they do not share the same points of view throughout *Gulliver's Travels.* Although Swift first presents Gulliver to his readers as a sensible and intelligent man, he gradually allows Gulliver to show himself to be vain, subservient, and irrationally addicted to the rational. Thus Swift separates himself from his narrator, and uses his irony to demonstrate the emptiness of human pride.

Under the time pressures of an examination obviously you cannot worry about polishing a beginning paragraph. You should be sure that it clearly and solidly sets forth the general terms of your answer, that it indicates you know what you are about and have only to fill in the details.

Then fill them in. If you stay within the time limit of the question, you can hardly put in too many details—so long as they are accurate and relevant. Build a paragraph or so on each major point, and develop the paragraphs fully. The *C* student may have the generalizations all right, but he is too lazy or too ill-informed to put flesh on the bones. Answers which get good grades are rich in substance; they bristle with facts, figures, illustrations which will support their theses. Beware, however, of irrelevant and erroneous data; students sometimes throw away a good grade by going on to put in something that isn't necessary and is wrong. In literature courses particularly, quotations make a good impression—if they are pertinent; spraying an answer with hackneyed passages which you appear to have memorized for the occasion and seem bent on using regardless of their applicability will get no "brownie" points.

Although stylistic elegance is not expected on an examination, write as well as you can. Professors are likely to be pathetically grateful and give you the benefit of substantive doubts. If you can be bright and original, so much the better; but at all costs be clear and sequential. If a reader has to go back over an essay to make out what it says and tally up how far it answered the question, putting together pieces here and there, he is already ill-disposed and probably thinking of a grade from *C* down. For this reason be sure to indicate transitions; show the reader where you are going and why. This practice will not only smooth the path of the grader and improve his disposition; it also will tend to make him accept the relevance of points which he might consider tangential and be inclined to discount unless they were clearly shown to be pertinent.

HOW TO GET A GOOD GRADE ON A THEME

When Naaman, captain of the host of the King of Syria, was stricken with leprosy and, hearing of a mighty prophet in Israel, came to Elisha to be healed, he was greatly disappointed to be told only to wash seven times in the River Jordan. He was about to go home in a rage when his servants pointed out, "My father, if the prophet had bid thee do some great thing, wouldest thou not have done it? how much rather then, when he saith to thee, 'Wash, and be clean'?" The great things of writing, the basic principles, have been the subject of most of the preceding sections of this book. But it is often the little things of practical method that make the difference between a satisfactory paper and an excellent one. Some of these sovereign little things are the subject of this section.

So far we have been concerned chiefly with the initial writing process. Good grades come from a deliberate recognition of *three* stages: writing, rewriting, and proofreading.

The First Draft

Most of the agony, the threshing around, the false steps—but in addition most of the excitement, the thrill, and the pride of creation —come in the first draft. How dark is the floor-pacing despair when the whole composition seems hopeless, how exhilarating the feeling of power when the work goes swimmingly, inevitably ahead. In such moments it is desirable—and difficult—for the writer to realize that the product *is* a *first* draft. Try to encourage yourself to remember that it is: the effect may be to relax you and condition you not to become married to your first formulations. Some writers prefer to write the first draft by hand because they believe that the typewriter tends to freeze an expression in the formality of type. Other writers use the device of typing triple-spaced lines, thus allowing themselves inviting blank areas for additions and emendations. These there certainly ought to be, and the first draft should be hospitable to them. It should have an easy tentative air, a comfortable informality. A good rough draft is a messy-looking thing. John Henry Cardinal Newman, one of the smoothest and clearest of prose stylists, explained his practice in a letter to his sister:

> I write, I write again; I write a third time in the course of six months. Then I take the third: I literally fill the paper with corrections, so that another person could not read it. I then write it out fair for the printer.

I put it by; I take it up; I begin to correct again: it will not do. Alterations multiply, pages are rewritten, little lines sneak in and crawl about. The whole page is disfigured; I write again; I cannot count how many times this process is repeated. (Jan. 29, 1838)

Some fluent writers pour out overflowing first drafts, anxious to get everything down while the spirit is upon them, intending to prune drastically later. The hazard of this method is that one may become infatuated with one's rich beautiful prose and be reluctant to sacrifice even patent excrescences. Some less facile writers grind out bare sentences, expecting to expand in revision. This method is perhaps even more hazardous because of the proverbial difficulty of putting new wine in old bottles: the added pieces are likely not to match. If a paragraph is well written in the first place, often a sentence cannot be added without spoiling the rhythm. Interpolations require adjustment of transitions and special attention to avoid separating pronouns and referents and unintentionally repeating key words. Still, do whatever comes easiest to you. Only get on with it. Take a break occasionally, but beware of rationalizations for delay: don't let anything stop you for long. Of course it is better not to be slovenly, not to put down inaccuracies which will plague you later. On the other hand, don't wait for perfection either. Get on with it. This is the *first* draft, but until you get it on paper there can never be a second.

The important element in revision is distance. Somehow the writer has to get far enough away from his work to acquire some objectivity. For when the words are still warm from the mind it is almost impossible to deal harshly with them. In fact, it is even difficult to read them as they actually are; they still carry the aura of their cerebral company and bear rich meanings which the outside reader would never realize. The partial eye of the fond author can unconsciously supply transitions, add punctuation, and even correct spelling.

One means of getting distance is to put time between you and your draft, as Newman said, to "put it by." Let it cool a bit. This counsel, I know, is difficult to follow in college, where one assignment comes hard on the heels of another and the flesh is weak. Too many papers are written on the last night and the rough draft copied over in the wee hours of the morning. With a little will power, however, it is usually possible to finish the draft at least a day before the paper is due, sleep on it for one night, and have one day to look it over.

Another means of getting distance is to take the words out of the visual realm in which you created them and listen to how they sound. Read them aloud. Often you will find that what your eyes slid over unquestioningly sounds pretty silly when you hear it. Even better, if you have an obliging roommate, stick the essay in his hands and, without giving him time to look it over, ask him to read it aloud to you. Just hearing it in another's voice will give you some objectivity. If the passages are not clear, the reader will probably show perplexity on his face or in his voice; if the punctuation is inadequate, he will probably stumble.

The Process of Revision

Again, remember that the first draft is just that, and nothing in it is exempt from change. Revision is not simply a matter of tidying up. It should be a genuine rewriting, a real effort to make the essay as good as you can make it. College assignments, sometimes verging on busywork, sometimes dealing with subjects in which you are not vitally interested, and always bustled by other assignments and activities, can generate an atmosphere in which high personal standards of craftsmanship seem unrealistic and extravagant. Even so, allow yourself the luxury of excellence as often as you can, or you will lose the capacity to enjoy it. And the man who cannot enjoy doing something right, who cannot feel the glow that comes from surveying his finished work—really *finished* work—is cheating himself.

Revision includes a close scrutiny of the substance of the essay. Now you are for the first time in a position to see what you have said. Really look at it and see if it makes sense. Sometimes not until you have a complete draft can you tell whether it hangs together or discover whether there are any holes or any excrescences. Be willing to believe that there can be such imperfections, that indeed the overwhelming likelihood is that there are. Be critical—constructively if you can, but destructively if necessary. Face the possibility that the only thing to do is to throw away great chunks of your essay and start over. Sometimes this drastic course is in the long run easier and more satisfactory than painful patching.

When you read the draft and get the feeling of the whole you may have flashes of revelation. You may see, for instance, that if you simply reverse the order of points two and three, the transitions are greatly improved and the essay builds to a stronger climax. For such surgery a pair of scissors is useful, and a second draft can be constructed economically and effectively by pasting or stapling rewritten sections or rearranged original sections and additions to new sheets of paper. At this stage don't type your paper over just to make it look neat; so long as it is legible enough for you to tell what you are doing, that is satisfactory. Keep the work fluid, be willing to juggle. You might rewrite the last paragraph, or even put on and take off again slightly different versions of the same paragraph, several times before you decide what is right, what fits.

Now is the time to check your paragraphing. To start with, look down the page and see how many indentations you have. If there are more than three or less than one, find out whether you can justify that condition. Look for transitions within and between paragraphs. Keep asking yourself, how could a reader, even a sleepy reader, get from there to here? Usually you will need to do something in this area, for all the transitions rarely get put in the rough draft; part of its roughness is the choppiness, the lack of connections which comes from working piecemeal. Now that you see the whole, smooth it out.

Look at your sentences. Probably you turned them out, one by one, with your attention on the development of your point rather than the shape of your sentences. When you see them now as sentences, is there a monotonous sameness about them? A childish simplicity? A breathless stringing out or a laconic chopping off of ideas? If you have taken the freshman's insurance policy of using only simple sentences to avoid the danger of making mistakes in constructions, now is the time to see if you cannot be a little more sophisticated. Undoubtedly some of the simple sentences ought to be combined into compound and complex sentences. Not all of them, of course; the point of revision is not to elaborate your syntax. Variety is good, but never at the cost of clarity. Be sure that after you have tried to make your sentences more presentable they still say to your reader exactly what you intend.

Examine your diction. Have you unconsciously been using the same words over and over when synonyms or maybe even pronouns will better serve your purpose by providing variety, precision, and continuity? Do you actually know what all the words you have used mean? This question may seem odd, but students frequently use words which *sound* something like the words they intend—"immolate" for "emulate," "humanism" for "humanitarianism"—or *mean* something like what they intend—"atheism" for "agnosticism," "capacity" for "competence." This is the time to look up any word about which you are not absolutely certain. Even experienced writers keep a dictionary at hand for this purpose.

It is probably best to start your revision of the paper by addressing yourself to its unique problems and finding the most effective way of saying what you want to say in this particular essay to these particular readers. But you have written papers before, and ultimately you should direct your revision specifically at your known weaknesses. We all have our slippery places: you should recognize yours. If necessary, look back over a few of your returned essays and remind yourself of what sort of corrections and suggestions your instructor has been making.

Check List of Common Errors

Here are a few typical mistakes and dangerous areas of the kind you want to look for in your drafts.

MISTAKES IN CONSTRUCTION

Most of the syntactical difficulties which bother college students fall into the following categories. Until you are sure that you are immune, read every draft through once looking particularly for these slips.

Faulty modifiers Sentences often go askew because of some failure in modification, frequently because either the modifier has slipped so far away from its subject that it seems to modify something else, or because it actually has nothing in the sentence to modify. We can see this fault in obvious examples:

> Opening the telegram a chill ran through me.

We are likely to miss it in more complex sentences:

> Taking into consideration the infinite variety achieved within a small range, Pope's use of the heroic couplet is a remarkable virtuoso performance.

Constructions of this sort relate to the Latin absolutes, but in English they are usually considered "dangling participles." They can, of course, be mended by the addition of a logical agent:

> Opening the telegram, I felt a chill run through me.

Taking into consideration the infinite variety within a small range, we can appreciate that Pope's use of the heroic couplet is a remarkable virtuoso performance.

Still, the constructions are not natural or particularly effective. It would be better to say:

As I opened the telegram I felt a chill run through me.

Or one might emphasize the duration of the suspense:

As I was opening the telegram, I felt a chill run through me.

In the mended second sentence above, the "Taking into consideration . . . we can appreciate" simply distracts attention from the central point. Why not:

Infinite variety within a small range marks Pope's use of the heroic couplet as a virtuoso performance.

Generally it is a good idea to be suspicious of introductory participial constructions.

Confusing changes of direction One of the difficulties with dangling modifiers is the change in subject: in the original version of the first sentence above trouble sprang from the fact that while "I" was the implicit subject of the first element, "chill" was the subject of the second and in a position to appear ludicrously to be the subject of the first. Avoid any change in subject, voice, or tense for which there is not apparent good reason. Observe the difference between the following two sentences:

In your first draft, when you move ahead by spurts and amidst interruptions, you are almost certain to make some unintentional shifts.

In your first draft, when you move ahead by spurts and amidst interruptions, some unintentional shifts are almost bound to occur.

In the second there is a probably unconscious change of subject, reflecting an unfortunate tendency to give the "shifts" a kind of autonomy; it is better to face squarely the fact that the first subject in the sentence makes the "shifts" and must be responsible for them. Possibly the note of impersonal inevitability in the second sentence is correct, and a writer need not feel guilty but simply resign himself to combating the gremlins. The point is debatable; the necessity of being alert to these distinctions is not.

Mistakes in agreement Normally, college students have little trouble in seeing to it that subjects and predicates agree in number, the principal vestige of inflection left in the English language. Mistakes in agreement can creep into rough drafts, however, particularly when a prepositional phrase with an object of a number different from the subject comes between the subject and the verb:

> The sound of stirring birds, rustling winds, and all the Spring's varied voices was pleasant to the ear.

"Sound" is so far from "was," and so many plural nouns come in between, that it is easy to slip into "were," although the singular verb is grammatically correct. Since a number of different sounds are actually mentioned, perhaps it would be better to make the subject plural. Revision is your opportunity to catch this kind of thing.

Sentence fragments The best protection against unintentional sentence fragments[1] is to check to make sure that each sentence has an independent clause with a finite verb. In a fragment such as the following, students may be misled by the two finite verbs "wrote" and "was" into thinking the sentence to be complete:

> When Aldous Huxley wrote *Brave New World* in 1931, thinking his ironic Utopia was perhaps 600 years off.

This combination is made up of an adverbial clause ("When . . . Huxley wrote . . .") and a noun clause ("[that] . . . Utopia was . . .") connected by a participle ("thinking"); it has no independent clause. Changing "thinking" to "he thought" would make an acceptable sentence.

POOR PROOFREADING

Most students can raise their theme scores by at least half a mark just by careful proofreading. For the instructor can grade only what is on the paper before him, although he may be sure that the author "really knows better." And yet, from press of time, an impatient desire to be through with the chore, or a naïve confidence in their own or their typists' accuracy, students often turn in papers which do not represent fairly their competence or their achievement. Some mistakes even result from students' hurriedly miscopying their drafts! Proofreading should catch these mistakes.

[1] See pp. 148–149.

Proofreading is largely an acquired skill. It comes from patience, a detached objectivity, and a meticulously followed system. The good proofreader has to pay attention to the meaning of what he is reading, else he cannot catch plausible errors and omissions. He must not, however, allow himself to be swept up into the content and rhythms so that he makes corrections mentally while leaving the mistake on the page. A recognized system is to read the work twice from top to bottom—once with special attention to the rhetorical flow, and once, more slowly, with special attention to the grammatical details and punctuation—then once from bottom to top, thus isolating the words and paying particular attention to spelling. It is important to have clearly in mind what you are looking for when you proofread. You want to be receptive to any rhetorical and grammatical corrections or refinements that might seem necessary or desirable; but if you did a good job on your revised draft, you ought not to have much left to do in that area, and you need to be careful that you do not undo something. You may be tempted into making changes in diction or syntax as you read through, only to discover a little later that there was good reason for the original form and that you have now introduced repetition or contradiction. Last minute changes of style should be made cautiously, and emphasis in proofreading laid on accurate transcription and correct spelling and punctuation.

Spelling Errors

Spelling is ironically one of the most insignificant and yet conspicuous elements in writing: correct spelling can never of itself make a good paper, but poor spelling all by itself can ruin one. Mistakes in spelling can interfere directly with communication when they result in the unwitting substitution of a homonym—"discrete" for "discreet," "imminent" for "eminent." More often they merely disrupt the rapport with the reader, who probably recognizes what word is intended, but is offended or amused at errors which suggest carelessness or illiteracy. Accurate spelling, therefore, is simply a necessity. Although misspellings should be corrected whenever they are recognized—in order to reduce the repetition of error and establishment of false patterns—attention to spelling must not be allowed to interfere with the creative process. Looking up a word in the dictionary can be disrupting; I usually find myself fascinated by illustrations of aardvarks and tumbrels. The place to concentrate on spelling is in the proofreading.

You know whether you are a reliable speller or not. If you are, count your blessings and look especially for typographical errors, metatheses, and such mechanical matters as italics (underlining in manuscript) for titles of books or other works published individually and quotation marks for titles of works published as part of a book. If you are not a safe speller, admit the fact frankly and resign yourself to looking up every word you cannot swear by. You have no alternative. Possibly by studying the rules of spelling, by keeping a notebook in which you copy down the words you look up, by encouraging yourself to find opportunities to reuse these words several times in succession, by glancing over this list as you stand waiting for a bus and spelling out words from it as you brush your teeth, by experimenting to see whether you learn to spell from auditory or visual images and exploiting your strength, by using mnemonic devices (e.g., *al*ways *al*most is *all* right)—possibly by all these devices you might improve your spelling and in time have less looking up to do.

The trouble is, however, that if you are an unsafe speller, you will think you can swear by the wrong words and not do enough looking up. Be especially suspicious of words with the following endings:

-ance or -ence
-tion or -sion
-ary or -ery
-ate or -ite
-able or -ible
-al or -le ("principle" and "principal" are commonly mixed up)
-cede or -ceed ("proceed" and "precede" are also frequently confused)

Watch out too for "ei" and "ie" combinations, a silent "e" before a suffix, and doubled consonants. The following rules have a number of exceptions but will help some.

1. To distinguish between "ei" and "ie" remember the old rhyme:

Write "i" before "e"
Except after "c,"
Or if sounded like "a,"
As in "neighbor" or "weigh."

The following sentence will help you to catch most of the exceptions: Neither foreign sovereign seized either height, forfeiting the counterfeit heir's leisure to a weird species of financier.

2. A final silent "e" is generally dropped before a suffix beginning with a vowel ("movable"), retained before a suffix beginning with a consonant ("sincerely"), but note especially these exceptions: "ninth," "wholly," "truly," "duly," "argument." Note also that before a vowel the final silent "e" is sometimes kept to prevent confusion with other words ("dyeing," "dying") or mispronunciation ("canoeist," "mileage"), and is usually retained after "c" or "g" before suffixes beginning with "a," "o," and "u" to preserve the soft consonant sound ("advantageous," "changeable," "peaceable").

3. When the prefixes "un-," "dis-," and "mis-" are added before words beginning with "n" and "s," the root consonant remains, resulting in a double consonant: "unnatural," "dissimilar," "misspell."

4. Nouns ending in a consonant plus "y" change the "y" to "i" before suffixes except those beginning with "i" ("babies," "tried," "busily," "weariest"; but "flying"). Nouns ending in a vowel plus "y" keep the "y" before a suffix ("volleyed"). Notable exceptions are "paid," "said," "laid."

5. When a suffix beginning with a vowel is added to a word ending in a single consonant preceded by a single vowel, the consonant is doubled provided the accent falls on the last syllable of the root word: "omitted," "occurrence"; but "commitment" (suffix begins with a consonant), "sleeping" (not preceded by a single vowel), "preference" (accent not on last syllable of root).

6. Words ending in "c" usually add a "k" before a suffix beginning with "e," "i," or "y": "mimicking," "panicky."

Punctuation Errors

Punctuation is another element which assumes disproportionate but real importance: long legal battles have been fought over the presence or absence of some crucial comma in a will or contract. Most of us are not called upon to point with such care; our punctuation is chiefly for the comfort and convenience of the reader. If we irritate or confuse him by punctuation that seems capricious, misleading, or illiterate, we have thrown away our effort on the paper. Here are a few situations which seem most likely to cause trouble to students. If you want information on any point not covered here, try the appendix on punctuation in your college dictionary.

Commas Commas should be used only where they are necessary to keep words and ideas from piling up on each other. Students usually have little trouble with this obvious function in separating appositives (Mr. Jones, the milkman); numbers in dates (April 24, 1963); elements in addresses (76 Longridge Road, Earls Court, London); and items in series (high, wide,[2] and handsome). They are likely to be confused about the similar role of commas in separating clauses and phrases, for here the situation is less clear-cut. A decision must be made concerning whether the elements are closely enough related to flow together or whether they need some separation. Introductory dependent clauses are more likely to seem to need a comma to hold them off than are concluding dependent clauses:

As soon as I could, I came.
I came as soon as I could.

Even introductory clauses may not require to be separated if they are relatively brief:

When I heard the news I immediately made plans to fly home.

When I heard the news that my only sister was getting married, I immediately made plans to fly home.

On the other hand, even introductory phrases may require to be set off, especially when they are several words long or make up absolute constructions:

Having at last made my point, I sat down.

Regardless of length, relative clauses must be set off if they are nonrestrictive, that is, if they are essentially parenthetical:

A spidery chair, which by its fragility seemed to suggest an aristocratic nonutility, stood primly against the wall.

A chair that once belonged to Henry James is now in our library.

The difficulties with commas in compound sentences usually come when the coordinating conjunction is "but" or "for." When the conjunction is "and" convention allows the writer leeway. No comma is necessary if the clauses are short and the connection is close:

We tried hard and we won first place.

[2] Informal style allows omission of the comma before "and" in series, provided the meaning is quite clear.

Yet if the writer wished a dramatic pause for the sake of emphasis, he could put a comma before "and," or even a dash. Before "but" a comma is normal.

> We tried hard, but we lost.

Before "for" a comma is necessary, to prevent the reader from thinking momentarily that the "for" might be a preposition.

> We tried hard, for first place is a coveted honor.
> We tried hard for first place.

The *comma fault* or *comma splice* results when a comma is asked to do too much—to hold apart long independent clauses not connected by a coordinating conjunction:

> After a trying day I just could not get to sleep, all night I squirmed and twisted and switched on the light to see what time it was.

This situation calls for a stronger mark of separation—either a period or, perhaps preferably, a colon, since the second clause can be regarded as an explanation or illustration of the first. The comma can be used, however, to separate short, closely connected, independent clauses:

> He came, he saw, he conquered.

Students should watch particularly that commas do not sneak in unnecessarily to separate subjects from their verbs and verbs from their objects:

> The delighted backer of the show proclaimed loudly [*no comma*] that everybody who had been involved in the whole production [*no comma*] most certainly should work in his next play.

No comma is required after "loudly" in this example of indirect discourse, although students may be led astray by the analogy with the role of commas in direct discourse:

> The delighted backer proclaimed loudly, "Everybody has a job in my next show."

Another complication is that subjects, verbs, and objects *may* be separated by pairs of commas or dashes used to set off parenthetical elements or by commas required to separate elements in a series:

The delighted backer proclaimed loudly, in a joyous voice which seemed to warm the theater, that everyone—actors, extras, stand-ins, and stagehands—most certainly should work in his next play.

Semicolons Student uncertainty in the use of semicolons usually stems from a failure to recognize that the semicolon is a sort of balance point which requires *somewhere* on either side units of the *same grammatical weight.* The most frequent uses are in compound sentences in which no coordinating conjunction is employed, and in complicated series in which the items have commas within them.

I came running at the sound of the crash; I was still too late to help.

Ind. cl.; ind. cl.

balance point

Real teaching requires lively, penetrating intelligence; unselfish, undeviating dedication; and warm, sympathetic humanity.

Modifiers, noun; modifiers, noun; modifiers, noun

balance points

Students get into trouble by using semicolons when there are no grammatically equal elements on opposite sides, as in involved complex sentences:

Since I had seen him somewhere before, although I could not remember where, I had to be careful that I did not reveal my identity, at least not yet.

When a sentence has as many commas as the above, a student is tempted to put in a semicolon somewhere on general principles, perhaps after "where." Since, however, there is only one independent clause, the effect would be lopsided:

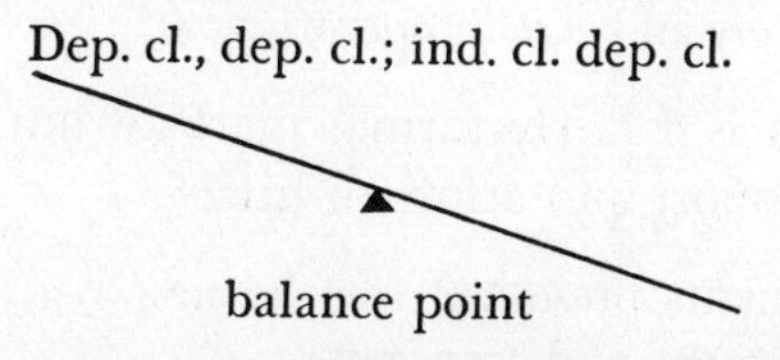

For the balance is not made by the weight of words or ideas on a given side but by the weight of equal grammatical structures.

Compound complex sentences frequently require semicolons between independent clauses, either where the coordinating conjunction is omitted, or where the presence of many other commas makes a semicolon useful before the coordinating conjunction to distinguish the major break from the minor ones:

Wordsworth and Coleridge worked together most fruitfully when they lived in Somersetshire in 1797; but although both men seemed to try, they were not able to retain that productive relationship.

Ind. cl. dep. cl.; dep. cl., ind. cl.
▲

Note, however, that the balance point of the semicolon does not depend on general symmetry. It makes no difference whatever else is on either side, so long as a grammatical unit of the same value is on each side.

Shakespeare is a very great poet; but nineteenth-century bardolatry is nevertheless incomprehensible to anyone who reads carefully, and who, while sympathetic, is still critical.

Ind. cl.; ind. cl. dep. cl., dep. cl.
▲

Colons Students sometimes try to use colons as if they were super semicolons, having a terminal force close to periods. This attitude may be fostered by the practice, not now common except in long quotations and examples, of capitalizing the first word following a colon. Actually, however, colons have a function quite different from that of periods: they are marks of introduction and anticipation. In a formal style a colon is used, where less formal writing allows dashes and commas, before introductory phrases: "for instance," "especially," "such as," and "namely." Its classic use is after "follows," expressed or implied, as in introducing a long series:[2]

The chief arguments presented for the new registration system were what might have been expected: [i.e., *as follows*] its speed, versatility, adaptability, economy and ease of operation.

Since the colon is a fairly formal mark of anticipation, it is not used to introduce short quotations or lists:

The chief arguments presented for the new registration system were [*colon unlikely*] its speed and economy.

Usually the colon is not employed unless there is a noun or noun clause before the colon to be in apposition with what comes after:

[2] Note that the colon here means an example follows.

We argued that the new registration system promised [*colon unlikely*] speed, versatility, adaptability, economy, and ease of operation.

Because the colon regularly means that what comes after somehow illustrates, justifies, or sums up what went before, it can be used between independent clauses when one introduces the other so that the colon virtually says "that is":

The price of liberty is high: it is no less than eternal vigilance for the freedom of all men.

In direct discourse the colon is used to introduce elaborate speeches, usually of more than one sentence in length.

Apostrophes The most slighted mark of punctuation in contemporary student writing is the apostrophe in possessives. Students, perhaps inspired by modern advertising, seem bent on dropping this use of the apostrophe. Such a development may eventually take place, for the apostrophe in the possessive singular represents an elided "e" of the Middle English genitive "es" which had ceased to be pronounced, and to drop it would be consistent with the loss of inflections in English. At the present the apostrophe still provides a useful differentiation in the written language: " 's" is required for the singular possessive, "s' " for the plural. Ironically, students are also wont to put the apostrophe in where it is not now used (it was once), in the possessive pronoun "its." Now "it's" is reserved for the contraction of "it is," where the apostrophe represents the omitted letter "i."

A common mistake is the failure to use the possessive form of nouns required with gerunds:

The new regulations will result in the students' taking three courses a quarter term.

The difficulty rises from confusion with participial constructions which take the objective case:

I heard the boy singing.

I enjoyed the boy's singing.

A test for doubtful instances is to try changing the noun to a personal pronoun; if "my," "his," or "their" sounds right, use the possessive form of the noun.

The apostrophe is also used in forming plurals of letters, numbers, and sometimes of words used as words, particularly of foreign words or English words which might be misread without the apostrophe.

We made our X's and left quietly, without any and's [or ands], but's [or buts] or so's in elections of the 1940's.

Punctuation of quotations College students usually have little trouble putting direct quotations in quotation marks, but they are vague on quotations within quotations, punctuation of quotations which extend over more than one paragraph and—particularly—the position of punctuation marks at the end of quotations. The rules are simple, and must simply be memorized. Quotations within quotations are in American usage placed in single quotation marks—British practice is reversed. When a quotation includes more than one paragraph, quotation marks appear at the beginning of each paragraph and at the end of the last only. Long quoted passages which are indicated by indentation do not require quotation marks at all. Punctuation at the end of quoted materials follows typographical practice and is not always logical:

1. The comma and the period are placed before the quotation marks.

"I remember distinctly," said the witness, "that he left muttering to himself."

2. The colon and the semicolon are placed after the quotation marks.

We have not yet exhausted the force of Washington's injunction against "foreign entanglements": its influence continues.

3. Dashes, question marks, and exclamation points are placed before the quotation marks when they apply to the quoted matter and after when they apply to the whole statement. When they come after the quotation mark no punctuation is used before the mark, even though the actual quote would have had other punctuation.

What else could I do, when the officer said, "Follow me"?

The distraught man kept asking, "Is my wife all right?"

ASSIGNMENTS

1. Bring in an examination that you have written for another class that has essay-type questions. Then do the following:

a. Write a critique of your answer as an essay.

b. Rewrite your answer, being concerned not with adding material which you did not know when you took the test, but with making the most of what you did know.

2. Analyze as many of the following questions as you can into their constituent questions:

a. Discuss Hamlet's reactions to the revelations made to him by the Ghost.

b. Explain the dramatic significance of the fact that Lady Macbeth actually got some of Duncan's blood on her hands.

c. Discuss the effects of having the story of *Treasure Island* told by Jim Hawkins.

d. Explain the use of figures in Wordsworth's sonnet, "The Earth hath not anything to show more fair."

e. Describe the current position of the United States on foreign aid.

f. Examine the athletic policy of your college.

3. Pick one of the above questions and write an essay on it in the following manner:

a. Force yourself to finish the rough draft at least three days before the essay is due.

b. Turn in both the rough draft and the final essay, with an appended paragraph in which you analyze the differences between the draft and the final form.

4. Look back over at least the last four papers you have turned in and do the following:

a. Make a list of your errors, trying to classify them according to kind and frequency.

b. Construct for yourself a check-list of points you think you ought to look for especially in your proofreading.

5. Proofread the front page of today's newspaper, make a list of the errors, and write a paragraph describing the experience. How did you go about it? Do you recognize any distractions or difficulties? How would you describe the "proofreader's mentality"?

6. Punctuate the following sentences:

a. Hanging on the ropes the weary fighter waited for the knockout.

b. His knees buckled his eyes glazed his arms limp he had no more strength left in him and even the will to go on was blurred.

c. His white trunks once fresh and sparkling were sweaty and blood-spotted his mouth protector half hung out of his slack jaw and his hair which gave him his name Pretty Boy had lost its proud lustre.

d. His opponent the underdog the man who was supposed to lose in three rounds looked inquiringly at the referee maybe he would stop the fight.

e. The promoter who was happy with his full house was already thinking about his next fight and wondering about a return match.

f. The battered fighters manager fingered his towel even though he had told the reporters my boy is way up he had feared this he knew that the boy was not in condition.

g. Each according to his temperament the spectators reacted some yelled for the kill some watched silently some cursed their unlucky bets.

7. Revise the following sentences:

a. Receiving an *F* on the paper, her face turned red and she started to cry.

b. She deserved a better grade, she thought, but the teacher did not.

c. This series of brief vignettes, descriptive pieces and narrative snatches were the best of her career, according to her brother, who might be prejudiced.

d. At the early age of ten her talent has revealed itself by entering a short story contest, the youngest entry.

e. All this flashed through her mind while returning to her seat crushed and weepy.

8. Suppose that on an examination you were given this question: "Discuss the contention that popular music usually has an anti-intellectual element." How would you decide which of the following items you would consider essential to your answer? Make the kind of rough outline you might jot down inside the cover of a blue book to organize your answer.

a. Definition of "popular."

b. Definition of "anti-intellectual."

c. List of examples of popular music.

d. List of anti-intellectual elements which may appear in music.

e. Ways in which music can be intellectual.

f. List of popular musicians.

g. Intellectual background of popular musicians.

h. Symphonic variations of popular music.

i. Analysis of musical themes in popular music.
j. General statement on anti-intellectualism in popular music.
k. Analysis of ideas in lyrics of popular music.
l. Analysis of metrical structure of lyrics of popular music.
m. Limitation of time period to be covered.

9. Here is a list of thirty-five frequently misspelled words:

accommodate	counsel	parallel
achieved	definite	personnel
apparent	dependent	procedure
appetite	embarrass	recommend
attendance	exhilaration	separate
believe	exuberance	soliloquy
cemetery	familiar	succeed
changeable	irresistible	temperament
coarse	loneliness	usage
committed	murmur	villain
competent	omission	writing
conceive	optimism	

Look at each and see if you can explain why it is likely to be misspelled. Cite any rules which can help you to remember to spell these words correctly. Can you think of any mnemonic devices for these words, such as "There's *a rat* in *separate*"?

10. What is wrong with the following sentences? Correct them.

a. As it twisted and writhed, its futile efforts becoming ever weaker, the animal in the trap mimicking modern man.
b. Whatever the Savage may have to teach us, when finally he speaks back to his civilizers.
c. Perhaps a lesson of feeling, a vital spirit in our computing world.
d. Since we have gone from wheels under us to wheels around us and within us—and far different wheels from those Ezekiel saw "turning up yonder."
e. The future, assuming there will be a future, one in which plowshares and pruning hooks, like swords, will be obsolete.

CHAPTER TWELVE

How to Write a Research Paper

Students often react unfortunately to an assignment to write a term paper, particularly if it is called a "research paper." Intimidated or stultified by the impressive term, they go scuttling off to the library and produce something pompous and rigid which fits their image of research, an arcane activity associated with white-coated scientists peering intently at test tubes and hunched greybeards pouring over musty tomes. Sometimes an instructor is tempted to think that for many students "research" is synonymous with "weary, stale, flat, and unprofitable."

Research ought to be at least rewarding and at best exciting. On the highest levels research is the search for truth, the making of contributions to the sum of human knowledge. Such expectation is, of course, unrealistic for most undergraduate papers. On any level, however, research is investigation for the establishment of some truth. Such activity is possible even to freshmen and is, in fact, commonplace: to find out what day Easter comes on this year is to perform an act of research. Deprived of its halo, the research paper can be recognized as not different in kind from any other piece of exposition, and it is salutary to put it in its place.

The research paper is usually expected to be longer than most essays. This requirement introduces nothing essentially new. A twenty-story building, however, needs a better foundation than a three-story building; and a long paper requires more advance planning. The research paper, or term paper, demands more system, more attention to preliminaries simply because it has to deal with more material.

The research paper is also concerned primarily with objective truth, and therefore requires more overt and demonstrably responsible treatment than do some other kinds of writing. Although the author must put his own stamp on the material, not simply compile paraphrases, he is frankly expected to get much of that material from outside himself. He must, then, be able to cite his sources, and he must also be sure that these are reliable and representative. He must, therefore, do a good deal of looking up sources: this is the "search" in most undergraduate "research." Its distinguishing characteristic is the great leap from dependence on the maternal encyclopedia; its insignia is the bibliography.

THE BIBLIOGRAPHY

What a freshman needs for his research paper is a *working* bibliography, a list which does not pretend to be exhaustive or critical, but is adequate to his purposes—a list of books and articles which are sound, pertinent, and available. This bibliography should be long enough and representative enough to protect him from a parochial point of view, still short enough for him to be able to use it. Such a list is not hard to come by if the student goes at it gradually. Bibliographies are self-creating; one item leads to another. The best place to start is with some authority's selective tabulation. For this purpose a good encyclopedia—provided it is of fairly recent vintage—is excellent, since the references at the end of most articles probably include the important works on the subject, and undoubtedly some of them are in the library. Each of these will in turn probably have a bibliography, or at least refer to other works. And so the list gets built up quickly. This method is safer than thumbing through the subject catalogue or browsing along the library shelves and selecting books because of some attraction in their titles or covers. Thumbing and browsing, particularly the latter, have the advantage of assuring that the books are available and even actually in hand, but they do not guarantee getting the best books. Students sometimes have difficulties because the fortunes of availability led them to base their papers on a few idiosyncratic works—everything in print is not equally reliable.

Once the student has accumulated a working bibliography, and read enough in it to begin to see where he is going and find out what else he wants to know, he will need to supplement his bibliography more systematically. He can make it as elaborate and complete as his time and library facilities permit; but the undergraduate should aim modestly at soundness rather than comprehensiveness—always remembering that the bibliography is made for the paper.

For the more systematic filling out of the bibliography some of the following should be helpful. This list, although it calls attention to some of the principal bibliographical and reference tools, is narrowly selective. Its purpose is to suggest something of the range of assistance available. The student who has not looked for himself through even a modest research library can have no real ideal of the conveniences for him which have been produced by the painful labors of dedicated bibliographers and librarians. When he does, he will wonder at such consecrated drudgery and be grateful.

Encyclopedias When we were children we were enjoined, "Look it up in the encyclopedia," as if there were just one encyclopedia and it were infallible. Disillusioning but salutary is the recognition that there are many enclopedias and that they disagree and can be wrong. They serve us now chiefly as places to start from in our investigations. The *Encyclopaedia Britannica* and *Encyclopedia Americana,* both now published in America, are useful general works, kept more or less up-to-date and supplemented by yearbooks. For most humanistic purposes, however, the eleventh edition (1910–1911) of the *Britannica* is to be preferred to the current edition. It is better to use a specialized encyclopedia if one is available in the area of your interest, since these can be expected to give fuller treatment than general encyclopedias. Be alert, however, to recognize slanted treatment which can come with special orientations. Here are some convenient specialized encyclopedic works:

The Catholic Encyclopedia. 16 vols. New York, 1907–1914. Supplements 1 and 2. New York, 1922, 1951.

The Jewish Encyclopedia. 12 vols. New York, 1901–1906.

Encyclopedia of Religion and Ethics, ed. James Hastings. 13 vols. New York, 1908–1927.

Encyclopedia of the Social Sciences, ed. Edwin R. A. Seligman and Alvin Johnson. 15 vols. New York, 1930–1935.

Grove's Dictionary of Music and Musicians, ed. Eric Blom. 5th ed. 9 vols. London, 1954. Supplement, London, 1961.

Dictionary of Philosophy and Psychology, ed. James Mark Baldwin. 3 vols. New York, 1901–1905. Rev. ed., 1918.

Encyclopedia of the Arts, ed. Dagobert D. Runes and Harry G. Schrieker. New York, 1946.

Oxford Companion to Classical Literature, ed. Sir Paul Harvey. Oxford, 1937.

Oxford Companion to French Literature, ed. Sir Paul Harvey and J. E. Heseltine. Oxford, 1959.

Oxford Companion to English Literature, ed. Sir Paul Harvey. 3rd ed. Oxford, 1946.

Oxford Companion to American Literature, ed. J. D. Hart. 3rd ed. London, 1956.

Oxford Companion to the Theatre, ed. Phyllis Hartnoll. 2nd ed. London, 1957.

Motif-Index of Folk-Literature, ed. Stith Thompson. Rev. ed. 6 vols. Bloomington, 1955–1958.

Dictionaries As a desk dictionary any of the so-called "College Editions" will do: *Webster's New Collegiate Dictionary, Webster's New World Dictionary, The American College Dictionary* or *Standard College Dictionary.* Some of them also contain such useful appendices as lists of colleges and universities, rules of spelling and punctuation, and hints on preparing copy for the press. For serious investigation of points of meaning or etymology, use something more complete:

The Oxford English Dictionary, 13 vols. Oxford, 1933. Originally published 1888–1928 as *A New Dictionary on Historical Principles,* hence called both *OED* and *NED.* Fullest English dictionary and best for citations.

A Dictionary of American English on Historical Principles, ed. William Craigie and James R. Hubert. 4 vols. Chicago, 1938–1944.

Webster's Third New International Dictionary. Springfield, 1961. Latest "unabridged" dictionary; does not regularly distinguish colloquial usage.

A Dictionary of Modern English Usage, ed. H. W. Fowler. London, 1926. An old stand-by, still useful.

A Dictionary of American-English Usage, ed. Margaret Nicholson. New York, 1957. An Americanized Fowler.

A Dictionary of Slang and Unconventional English, ed. Eric Partridge. 5th ed. 2 vols. London, 1961.

Indexes The subject index in the library card catalogue will probably find you all the books on a subject you need. But if you are also after shorter and perhaps more current treatments in periodicals and general books, the following can be helpful. Note, however, that despite comprehensive titles each work actually indexes a limited and changing list of periodicals which is usually given in the introduction. To find in what work a given periodical is indexed, consult the ninth edition of *Ulrich's Periodicals Directory,* edited by E. C. Graves, New York, 1959. To find where issues of a given periodical may be located, check the *Union List of Serials.*

Essays and General Literature Index. 1893–. Indexes books in English "which treat several subjects under one title," by author, subject, and sometimes title.

Poole's Index to Periodical Literature. 1802–1906. Subject index only.

International Index to Periodicals, A Quarterly Guide to Periodical Literature in the Social Sciences and Humanities. 1907–. Author and subject index to works in English only.

Readers' Guide to Periodical Literature. 1900–. Gives author and subject index; issued semimonthly September–June, monthly in July and August.

The Art Index. 1929–. Subject and author index to certain fine arts periodicals and museum bulletins; quarterly.

Engineering Index. 1884–.

Granger's Index to Poetry, ed. William F. Bernhardt. 5th ed. 1962.

Biography Index. 1946–. Indexes biographical material in books and periodicals; quarterly.

Book Review Digest. 1905–. Monthly except February and July.

The New York Times Index. 1913–. Useful also for references to local newspapers, which usually report events on about the same dates as those shown in the *Times* reference; twice a month.

Palmer's Index to the [*London*] *Times Newspaper.* 1790–1941.

The [*London*] *Times. Official Index.* 1906–. Every two months.

Bibliographies

Bibliographic Index, A Cumulative Bibliography of Bibliographies. 1937–. Annual volumes, 1960–.

A World Bibliography of Bibliographies, ed. Theodore Besterman. 3rd ed. 4 vols. Geneva, 1955.

Cambridge Bibliography of English Literature, ed. F. W. Bateson. 4 vols. Cambridge, 1941. Supplement, 1957.

Bibliography of American Literature, ed. Jacob Blanck. New Haven, 1955–. Appearing volume at a time alphabetically; currently 4 vols. have been published: *A–Ing.*

Cumulative Book Index. 1898–. "World list of books in English."

A Concise Bibliography for Students of English, ed. Arthur G. Kennedy and Donald B. Sands. 4th ed., Stanford, 1960.

Bibliographies in American History, ed. Henry P. Beers. New York, 1942.

Miscellaneous useful reference works

Dictionary of National Biography. 1885–1900. 63 vols. Supplements, currently to 1950. Most useful biographical reference on British citizens.

Dictionary of American Biography. 1928–1936. 20 vols. Supplements.

Who's Who in America. 1899–. Most useful for contemporary biographical data. There are also "Who's Whos" in specific fields and localities, even a *Who's Who in Atoms.* London, 1959.

World Almanac. Published annually. One reference work which is inexpensive enough for any student to own and which includes an incredible amount of factual information.

Bartlett's Familiar Quotations. 11th ed. 1937. Best known of many dictionaries of quotations. Will enable you to find a frequently quoted passage if you know one significant word in it.

Roget's Thesaurus. Best known of many dictionaries of synonyms and antonyms.

Concordances. For the Bible and the works of most major poets there are available alphabetical listings of all important words, which are useful both as a means of locating a known passage and as rough subject indexes.

NOTES

Backs of old envelopes, flyleaves of textbooks, insides of matchbook covers, and assorted odds and ends of loose-leaf sheets may well enough hold memoranda for informal essays; a research paper requires serious and systematic note-taking. If you have never thought about the problem of recording data and never developed a system of your own, now is the time to do it. The right system can contribute significantly to your success in college and later on in making reports and after-dinner speeches. Your system should ensure notes that are accurate, full, and accessible.

Accurate notes Accuracy is the mark of the responsible man. Always desirable, it is imperative in anything which claims even a distant relationship to the search for truth. For the research paper deals in large measure with facts, with information which is verifiably right or wrong, which either enlightens or misleads the uninformed reader, which either satisfies or disgusts the knowledgeable reader. A frequent cause of inaccuracy in the final paper is careless notes. If you make a mistake in recording a date or a name in your notes, the odds are that you will never catch the error through all your drafts. It pays to check the details of any note before you close the source book. If you do not, the book will invariably be out of the library when you want it again.

More serious inaccuracies often result not from factual errors in what the note-taker recorded, but from what he did not take down, from crucial omissions which encourage incorrect interpretations of the data collected. Notes must be full enough to serve your purpose, which probably means that they should be a little fuller than you will be tempted to make them. Since you do not know until you get your subject focused and outline your paper just what tack your study will take, you cannot be sure just how much material is relevant. If you are too restrictive in your initial note-taking, you may find when you determine your direction that you have to go back to your sources for data you dimly remember but did not record. Probably some going back for additional material is almost inevitable, and it may be better than spending time taking wastefully excessive notes. The danger is, however, that you might not remember even dimly certain crucial material, and the absence of notes might lead you to decide on an unwarranted thesis or produce a distorted treatment. If your notations showed that the Eighteenth Amendment to the Constitution of the United States forbade the manufacture, sale, and transportation of intoxicating beverages, and did not show that the Twenty-first Amendment repealed the Eighteenth, you might write a paper seriously in error.

How to translate your sources into notes Source materials are generally of two different sorts although both may be found in the same document. Facts—dates, locations, cost figures, statistics—may be scattered through sources and can be picked out piecemeal. They pose few problems beyond accuracy of transcription. Ideas and opinions are something else again: they may be paraphrased, summarized, précised, or quoted verbatim. Which should you do?

To paraphrase a passage is to put it into your own words almost as if you were translating it from a foreign language. You probably would not want to do this with a very long passage, because the method results in almost no reduction in bulk. Paraphrasing shorter passages at the outset helps you to assimilate the material and protects you against unconscious plagiarism. It is safer to translate into your own words when you have the whole text before you and can look at the context rather than later when you are working with an isolated passage.

Generally, however, you want in your note-taking to find some means of condensing your sources. Most useful is to sum up the main points. The *summary* is interpretative; it pays little attention to the rhetorical organization of the original, cuts through the supplementary and illustrative material, and gives the ideas the emphasis which seems valid to the note-taker. A summary of the second paragraph in the section above entitled "Accurate Notes" might be:

> Notes should be full enough to protect you against unnecessary going back to sources and, more important, against reaching unwarranted conclusions from incomplete data.

A *précis* makes an effort to stick to the order of the original and to reproduce accurately its tone and emphasis. The same paragraph précised might be:

> Important inaccuracies can result from significant omissions in notes. Just how full notes should be is hard to determine before the subject of the essay is definite. Too brief notes can send you back to the source; too full notes are a waste of time. But they should be at least full enough to keep you from drawing wrong conclusions.

You might decide to précis a passage which you considered too long to paraphrase or to quote but important enough to represent faithfully.

Exact *quotations* from your sources are valuable for authority and color. If the style of your author is such that he provides convenient and reliable summaries of his ideas, then get them in his own words, being sure not to forget the quotation marks. His words will probably be more effective than yours and you might as well have it "from the horse's mouth." If you think that a passage might be important but find it ambiguous, don't risk misinterpreting it—copy the whole thing. In any event, even if summary and paraphrase will generally suit your needs, include a few striking quotations for possible use in your essay when you want to call an authority to your aid. Be sure, however, that you take careful note of the contexts so that you will not use the quotations misleadingly. It goes without saying that quotations should be copied exactly, including spelling and punctuation.

Notice how John Fischer, in an essay entitled "Why Nobody Can't Write Good" (*Harper's Magazine,* February, 1964, pp. 16–22), uses quotations and facts from his sources:

> Such complaints are becoming frequent enough to suggest that the almost-vanished art of writing has become an expensive problem for American business. The dean of the Harvard Business School, for example, reports that "an incredible number of college graduates who apply for admission can't write a passable sentence"—and he is supposed to get the cream of the crop. Langley Carleton Keyes, the head of a Boston advertising agency, has deplored the "enormous wastefulness" which results from "the great amount of dull, difficult, obscure, hackneyed, wordy, writing in business." Several of the better law schools have started intensive programs in writing because—as Thomas M. Cooley, dean of the University of Pittsburgh law school put it—"the graduates of our colleges, including the best ones, cannot write the English language," much less draft a cogent brief. The State Department has just launched a course in elementary composition for its officers, who frequently cannot comprehend one another's memoranda. And Washington University in Saint Louis is starting a special project, at the cost of $135,000 a year, to translate the incomprehensible jargon of social scientists into English.

No note is complete unless it contains all information necessary to identify the source and to permit you or anybody else to find it again as easily as possible. Always record the author, title and place and date of publication of the source book. Be sure that it is the date of the edition that you used, which may not be the date in a bibliography you constructed from secondary materials. Get in the habit of putting down automatically the exact number of the page on which you found an item as soon as you finish writing the note. Nothing is so frustrating as the certainty that a desired fact or phrase is somewhere in a 500-page book, but you don't know where—except for an impression that it is on a lower left-hand page. If the item has a universal reference point, such as chapter and verse in the Bible, record that as well as the page number, so that you and your readers can find the reference in any edition.

Note form No matter how accurate and full your notes are, they will avail you little unless you can use them easily. And the fuller they are the more difficult this is likely to be. I have over the years tried nearly every possible system of note-taking, and have settled on unruled 4 × 6 cards as the most convenient device for the most readily accessible notes. The unruled cards accommodate diagrams and typing; the 4 × 6 size fits handily into pocket or purse, ready for anything worth setting down, and yet is large enough for most entries. The 3 × 5 size is not, and 5 × 8 is bulky and wasteful. Key punch and IBM cards, which admit of multiple classification and automatic sorting, are something to consider. It is most important to limit yourself to only *one* entry to a card and resist the impulse to save time or paper by putting two different points from the same source on the same card. You will only find yourself mentally or physically shuffling the card back and forth, and frequently forgetting to take into consideration one point because the card is filed under the other. A useful format is the one shown below. Such a card

POETRY [Subject key]	WORDSWORTH [Author key]
"poetry is the spontaneous overflow of powerful feelings"	
Preface to the Lyrical Ballads, The Poetical Works of William Wordsworth, ed. E. de Selincourt (Oxford, 1944), II, 400. [Source]	

can be filed under the subject or the author. Or it can be copied and filed under both, or filed under one with a cross-reference card under the other. These more elaborate procedures are more appropriate for later stages of a research career. At first the "file" may consist of a rubber band, then a small portable file box, and eventually a substantial file cabinet. Such a system pays cumulative dividends: notes taken for one paper can be used for another and notes taken from incidental reading or lectures can be preserved for future needs. And all the while, whether the notes are few or many, they are readily accessible. They can be separated and arranged and rearranged until a pattern emerges. When it does, the ordered cards constitute virtually an outline for writing the paper.

When material from notes is finally transferred to the rough draft, the source reference should go with it as well. Work out a simple but foolproof system of shorthand—the reference shown in the diagram, for instance, might be identified as WW II, 400—and put such notations in your draft. I usually put them between the lines, just above the relevant passage. Looking back through your notes later to find sources of unidentified material is wastefully time consuming and often produces frustration and error.

DOCUMENTATION

After a student has accumulated a collection of notes from a variety of sources, he sometimes wants to show them off. I have a painful memory of having put over 150 footnotes in my first term paper. A sort of pedantic pride can drive any writer to overdocument. Even editors of learned journals have to fight the invasion from the bottoms of the pages, and some as a result have gone too far in discouraging documentation. The only remedy for both the display and the reaction against it is to recognize the legitimate uses of footnotes.

Footnotes have three valid functions, two having to do with documentation and one with supplementation; one is primarily for the benefit of the reader, and two largely for the convenience of the writer.

For the reader Footnotes ought to give for any statement of fact or opinion any source which a reader might be interested in knowing or might wish to check. If the information is more or less common knowledge or can be found in any of several neutral sources, a footnote is not necessary. Should you find yourself led to write "A stitch in time saves nine," you would accomplish nothing by footnoting, "Old proverb." Similarly familiar quotations from Shakespeare and the Bible can usually go without documentation, as can noncontroversial facts, such as the height of the Eiffel Tower or the date of George Washington's death. The date of Shakespeare's birth or the maximum thickness of the earth's crust, on the other hand, would probably require an authority.

For the writer For his own protection, and out of simple honesty, the writer uses specific footnote references to give credit where credit is due for ideas or formulations which are not his own and in which someone else clearly has property rights. Some ideas are in the common domain, some are available in one form or another in so many places or have been so modified that a writer feels no specific indebtedness. Others, however, have a very clear provenience which should be acknowledged. Students sometimes seem to feel that they have done their duty by property rights in words and ideas if they have simply listed in their bibliographies works they have pillaged. Often they even use this listing as an excuse to be a little careless with quotation marks. A good rule for the student is that any "paraphrase" which changes only a few words in the original should be made an accurate acknowledged quotation. If by this process you find that the paper is almost all quotations, you ought to realize that you have not written a paper, merely assembled other writers' passages. A scrupulous acknowledgement is not the remedy: you need to assimilate the material and come up with a selection and organization which is your own.

Vanity and pedantry aside, then, the writer legitimately uses footnotes to give his sources. He may, however, also make them serve a quite different purpose and use them, sparingly, for additional facts or corollary points which he thinks might interest the reader but which would have been excessive or obscuring in the text of the paper. He must, however, avoid a situation—amusingly caricatured by Frank Sullivan's "A Garland of Ibids"—in which the footnotes seem to be taking over or, as a depository of the author's afterthoughts, talking back to the paper. When the footnotes begin taking on a substantive character, they at least raise the question of whether the paper should not be rewritten to a different focus. Their chief function for the reader and the writer must remain documentation.

Footnote form The form of documentation should be as inconspicuous and as accessible as possible. It should be full enough to identify the source precisely, yet still simple and clear. Any form which satisfies these criteria and is used consistently ought to serve, but in practice it is much easier and safer for the writer to accept a standard style. That laid down by the Modern Language Association *Style Sheet* is now generally used. Documentation, if not placed in footnotes, may be put in parentheses immediately following the element to which it refers. When citations are few and short, the latter system is preferable. A series of page or verse references to the same work are most conveniently interpolated: "With 'Lay on, Macduff' (V, viii, 33), Macbeth bravely faces the inevitable."

Footnote references are usually indicated by Arabic numbers, running consecutively through the essay or chapter. The numbers are superscripts, written a little above the line, and placed after the punctuation at the end of the passage to which they refer. They do not have periods after them, nor are they put in parentheses or brackets or slant lines or circles—they just stand there naked like this:

The following quotation is taken from a recent novel.[1]

They stand in the same way at the beginning of the footnote. The footnotes themselves may be placed at the bottoms of the pages to which they apply, or all together at the end of the paper. The latter system is more convenient for printers and is often required of manuscripts submitted for publication; it is a good deal less convenient for the reader and ordinarily should not be used in student papers. The number of footnotes can be reduced by putting in the same footnote several references which come close together in the text, generally in the same paragraph—always provided that the citation remains clear and easy to use. The footnotes are indented and have periods at the ends, whether they are normal complete sentences or not. The conventional form can be seen in the table which follows.

FOOTNOTE FORM

[1] William Wordsworth, "Advertisement to the Lyrical Ballads, 1798," *The Poetical Works of William Wordsworth,* ed. E. de Selincourt and Helen Darbishire (Oxford, 1940–1949), II, 383–384.

Entry	*Description*
William Wordsworth,	Author's name, as normally written, not last name first as in bibliography form, followed by a comma.
"Advertisement to the Lyrical Ballads, 1798,"	Title of a chapter or section in a larger work or of an article in a journal, in quotation marks, followed by a comma within the quotation marks.

The Poetical Works of William Wordsworth,

Title of the book or journal in italics, followed by a comma. Very long titles can be shortened intelligibly; use three periods (ellipses) to indicate internal omissions. If the book is part of a series, the series title is given without italics or quotations marks.

ed. E. de Selincourt and Helen Darbishire

Names of editors or translators, if any, preceded by "ed." or "trans." and followed by a comma, which is delayed, however, until after any parenthetical element that may follow. The editors of journals are not usually given.

(Oxford, 1940–1949),

Place and date of publication, separated by a comma, in parentheses, followed by a comma. The name of the publisher may be included as follows: (Oxford: Clarendon Press, 1940–1949). For references to periodicals the place of publication is usually omitted, and the date of publication follows the volume number:

Wilfred S. Dowden, "Thomas Moore and the Review of *Christabel,*" *Modern Philology* [usually abbreviated *MP*], LX (August, 1962), 47–50.

II,

Volume number, if there are two or more volumes in the work, in capital Roman numerals, followed by comma.

383–384.

Page number, in Arabic numerals unless the text cited uses some other system, followed by a period unless the reference goes on to identify line or footnote number on that page: "p. 17, 1.9" or "p. 18, n.5." Note that when a volume number is given, the page reference is made by figure only; but when there is only one volume in the work, the page reference is preceded by "p." if single, "pp." if plural. This citation could also be written "pp. 383 f."—meaning page 383 and the page following. If more than two pages had been indicated, the notation could have been "pp. 383 ff." —meaning page 383 and the pages following. The specific reference is generally preferred.

Footnote form permits and indeed encourages abbreviations. A student with a few footnotes and no printing costs to worry about, however, should err on the side of fullness until he is conversant enough with his field to know which abbreviations are generally accepted. Latin words and abbreviations were once almost hallmarks of learning, but now their English equivalents are often preferred. Note that these common Latin terms are now considered sufficiently Anglicized not to require italicization although they frequently appear in italics:

ca. or c. (*circa*)—about
cf. (*confer*)—compare
e.g. (*exempli gratia*)—for example
ibid. (*ibidem*)—in the same place
vs. (*versus*)—against, but also sometimes used as an abbreviation for "verse"
i.e. (*id est*)—that is
infra—below
loc. cit. (*loco citato*)—in the place cited
passim—here and there throughout
sic—thus
sup. (*supra*)—above
viz. (*videlicet*)—namely

"Ibid." should be used only where it results in a clear advantage. If you have been citing a book by Jones and want to refer to it again, it is just as easy to write "Jones, p. 161" as "Ibid., p. 161"—and generally more helpful.

Bibliography form The standard bibliography form provides about the same information as the footnote form, but shows some differences for practical reasons. The items in a bibliography are usually arranged in alphabetical order, author's last name first, followed by a comma, his first name, and a period. And since bibliography items refer to whole works, and are not designed as are footnotes to locate a source precisely, book entries need not end with a specific page reference, and therefore do not interpolate the place and date of publication in parentheses as do footnotes. The order of a book entry is:

Author's last name, first name. Title, editor or translator. Number of volumes if more than one. Place of publication, date of publication.

Wordsworth, William. *The Poetical Works of William Wordsworth,* ed. E. de Selincourt and Helen Darbishire. 5 vols. Oxford, 1940–1949.

Notice that the book entry frequently separates elements by *periods,* but still uses commas after the author's last name, between the title and the editors or translators if there are such, and between the place and date of publication. If an item has multiple authors or editors, the name of the first only is reversed, and the names of the various individuals are separated by commas as are other items in a series:

Thorpe, Clarence D., Carlos Baker, and Bennett Weaver, eds. *The Major English Romantic Poets: A Symposium in Reappraisal.* Carbondale, 1957.

The bibliography entry for an article, however, still needs page references to locate the article in the journal or book in which it appears, and therefore the form for an article entry can be the same as for a footnote except for the reversal of the author's name and the period after his first name:

Dowden, Wilfred S. "Thomas Moore and the Review of *Christabel*," *MP*, LX (August, 1962), 47–50.

Usually the bibliography of an undergraduate paper is intended as a list of works cited or used in the work to which it is attached. Don't be tempted to pad it with books you perhaps leafed through or titles you got out of the card catalogue. If for valid reasons you want to present a selective bibliography of significant works on the subject, whether you have been able to use them or not, make this fact clear in the heading of the bibliography. Your instructor may ask you to submit a critical bibliography, which is merely a listing with a brief comment on the character and value of each entry.

A sound bibliography is of first importance to the production of a good term paper, but the tail ought not to wag the dog. The bibliography is only an appendix to the essay, which should be in itself a complete and satisfying whole.

ASSIGNMENTS

1. A research paper for an English course may well serve also as a paper for a course in another department—if both instructors agree. Consider the possibilities in your program and see if you can negotiate a double assignment.

2. Write a précis of one of the following:

a. Chapter One of this book.

b. A chapter or an essay in your reading text.

c. An essay in a recent issue of *Harper's Magazine* or similar journal. If your instructor approves this option, you will need to turn in the article with your précis.

3. Read carefully the following passage from the foreword to Aldous Huxley's *Brave New World:*[1]

Assuming, then, that we are capable of learning as much from Hiroshima as our forefathers learned from Magdeburg, we may look forward to a period, not indeed of peace, but of limited and only partially ruinous warfare. During that period it may be assumed that nuclear energy will be harnessed to industrial uses. The result, pretty obviously, will be a series of economic and social changes unprecedented in rapidity and completeness. All the existing patterns of human life will be disrupted and new patterns will have to be improvised to conform with the nonhuman fact of atomic power. Procrustes in modern dress, the nuclear scientist will prepare the bed on which mankind must lie; and if mankind doesn't fit—well, some stretching and a bit of amputation—the same sort of stretching and amputations as have been going on ever since applied science really got into its stride, only this time they will be a good deal more drastic than in the past. These far from painless operations will be directed by highly centralized totalitarian governments. Inevitably so; for the immediate future is likely to resemble the immediate past, and in the immediate past rapid technological changes, taking place in a mass-producing economy and among a population predominantly propertyless, have always tended to produce economic and social confusion. To deal with confusion, power has been centralized and government control increased. It is probable that all the world's governments will be more or less completely totalitarian even before the harnessing of atomic energy; that they will be totalitarian during and after the harnessing seems almost certain. Only a large-scale popular movement toward decentralization and self-help can arrest the present tendency toward statism. At present there is no sign that such a movement will take place.

a. Write a paraphrase of the passage.

b. Write a summary of the passage.

c. Under what subject headings could you conceivably file notes taken on this passage?

4. Make a rough diagram of the open-shelf area of your campus library, showing the location of the different classifications of books.

5. Choose one of the reference works listed in this chapter, examine it carefully and write an essay describing its contents and discussing its usefulness.

[1] Aldous Huxley, *Brave New World* (New York: Harper & Row, 1946).

6. Consider the problems involved in writing papers on the following subjects. What would you need to find out? Where would you go to look?

a. The origins of New Orleans jazz.

b. The relation of football to soccer.

c. The folk voice of Robert Frost.

d. United States foreign policy concerning Laos.

e. The application of jet engines to automobiles.

f. Limiting factors in color television.

g. Theatrical interpretations of Caliban.

7. For one of the following general subjects do enough investigation to find out an area of disagreement among authorities, and then write an essay on the crux of that disagreement:

a. The Dead Sea Scrolls.

b. Fluoridation of drinking water.

c. Shakespeare's sonnets.

d. The automobile's contribution to air pollution.

e. Federal support of the creative and performing arts.

f. Pay television.

g. Trout fishing.

h. Football rules.

i. T. S. Eliot's poetry.

8. Go to your library reference room and try to find and handle as many as possible of the reference books mentioned in this chapter. List those that you looked into and next to each write the titles of at least two other interesting and helpful works you found on the same shelf.

9. Compare the treatment of John Calvin in the *Encyclopaedia Britannica,* the *Catholic Encyclopedia,* and the *Encyclopedia of Religion and Ethics.*

10. Write a research paper in the following steps. This will take time; do not put it off until the last minute.

a. Choose a subject area in which you are interested and begin looking for a manageable subject.

b. Turn in a focused subject for the approval of your instructor.

c. Once your subject is cleared, begin reading and assembling a working bibliography. Submit it to your instructor to see whether he thinks that it is full enough, representative enough, and reliable enough.

d. Start accumulating careful notes.

e. Read over your notes and determine whether now that you know more about your subject you think it might be desirable to make any changes in your focus.

f. Start making a topic outline of your paper, stopping to do further reading in order to fill in any gaps that develop.

g. Submit your outline to your instructor for his suggestions.

h. Write a rough draft and give it time to cool.

i. Read over the rough draft and revise and correct, rewriting any sections that seem to require it. Check your documentation and bibliography.

j. Prepare your final version.

k. Proofread your final version at least twice.

l. Turn it in and take the night off.

INDEX